D0850331

ABRAHAM LINCOLN WAS A LIBERAL.
JEFFERSON DAVIS WAS A CONSERVATIVE

❧ THE LOCHLAINN SEABROOK COLLECTION ❧

Five-Star Books & Gifts From the Heart of the American South

❧ SeaRavenPress.com ❧

ABRAHAM LINCOLN WAS A LIBERAL

JEFFERSON DAVIS WAS A CONSERVATIVE

The Missing Key to Understanding the American Civil War

GENEROUSLY ILLUSTRATED BY THE AUTHOR,
"THE VOICE OF THE TRADITIONAL SOUTH," COLONEL

LOCHLAINN SEABROOK

JEFFERSON DAVIS HISTORICAL GOLD MEDAL WINNER

Diligently Researched for the Elucidation of the Reader

2017

Sea Raven Press, Nashville, Tennessee, USA

ABRAHAM LINCOLN WAS A LIBERAL,
JEFFERSON DAVIS WAS A CONSERVATIVE

Published by
Sea Raven Press, Cassidy Ravensdale, President
The Literary Wing of the Pro-South Movement
PO Box 1484, Spring Hill, Tennessee 37174-1484 USA
SeaRavenPress.com • searavenpress@gmail.com

1ˢᵗ SRP paperback edition, 1ˢᵗ printing: March 2017, ISBN: 978-1-943737-44-4
1ˢᵗ SRP hardcover edition, 1ˢᵗ printing: March 2017, ISBN: 978-1-943737-45-1

ISBN: 978-1-943737-45-1 (hardcover)
Library of Congress Control Number: 2017933475

Abraham Lincoln Was a Liberal, Jefferson Davis Was a Conservative: The Missing Key to Understanding the American Civil War, by Lochlainn Seabrook. Includes an index, endnotes, and bibliographical references.

Front and back cover design and art, book design, layout, and interior art by Lochlainn Seabrook. All images, graphic design, graphic art, and illustrations copyright © Lochlainn Seabrook. Cover images & design copyright © Lochlainn Seabrook. Portions of this book have been adapted from the author's other works

The views on the American "Civil War" documented in this book are those of the publisher.

Dedication

To my favorite early American Conservatives: Thomas Jefferson, Thomas Paine, George Mason, John C. Calhoun, Alexander H. Stephens, Robert E. Lee, Stonewall Jackson, Nathan Bedford Forrest, and Jefferson Davis.

Epigraph

"Only in name are the Republican and
Democratic parties of today like their
predecessors. The Democrats who
annually dine in memory of Jefferson
and Jackson cherish political notions
which Jefferson and Jackson would have
repudiated. The Republicans who
celebrate Lincoln's birthday are for the
most part a party in whose company
Lincoln would have been ill at ease."

WILLIAM MACDONALD, 1921

CONTENTS

NOTES TO THE READER

THE TWO MAIN POLITICAL PARTIES IN 1860

☞ In any study of America's antebellum, bellum, postbellum, and interbellum Civil War periods, it is vitally important to understand that in 1860 the two major political parties—the Democrats and the newly formed Republicans—were the opposite of what they are today. In other words, the Democrats of the mid 19th Century were Conservatives, akin to the Republican Party of today, while the Republicans of the mid 19th Century were Liberals, akin to the Democratic Party of today, facts which form the central theme of this book.

THE TERM "CIVIL WAR"

☞ As I heartily dislike the phrase "Civil War," its use throughout this book (as well as in my other works) is worthy of explanation.

Today America's entire literary system refers to the conflict of 1861 using the Northern term the "Civil War," whether we in the South like it or not. Thus, as all book searches by readers, libraries, and retail outlets are now performed online, and as all bookstores categorize works from this period under the heading "Civil War," book publishers and authors who deal with this particular topic have little choice but to use this term themselves. If I were to refuse to use it, as some of my Southern colleagues have suggested, few people would ever find or read my books.

Add to this the fact that scarcely any non-Southerners have ever heard of the names we in the South use for the conflict, such as the

The American "Civil War" was not a true civil war as Webster defines it: "A conflict between opposing groups of citizens of the *same* country." It was a fight between two individual countries; or to be more specific, two separate and constitutionally formed confederacies: the U.S.A. and the C.S.A.

"War for Southern Independence"—or my personal preference, "Lincoln's War." It only makes sense then to use the term "Civil War" in most commercial situations, distasteful though it is.

We should also bear in mind that while today educated persons, particularly educated Southerners, all share an abhorrence for the phrase "Civil War," it was not always so. Confederates who lived through and even fought in the conflict regularly used the term throughout the 1860s, and even long after. Among them were Confederate generals such as Nathan Bedford Forrest, Richard Taylor, and Joseph E. Johnston, not to mention the Confederacy's vice president, Alexander H. Stephens.

In 1895 Confederate General James Longstreet wrote about his military experiences in a work subtitled, *Memoirs of the Civil War in America*. Even the Confederacy's highest leader, President Jefferson Davis, used the term "Civil War,"[1] and in one case at least, as late as 1881—the year he wrote his brilliant exposition, *The Rise and Fall of the Confederate Government*.[2]

Confederate General James Longstreet.

Authors writing for *Confederate Magazine* sometimes used the phrase well into the early 1900s,[3] and in 1898, at the Eighth Annual Meeting and Reunion of the United Confederate Veterans (the forerunner of today's Sons of Confederate Veterans), the following resolution was proposed: that from then on the Great War of 1861 was to be designated "the Civil War Between the States."[4]

CLARIFICATION

☞ To assist the reader in keeping track of the often confusing two-party political system referenced by early American writers and speakers before, during, and after Lincoln's War, I have inserted brackets identifying Victorian party affiliations where I deem appropriate. Brackets also include my additional comments and notes.

Additionally, to further aid in simplifying an overly labyrinthian topic, I identify our U.S. presidents with their specific party affiliation rather than with their own personal political views—which rarely fully accord with the former.

Finally, I have provided a detailed set of Appendices which will help the reader demystify and more fully understand the subject of this book.

PERSPECTIVE

☞ Few areas of human thought are as fraught with ambiguities, uncertainty, and questions marks as American political history. Indeed, no two historians or presidential scholars even agree on which of our chief executives were "liberal" or "conservative," or something else altogether.

Debate continues, for example, over the influences, outcomes, and consequences of our various elections, dating all the way back to our first U.S. president, George Washington. There is no consensus regarding the definition of a "party," or even the number of popular votes our presidential candidates received at each election. There is not even agreement on the number of popular votes accorded in our most recent election: the bitter 2016 contest between Donald J. Trump and Hillary Clinton. Thus in most cases no definitive answer can be given to even our most basic questions.

Some of this confusion results from the fact that, as studies have shown, no single issue can explain party divisions.[5] Also, in many cases men, such as Alexander Hamilton, changed their views and statements over time, making it difficult to ascertain their true political beliefs, while others, like ultra demagogue Abraham Lincoln, purposefully and constantly altered their words to fit their audiences.

U.S. President George Washington.

Still others, such as Edmund J. Randolph, were known to frequently switch parties, making it nearly impossible to categorize their party affiliation.[6] John Quincy Adams, as another example, changed parties so many times—in some cases, to the opposing side—that it was said of him, "he was not a reliable party man."[7]

Our first United States attorney general, Edmund J. Randolph.

Another difficulty is that many early American political documents, conditions, and traditions have not yet been studied;[8] just as problematic, the definition of the words "conservative" and "liberal" have been different at different periods in our history—completely the opposite at times. Some scholars, for instance, refer to all Federalists (early American Liberals) as "conservatives,"[9] and all Democrats (early American Conservatives) as "liberals"—which, *concerning the definitions of that time*, is accurate, but would be confusing to most modern readers.[10]

Finally, the candidates and presidents themselves have added considerably to the disorder by blurring the lines between conservatism and liberalism. President Thomas Jefferson, though a Republican (a Conservative at the time), adopted a number of Federalist (Liberal) policies and strategies,[11] and was a proponent of Adam Smith's philosophy of *laissez-faire* (literally "let to" or "leave alone"), an economic theory once considered a "liberal" concept—but which is now seen as "conservative." He became moderate enough in various areas that some of his more conservative followers formed an anti-Jefferson party known as the "Quids."[12] He once went as far as to wrongly call the U.S. a "nation" (it is a republic), and even appeared to contradict his advocacy of states' rights and the right of secession, saying to James Madison in 1786:

> The policies of Europe render it indispensibly necessary that with respect to everything external we be one nation only, firmly hooped together.[13]

President John Adams, though a Federalist (a Liberal), and thus a proponent of elitist aristocratic government, was distrusted by

Republicans (Conservatives) for his "conservatism," and disliked by
fellow Federalists (Liberals) due to his "cold" personality.[14]

U.S. President Woodrow Wilson and his cabinet.

President Woodrow
Wilson, a staunch Democrat
(a Liberal in that period), in
opposition to the
Constitution, once
advocated strict censorship
of the press, a trait still
common among modern
Liberals. Yet, at the same
time he aggressively
defended the Southern
Confederacy and her fight for independence during Lincoln's
War—something few if any Democrats or Liberals would do today.[15]

Then there was President Theodore Roosevelt, a Republican *after* the
party had become conservative in 1896. Yet he claimed to be a "liberal,"
and even referred to himself as a "progressive," writing in 1911:

> I am a progressive; I could not be anything else, for the Progressives are really
> those who believe in the people, who stand for the fundamentals of popular
> rule. We must work and we must fight for the restoration of popular rule,
> secure the adoption of such instruments of popular rule as direct primary,
> strict election law, corrupt practices act and the popular election of United
> States senators. These means are only good if, when they are adopted, we use
> them so as to secure the true object of government, by the people, which is
> the welfare of the people.[16]

Despite these words, actual progressives and socialists did not consider
Roosevelt a true progressive, but rather what he actually was: "Just
another capitalist competing with other capitalists."[17]

A majority of our other presidents gave mixed impressions of their
political views as well. Indeed, it would be difficult if not impossible to
find a single U.S. chief executive who was either 100 percent
conservative or 100 percent liberal. Our parties have always been
comprised of people who held every manner of opinion, and who wrote
platforms containing policies that contradicted earlier ones, with little
consistency along the way.

The Democrats, the Conservative party during the Jacksonian Era (circa 1824-1845), as just one example, had wealthy members and poor members, Southern members and Northern members, Eastern members and Western members, slave owners and abolitionists—nearly all who clashed with one another over varying issues.[18] In a word, any attempt to pigeonhole our presidents, the leaders of such parties, is futile, forcing us to rely on their party identification, however obtuse their own personal political beliefs may have been.

Simply put, there is no single guide that all will agree on concerning the origins and history of America's two-party system. Thus, in this book I have used a wide variety of sources that I feel bring meaning, context, and lucidity to a complex subject; one which we must accept as a gargantuan jigsaw puzzle that will always be missing important pieces.

PRESENTISM
☛ As a historian I view *presentism* (judging the past according to present day mores and customs) as the enemy of authentic history. And this is precisely why the Left employs it in its ongoing war against traditional American, conservative, and Christian values. By looking at history through the lens of modern day beliefs, they are able to distort, revise, and reshape the past into a false narrative that fits their ideological agenda: the liberalization *and* Northernization of America, the strengthening and further centralization of the national government, and total control of American political, economic, and social power, the same agenda that Lincoln championed.

Judging our ancestors by our own standards is unfair, unjust, misleading, and unethical.

This book, *Abraham Lincoln Was a Liberal, Jefferson Davis Was a Conservative*, rejects presentism and replaces it with what I call *historicalism*: judging our ancestors based on the values of their own time. To get the most from this work the reader is invited to reject presentism as well. In this way—along with casting aside preconceived notions and the erroneous "history" churned out by our left-wing, South-shaming education system—the truth in this work will be most readily ascertained and absorbed.

IMAGES
☛ The images in this book all derive from one of the following sources: 1) public domain, 2) purchase from stock photo libraries, 3) creation of the author.

LEARN MORE
☛ Lincoln's War on the American people and the Constitution can never be fully understood without a thorough knowledge of the South's perspective. As this book is only meant to be a brief introductory guide to these topics, one cannot hope to learn the complete story here. For those who are interested in additional material from the South's perspective, please see my comprehensive histories listed on page 2.

PREFACE

Though this book contains much history about America's two-party system, it is not intended to be an in-depth history of our presidents' elections and party affiliations. Its sole purpose is to show how and why Abraham Lincoln, though a Republican, was not a Conservative, but rather a Liberal; and how and why Jefferson Davis, though a Democrat, was not a Liberal, but rather a Conservative.

U.S. President Dwight D. Eisenhower.

Along the way I will demonstrate why the Republican Party of Lincoln was not the Conservative Republican Party of Thomas Jefferson, Dwight D. Eisenhower, or Ronald Reagan, but instead why it was actually the Liberal party of Franklin D. Roosevelt, Jimmy Carter, and Barack H. Obama. Simultaneously, I will illustrate why the Democratic Party of Davis was not the Liberal Democratic Party of Franklin D. Roosevelt, Jimmy Carter, or Barack H. Obama, but instead why it was actually the Conservative party of Thomas Jefferson, Dwight D. Eisenhower, and Ronald Reagan.

In this way the politically confusing event we Southerners call the War for Southern Independence, our American "Civil War," will make sense for the first time, and will finally be seen for what it really was. Not a fight between "racist Southern slaver owners" and "egalitarian Northern abolitionists," as pro-North writers would have you believe—and which is as far from the truth as it could possibly be. But an archetypal battle between Conservatism and Liberalism, one of the most violent and large scale of such conflicts the world has ever known.

INTRODUCTION

The most serious impediment to a true and full understanding of the American Civil War concerns the two main political parties at the time, the Republicans and the Democrats. The confusion comes from the fact that their platforms were the reverse of what they are today. In other words, while the modern Republican Party is conservative, the Civil War Republican Party was liberal; and while the modern Democratic Party is liberal, the Civil War Democratic Party was conservative. This book explains how this reversal came to be.

For at least the past 100 years, the War for Southern Independence has been grossly misunderstood due to a lack of knowledge of our changing political party names and platforms.

We are so instilled with the 21st-Century notion that the Republicans and Democrats are conservative and liberal respectively, that most naturally assume that they have always been this way, all the way back to the 1860s, or even further, back to the founding of the U.S.A. in 1776. In my personal experience this false view has caused more confusion, more misconceptions, and more problems when it comes to the topic of the American Civil War than any other factor.

Because the average person assumes that Abraham Lincoln, being a Republican, was a Conservative, and that Jefferson Davis, being a Democrat, was a Liberal, the entire War itself has been turned on its head, and thus misconstrued. This means that the actual cause of the War, the identities of those who started it, the reasons they started it, and the consequences that came afterward, are all totally misunderstood by the majority of people—and I include in this list most Civil War scholars, authors, and educators, both pro-North and pro-South.

This misunderstanding has led to a host of political absurdities and outrages, such as when President Trump intentionally held his Inaugural Concert in front of the Lincoln Memorial (big government Liberal

Lincoln would have despised Trump), or when well-known conservative, independent, or right-leaning personalities and politicians continually and publicly praise Lincoln (a socialistic, anti-conservative who would have had them imprisoned for publicly promoting views that contradicted his).[19] Just as egregious, American society continues to wrongly attribute the abolition of American slavery to Lincoln and the "conservative" Republican Party,[20] and the founding of the original Ku Klux Klan to Davis and the "liberal" Democrats.[21]

Countless other oddities, absurdities, and scandals—the result of America's lack of even the most basic knowledge of our political history—abound throughout our society and culture.

An 1852 political cartoon with the Democrats' donkey symbol. The Democratic Party of the mid 19th Century was the Conservative party of that era. Thus the donkey should not be used by the 21st-Century Democratic Party, which is Liberal.

The Democratic Party mascot, for instance, is wholly incorrect: its familiar "donkey" emblem emerged during President Andrew Jackson's tenure (1829-1837), when the Liberal press and the Whigs began using the donkey as a sarcastic reference to Jackson's supposed "ignorance," snidely portraying him as a "Jack-ass."[22] At the time the Democratic Party happily adopted the symbol.[23] But 21st-Century Democrats should not be using it. Why?

Because the Democratic Party of the Jacksonian period is not the same as today's Democratic Party. Indeed, not only are the two not at all connected, their platforms are opposite one another. For Jackson's Democratic Party was the Conservative party then, the equivalent of today's Republican Party. The Whigs, on the other hand, were the Liberal party then, the equivalent of today's Democratic Party. Thus Jackson himself was a 19th-Century version of a Conservative Republican,[24] making the donkey symbol wholly inappropriate for today's Democratic Party (Liberal), but absolutely appropriate for today's Republican Party (Conservative).

An 1895 political cartoon using the Republicans' elephant symbol, with Democratic (Conservative) President Grover Cleveland in the center. The Republican Party of the late 19th Century (up until 1896) was the Liberal party of that era. Thus the elephant should not be used by the 21st-Century Republican Party, which is Conservative. (The Democratic Party mascot, the donkey, can also be seen here.)

The modern Republican Party symbol, the elephant, has the same problem. In 1874 Republican sympathizing cartoonist Thomas Nast[25] selected the pachyderm to represent his party,[26] probably due to its strength, power, and size.[27] But the Republican Party at the time of the Grant administration (1869-1877) was the Liberal party. Both Grant and Nast were in fact Liberals—the latter a German immigrant who grew up under the left-wing influence of Forty-Eighters and radical European Liberalism, and whose hero was Italian socialist-facist revolutionary Giuseppe Garibaldi.[28]

Why is today's Republican Party using a symbol that was created nearly 145 years ago by Liberals for a Liberal party? For the same reason that today's Democratic Party is using a symbol that was created nearly 190 years ago to represent the Conservative Party of that era, the Democrats of 1828. It all comes down to ignorance of our party history.

As with all truths, these particular simple and demonstrable facts are considered heresy; in this case, mainly by experts in the intellectual and political

By confusing the then Conservative Democrats and the Liberal Republicans of the 1860s, most Civil War scholars have wrongly interpreted the conflict.

spheres. Indeed, for even stating them I have been verbally attacked and insulted, my manuscripts have been rejected by academic publishers, and I have had my books banned from various retail stores and even so-called "educational" institutions and museums—usually by individuals with multiple degrees in American history. Such is the depth of this near universally confounded issue.

It can further be seen in the absurd and historically inaccurate manner in which Lincoln, Davis, and the War are commonly characterized by both professionals and the lay public. Republican Lincoln is held up as a *Conservative* who tried to "save the Union"; Democrat Davis is portrayed as a *Liberal* who tried to "destroy the Union"; the War itself is depicted as a fight between the "righteous North" and the "wicked South," a moral battle between the "Union and the Confederacy," the "Blue and the Gray," the "Abolitionists and the Slaveholders"; the "Good Guys (the pro-Constitution Union) and the Bad Guys (the anti-Constitution Confederacy)."

But because the view of the two main political parties of the Civil War era is wrong, all of these characterizations are false as well, and so have misled generation after generation of not only Americans, but people of every nationality. For this erroneous view of the War, which starts with a faulty view of 19th-Century politics, is taught in schools, colleges, and universities around the world, from Europe and Africa, to

Asia and the Middle East. Examine your children's textbooks and you will find Lincoln imaged as "that egalitarian, patriotic Republican who emancipated the slaves" and Davis as "that treasonous, racist Democrat who tried to maintain slavery."

In this book I set the record straight by providing a brief but assiduous study of America's two main political parties, showing how, why, and when they were formed, and more importantly why and when they became the parties they are today, namely Republican Conservatives and Democratic Liberals. Though I go through all 58 elections and 45 presidents (beginning with the election of President Washington in 1788 and ending with the election of President Trump in 2016), I give special emphasis to the years between 1828 and 1896, revealing how the events of this important 68-year period shaped the antebellum, bellum, and postbellum eras, and in particular how they affected the Great American War Between Conservatism and Liberalism—otherwise incorrectly known as the "Civil War."

It is my sincere hope that this knowledge will help dissipate the confusion surrounding the conflict, and finally provide a complete and thorough understanding of the conservative and liberal forces at work behind it. Only then can the conservative, patriotic, Constitution-loving South be vindicated and her true and honorable place on the stage of world history be established once and for all.

Lochlainn Seabrook
Nashville, Tennessee, USA
March 2017

1

FROM WASHINGTON TO ADAMS 1788 TO 1828

T HE EXACT DAY ON WHICH America's two-party system started is not known, just one of the numerous mysteries pertaining to the history of the Republican and Democratic Parties. In fact, as Francis Curtis noted in 1904, "party history and party names for some reason have become most complicated, and almost impossible of elucidation."[29] To those historians, and I include myself among them, who are intimately acquainted with the many different views regarding the development of American parties, this is certainly a vast understatement.

One historian has rightly called Washington politics "enigmatic," despite repeated investigation over the centuries—all which has only resulted in inadequately answered questions and increased speculation.[30] Another takes note of the many diverse schools of thought surrounding this topic, and the wide "variety of explanations" they produce. The shaping of our national party system, he proclaims, "is one of the most complex and perplexing developments" in our history, producing major disagreements as to the whos, whys, whats, whens, and wheres. What were the catalysts that spawned the Republicans and the Democrats? Were our two primary political parties the products of ideology, war, economics, or politics, or even mere chance? Maybe it was a combination of these and other unknown forces.[31]

Not even U.S. presidents have been able to unravel the many conundrums of our political history. One of these was our eighth chief executive Martin Van Buren, who penned the following in the opening pages of his book, *Inquiry Into the Origin and Course of Political Parties in the United States*:

> . . . to define the origin and trace the history of national parties is an undertaking of extraordinary difficulty; one from which, in view of the embarrassments that surround it in the case of our own political divisions, I have more than once retired in despair, and on which I now enter with only slight hopes of success.[32]

In the end no one can say for sure precisely how, when, or why our two-party began, a realization which has prompted another historian to state that "no reliable history of the process can ever be written."[33] As it is ultimately unknowable, this is true.

Still we may theorize. My own belief is that

> the origin of parties is to be found not in the nature of the governmental organization but in the nature of public opinion. It is because people think differently on public questions that they group themselves in parties; and it is in no sense a natural thing, and least of all an inevitable one, that they should array themselves in only two groups. The two-party system in this country is primarily historical in its origin. When the Constitution was before the States for ratification, there was a natural division into the two groups of those who favored the Constitution and those who opposed it. The Constitution must be either ratified or rejected; no middle course was possible. Hardly had the new government been put into operation before a violent controversy developed between those who favored a liberal interpretation of the Constitution and those who would restrict its scope, and party lines again formed on that question. The point at issue, however, was not at all one of governmental form, but the essentially legal one of constitutional interpretation . . .[34]

There is one thing we can be quite sure of, however, as Frederick J. Turner states:

> We may trace the contest between the capitalist [Conservative] and the democratic pioneer [Liberal] from the earliest colonial days.[35]

This would set the faint beginnings of our party system back to at least 1607, when the first American colonies began to be established, a time in which the bitter sectionalism between the Conservative South and the Liberal North was already becoming evident. As I am about to show, our two-party system developed around the two primary figures who represented these two sections and their intensely opposing views of the U.S. Constitution.

Nearly 200 years later, at the Philadelphia Convention of 1787, we find the earliest definitive traces of our party origins. It was during the debates here, where our first Constitution, the conservative Articles of Confederation, was replaced by the more liberal U.S. Constitution, that

> marked differences of opinion were soon developed, which resulted practically in dividing the body into two opposing parties. . . . These differences of opinion consisted, on the one hand, in a [conservative] tendency to maintain freedom of action for the individual citizen, and for the several states independence in legislation and administration, and in everything, indeed, except the foreign policy and the national defences of the Union. On the other hand, the [liberal] tendency was to subordinate the states to national authority and clothe it with powers commensurate with its responsibility and dignity as the ruling power of the nation.[36]

George Washington.

A year later, with our first quadrennial election in 1788, our first U.S. president, George Washington, appeared on the scene, serving two terms, from 1789 to 1797. Though, hoping to minimize conflict,[37] he belonged to no party, was strictly nonpartisan, often spoke out against the very idea of parties[38] and their "baneful effects,"[39] and was not elected—but instead was "made president by common consent,"[40] even as the ink was drying on the new U.S. Constitution in September 1787, America's citizens were now busily dividing themselves into two strongly opposing camps surrounding the central political party figures of the day,[41] Liberals Alexander Hamilton and John Adams, and Conservatives Thomas Jefferson and James Madison.[42]

This despite the fact that, notably, the U.S. Constitution does not include any provisions for party government;[43] that is, for operating the government according to political parties.[44] Further, says MacDonald: "Neither directly nor indirectly does it recognize or even assume the existence of parties."[45] Indeed, the Founders, including both Jefferson and Hamilton,[46] were essentially anti-party, and the Founders wrote the Constitution itself with this view in mind, filling it with party-inhibiting ideas and party-destroying

John Quincy Adams.

clauses. These include staggered elections, fragmented constituencies, the separation of governmental powers, and the division of powers between the nation and the states—all which were designed to prevent the rise of popular majorities while promoting conciliation and compromise.[47]

The commonly held opinion of the time was voiced by John Quincy Adams in 1816: "The existence of parties is not necessary to free government."[48] Some went as far as to hold that "faction is the madness of the many for the benefit of the few."[49] Writing to Judge Francis Hopkinson of Pennsylvania from Paris, France, March 13, 1789, Jefferson spoke for many of the Revolutionary Generation:

> You say I have been dished up to you as an anti-federalist, and ask me if it be just. My opinion was never worthy enough of notice to merit citing; but since you ask it, I will tell it to you. I am not a federalist [Liberal], because I never submitted the whole system of my opinions to the creed of any party of men whatever, in religion, in philosophy, in politics, or in anything else, where I was capable of thinking for myself. Such an addiction is the last degradation of a free and moral agent. If I could not go to heaven but with a party, I would not go there at all. Therefore, I protest to you, I am not of the party of federalists. But I am much farther from that of the anti-federalists [Conservatives].[50]

The prevalence of such early American anti-party attitudes notwithstanding, nothing, not even the efforts and wisdom of the Founding Fathers, could prevent the formation of political factions divided along sectional, cultural, and social lines, as well as various emotional, philosophical, and economic factors. Indeed, the gaping hole left by the Constitution concerning the nomination of candidates for governmental offices itself encouraged the formation of parties.[51] As McLaughlin writes, like it or not,

> party organizations were forming, and political prejudices and opinions were hardening in those days when the government of the new nation, peace, and domestic tranquility were at stake.[52]

Our first party, one that supported the powerful new Federal government over the sovereignty of the states, called itself "Federalist," or what we would today refer to as "Liberal." Our second emerging party, made up of those who preferred a small limited government and the associated policy of states' rights, was called by its opponents "Antifederalist,"[53] or what we would refer to as "Conservative." Of these two parties and names Van Buren says:

> When to these sources of opposition to the views of the [Liberal] party which had arrayed itself against the government of the [U.S.] Confederation [1781-1789] is added the natural and deeply seated hostility of those [Conservatives] who dissented from its views in respect to hereditary government in any form, and the suspicion of a reserved preference for such, or at least for kindred institutions, we cannot be at a loss in accounting for the origin of the first two great parties which sprang up and divided the country so soon after the establishment of our Independence.
>
> But the names by which these parties were distinguished are, it must be admitted, not so intelligible. The name of Anti-Federalists [small government Conservatives] was strangely enough given by their [Liberal] opponents to those [Conservatives] who advocated the continuance of the Union upon the principles which prevailed in its [original] establishment [as a confederacy in 1781], and according to which it was regarded as a Federal League or Alliance of Free States, upon equal terms, founded upon a compact (the Articles of Confederation) by which its conditions were regulated,—to be represented by a general Congress, authorized to consider and decide all questions appertaining to the interests of the alliance and committed to its charge, without power either to act upon the people directly or to apply force to the States, or otherwise to compel a compliance with its decrees, and without any guarantee for their execution other than the good faith of the parties to the compact.
>
> On the other hand the name of Federalists [big government Liberals] was assumed, and, what is still more extraordinary, retained by those who desired

to reduce the State governments, by the conjunction of which the Federal Union had been formed, to the condition of corporations to be intrusted with the performance of those offices only for the discharge of which a new general government might think them the appropriate functionaries; to convert the States, not perhaps in name, but practically and substantially, into one consolidated body politic, and to establish over it a government which should, at the least, be rendered independent and effective by the possession of ample powers to devise, adopt, and execute such measures as it might deem best adapted to common defense and general welfare.

That this was a signal perversion of the true relation between party names and party objects can scarcely be denied. Yet we who have, in later days, witnessed the caprices in respect to party names to which the public mind has been occasionally subjected, and the facility with which one party has, through its superior address or its greater activity, succeeded in attaching to its adversary an unsuitable and unwelcome name [that is, the Antifederalists], have not as much reason to be surprised at that perversion as had the [Conservative] men of that day who were subjected to it. The motive which operated in thus denying to men whose principles were federal [Conservative] the name which indicated them [the Federalists], and in giving it [that is, the name Federalists] to their opponents [the Liberals], must be looked for in the fact that federal [Conservative] principles were at that time favored by the mass of the people. This was well understood at the time, and was made still more apparent by the circumstance that those who really adhered to them, though compelled by the superior address of their adversaries to act under the name of Anti-Federalists [the Conservative Party of that day], maintained their ascendency in the government of the [U.S.] Confederation to its close [in 1789].

. . . It cannot be difficult to decide which of these parties was, in truth, federal, and which anti-federal, according to these authentic definitions of a federal government [in other words, the Liberal "Federalists" were actually Antifederalists and the Conservative "Antifederalists" were actually Federalists]. Between these parties, thenceforth distinguished by the misnomers of Federalists [Liberals] and Anti-Federalists [Conservatives], there was, from the close of the war to the establishment of the present government, an uninterrupted succession of partisan conflicts, in which the whole country participated.[54]

Though some historians claim that "there were no sharp party antagonisms" during the Washington administration, the facts state otherwise: not only did Jefferson, Hamilton, Madison, Elbridge Gerry, and even Washington himself believe that there were political parties at the time, but contemporary newspapers classified candidates as either "Federalists" or "Antifederalists."[55] In reality, as we have seen, "there

Elbridge Gerry.

were, even before Washington's election, two distinct and widely diverging political parties,"[56] which had already become evident at the 1787 Philadelphia Convention.[57]

Whatever the exact date of their respective births, from the start these two sparring groups operated more from passion and mutual hatred than from reason and political idealism, with an agenda seemingly aimed solely at the total destruction of the opposing party. Jefferson, for example, a pacifistic intellectual, wrote the following to Levi Lincoln concerning the countless savage insults he had received from Federalists (Liberals):

> I shall take no other revenge than by a steady pursuit of economy and peace, and by the establishment of republican principles in substance and in form, to sink Federalism into an abyss from which there will be no resurrection.[58]

Jefferson's hatred for his Liberal counterparts is obvious. The friction between them was so severe that it was said that no matter what area of life, from business to religion, men had separated themselves into Antifederalist (Conservative) and Federalist (Liberal) groups. The bitterness and hostility was such that many drank in separate taverns.[59] Of this period Brown writes:

> The [Liberal] advocates of a central national authority soon became known as Federalists. The opposite party [the Conservatives] took the name of Republicans, or Democrats, or Democrat-Republicans, Thomas Jefferson leading the latter, and Alexander Hamilton the former of these then recognized divisions of the political sentiment of the country. These new parties, though they did not possess the advantages of organization and the means of support which are so readily obtainable at the present day, nevertheless grew apace and shared the public confidence. They had their separate candidates for the Presidency and for the different State offices, and their party leaders in the Senate and House of Representatives.
> . . . Other issues began to arise between these parties of a commercial, economic, and diplomatic nature. There was much party bitterness, and malice even, manifested in the literature and discussions of the partisans of the day; a wholesale detraction of their opponents and a general disregard for

truth and common courtesy were the chief vices of the politicians of that period; but there was comparatively little of that tendency, afterwards exhibited in so many forms, to make merchandise of the powers and resources of the State and of the rights of individual citizens.[60]

Early American scenes.

As today, early American party lines fell largely along sectional lines, with most of the Federalists living in the North and most of the Antifederalists living in the South.[61] This is exactly what one would expect, since, from the beginning, the two regions have been described as "separate civilizations,"[62] whose citizens spoke, thought, believed, dressed, and acted differently,[63] producing "two systems of social and economic life, which had engendered two systems of political theory," one conservative, one liberal. In short, the South and the North represented two "irreconcilable, reciprocally contemptuous, mutually destructive" political factions;[64] factions which themselves were described as "clannish, selfish, and exclusive to a marked degree."[65] Should anyone be surprised that the conservative South seceded from the liberal North, or that Southern Conservatives and Northern Liberals eventually ended up going to war against one another in 1861? This regional separation over politics, as well as the subsequent cascade of Southern state secessions beginning in 1860, was predicted as early as 1792, when Abigail Adams wrote to her sister on April 20:

> I firmly believe if I live ten years longer I shall see a division of the Southern and Northern states, unless candor and less intrigue, of which I have no hopes, should prevail.[66]

As that very war was drawing to a close in early 1865, Confederate President Jefferson Davis would verbalize the anti-North sentiment that Conservative Southerners had been expressing for generations:

I can have no common country with the Yankees. My life is bound up with the Confederacy. If any man supposes that under any circumstances I can be an agent of the reconstruction of the Union, he mistakes every element of my nature. With the Confederacy I will live or die.[67]

In 1790, North Carolina Senator Samuel Johnston reported on the intense sectionality that had already begun to emerge, and which was growing more rampant each year:

The House of Representatives having taken up most of the business recommended by the President [Washington], there has not yet been much debating in the Senate. In some few instances where there has, it would appear that the sentiments of the Northern or Eastern [Liberals], and Southern members [Conservatives] constantly clash, even when focal interests are out of the question. This is a thing I cannot account for; even the lawyers from these different quarters cannot agree on the principles and construction of law, though they agree among themselves.[68]

That same year a Southern Federalist, North Carolina Congressman John Steele, wrote:

The Gentlemen from the Eastern States [that is, Northern states] differ from us in sentiments so much, on the excise bill and some others, and seem to be so unacquainted, or so regardless of the interests, the situation, the feelings, and I might add the poverty of the people in the Southern States, that there is little prospect of doing anything this Session that will terminate for the good of the whole.[69]

John Steele.

Of our perpetual American sectionalism Harvey writes:

> It was shown in the Convention of 1787, which framed the Constitution; it
> revealed itself in the Missouri admission discussion of 1819-21, in the middle
> of the period of treacherous surface calm called the "era of good feeling"; it
> was shown in the Democratic Convention of 1844, which defeated Van Buren
> for the presidency, and then and there helped to sow the wind out of which
> grew the whirlwind of the Charleston Convention sixteen years later; it
> caused the war with Mexico in 1846-48, and the contest against the admission
> of California that forced the compromise of 1850; it cut off the Southern
> section from the Whig party [Liberals] in 1852, and prepared the way for the
> party's destruction through the Kansas-Nebraska act of 1854; it erected what
> was virtually a geographical line in the vote on [Nathaniel P.] Banks for the
> speakership and [James] Buchanan for the presidency in 1856, a line which
> was made sharper and clearer in the canvass of 1860; it split the Democracy
> in that year and excluded it from the presidency for a quarter of a century; it
> caused eleven States to endeavor to get out of the Union, precipitated the
> war, put a solid South and a solid North in politics, and kept them in until
> 1895.[70]

In a word, hatred of the opposing faction is what distinguished our first
two political parties.[71] And here is why.

Federalists (Liberals) thought the Constitution was too weak,[72]
wanted to centralize or consolidate all political power in Washington,
D.C., and even eliminate the very concept of "states."[73] Antifederalists
(Conservatives), however, held that the Constitution was too strong, and
believed in decentralizing or diffusing the power of the national
government and giving it to the states.[74] Let us note here that Thomas
Jefferson and other early Conservatives viewed the original states as
individual "nations,"[75] independent self-governing countries operating
within the framework of the U.S.A., a government purposefully created
by the Founding Fathers as a *voluntary*[76] "Confederate Republic,"[77] and
which Jefferson rightfully referred to as "the world's best hope" for
happiness and prosperity.[78] He went on to explain the Antifederalist
(Conservative) position this way: "I would rather be exposed to the
inconveniences attending too much liberty than those attending too small
a degree of it."[79]

Some of the Liberal (or left-leaning) Federalists who supported the
new U.S. Constitution and, by association, big government, were
George Washington, Alexander Hamilton, Edmund Pendleton, John

Marshall, Henry "Light-horse Harry" Lee, Bushrod Washington, Richard Bassett, Gunning Bedford, John Blair, George Clymer, William R. Davie, Jonathan Dayton, Oliver Ellsworth, Thomas Fiztsimons, Nathaniel Gorham, Jared Ingersoll, Rufus King, William S. Johnson, James McHenry, Thomas Mifflin, Gouverneur Morris, Robert Morris, William Paterson, Charles C. Pinckney, George Read, John Rutledge, Roger Sherman, Caleb Strong, and James Wilson.[80]

Conservative (or right-leaning) Antifederalists who did not support, or at least questioned, the new Constitution, and were thus proponents of small government, included Thomas Jefferson, Patrick Henry, George

John Dickinson.

Mason, James Madison, James Monroe, John Tyler, John Dickinson, Richard Henry Lee, Elbridge Gerry, John Langdon, Pierce Butler, William Grayson, William Few, Alexander Martin, John Mercer, George Wythe, John Lansing, Luther Martin, Edmund J. Randolph, Robert Yates, and Benjamin Harrison.[81]

When the Bill of Rights, with its Ninth and Tenth Amendments (restricting the scope and power of the Federal government), was later added to the Constitution in 1789, most of the Antifederalists, such as Jefferson, began to grudgingly give their support to the document. This, our country's first official battle between Conservatives and Liberals, was, as one historian aptly described it, "truly a war of giants."[82]

This great political war did not end with the final ratification of the Bill of Rights in 1791, however. It is simply not in the nature of either true Conservatives or true Liberals to live harmoniously with one another, for their doctrines, beliefs, and principles are utterly incompatible. Thus, they are each compelled to scrap, claw, and fight in order to crush the opposing side. This is precisely what occurred that year, as the two parties became evermore mature, sectional, structured, concretized, and polarizing.[83] Jefferson himself once admitted:

The opinions of men are as various as their faces, and they will always find some rallying principle or point at which those nearest to it will unite, reducing themselves to two stations, under a common name for each. These stations, or camps, will be formed of very heterogeneous materials, combining from very different motives, and with very different views.[84]

Just what did the two main early American parties stand for?

The 18th-Century Federalists, headed by monarchist Alexander Hamilton, were akin to our modern day Democrats; elitist Liberals who held a loose interpretation, and a generally negative view, of the Constitution,[85] and believed that the common man was not intelligent or educated enough to govern his own life, and therefore needed the full assistance of the central government from cradle to grave. Neither was the average individual, so they claimed, capable of holding political office.[86] Such important positions must never be given to the "rabble," but should only be filled by those who are "qualified"; that is, college educated Liberals and left-wing intellectuals, the one and only proven arbiters of matters concerning government, business, the military, money, education, health, housing, and transportation. Of the Liberals or Federalists Hopkins writes:

Federalist Alexander Hamilton, an early American Liberal.

Those retaining the name of "Federalist" were extremists, and inclined to favor the establishment of a monarchy. John Adams declared that the British Constitution would be the most perfect if some of its defects and abuses were corrected. Hamilton went farther, and expressed his conviction that, as it stood, the British system was the most perfect ever devised, and that the correction of its vices would impair its power. He may not have wished a monarchy to be established here,—as many believed,—but he certainly advocated incorporating in the Constitution monarchic features.

. . . There were many with Adams who, if not monarchists, were earnestly in favor of perpetuating an aristocracy, and their action in forming the Constitution was colored by those views. They wanted the President to be called "Excellency," or "His Highness, President of the United States and Protector of their liberties." Jefferson, Samuel Adams,—John's cousin,—and those of their school, were opposed to all titles—even that of Esquire.[87]

In short, fearing anarchy, Federalists, an essentially pessimistic uninspired party, supported order at the expense of personal liberty.[88] Hence, they trusted only the privileged propertied classes, whom they expected to rule over a strongly consolidated centralized government.[89] As Wilson writes:

> Hamilton had no faith that the experiment of a government resting on the people could succeed. He aimed to make it rest on capital, seeking by his "financial policy," as a recent biographer, Mr. [Henry Cabot] Lodge, states it, "to bind the existing class of wealthy men, being, at that day, the aristocracy bequeathed by provincial times, to the new system, and thus, if at all, assure to the property of the country the control of the government."[90]

Republican Thomas Jefferson, age 35, an early American Conservative.

The 18th-Century Antifederalists, headed by Conservative Thomas Jefferson, of course, maintained the opposite view. Man, they believed, was perfectly capable of managing his own affairs, fully able to live under self-government.[91] McMillan comments:

> The [Antifederalists] . . . or Conservative party sought to strengthen the States as the best bulwarks of popular liberty. As it wished to preserve the greatest degree of liberty to the people, so it sought to repose many important powers which were necessary to government, in those agencies which were nearest to the people.[92]

Embracing a strict interpretation and positive view of our country's most sacred document, the Conservative Antifederalists

> intended that the Constitution which they were forming should rest equally and justly as to benefits and burdens on all the people; that there should be no privileged classes; that the machinery of government should not be wrested from its only rightful purpose, the common protection of all citizens, to add to the power and wealth of a limited number. Other governments had sought to keep the great masses of the people at unremitting labor by taking from them as from bees all their earnings beyond a scanty subsistence. Our Constitution was to establish a government resting on absolute [political] equality of citizenship.[93]

In essence, the Antifederalists, an energetic optimistic party,[94] fearing tyranny, supported personal liberty at the expense of governmental control.[95]

The Conservative doctrines of Jeffersonianism are alive and well to this day. Here, in an 1883 political cartoon, we see the various factions of the Democratic Party (then Conservative) splitting apart under "The Banner of Jeffersonian Principles."

It was in this heated atmosphere that the followers of Hamilton (known as "Hamiltonians") bestowed upon themselves the grand party designation "Federalists," after the Federalists of 1787, who had overseen the U.S.A. under the Articles of Confederation (1781-1789).[96] But this name had nothing to do with true Federal principles or policies. It was merely an intentional and prestigious misnomer meant to fool the public into thinking that Federalists were pro-Constitution and anti-government, when they were actually anti-Constitution and pro-government. This monarchical group also arrogantly invented the name for their opposition, the "Antifederalists," an attempt to discredit the conservative followers of Jefferson (known as "Jeffersonians") as "anti-Constitutionalists." The lie was exposed when Conservatives, lovers of the original U.S. Confederate Republic (1781-1789),[97] rejected this slanderous name and took on a more appropriate title, "Democratic-Republicans,"[98] for they were authentic supporters of the idea of republicanism, a government of, by, and for the people, making them the first true democrats.[99] Of this name Hopkins says:

> As many of the Anti-Federalists [Conservatives] had surrendered their views in order to secure the adoption of the Constitution, so now many of the leading Federalists [Liberals] joined with their former opponents to resist the aggrandizement of power in the general government. Under the leadership of Mr. Jefferson, they formed the new and distinctive organization called the Democratic-Republican party, which name has been retained through all the succeeding years, except that in 1825 the co-title, Republican, was dropped; and thenceforward the simpler name—Democratic—designated the [Conservative] party of strict constructionists founded by Jefferson. The original name, "Democratic-Republican" continued in use in some States, notably in Pennsylvania, until about 1840.[100]

It is important to note here that at that time the name of Jefferson's Conservative party, the Democratic-Republicans,

> was abbreviated into Democrats and Republicans, the latter used almost exclusively by members of the party itself, and the former by their adversaries, often with the adjectives "vile," "wild," or "Jacobinical" prefixed.[101]

It was due to this very opprobrium, a negative connotation that had been attached to the word "Democrat," that it fell into disrepute during the French Revolution (1789-1799), and which caused it to be dropped from the party name soon afterward,[102] not to be used again until the rise of right-leaning Andrew Jackson during the election of 1828.[103] Thus it is that most historians today refer to Jefferson's Democratic-Republicans as simply "Republicans," a party whose "primary object was the defense of unsurrendered rights against the monocratic doctrines and measures of the Federalists [that is, Liberals]."[104]

Monticello, the home of Thomas Jefferson.

In 1915 historian Allen Johnson noted of this period:

Party organization was visible only in its most rudimentary form—a leader and a personal following. The machinery of a modern party organization did not come into existence until the railroad and the steamboat tightened the bonds of intercourse between State and State, and between community and community.

In another respect political parties of the Federalist period [1789-1801] differed from later political organizations. Under stress of foreign complications, Federalists [Liberals] and Republicans [Conservatives] were forced into an irreconcilable antagonism. The one group [the former] was thought to be British in its sympathies, the other [the latter] Gallic [French]. In the eyes of his opponents, the Republican was no better than a democrat, a Jacobin, a revolutionary incendiary; and the Federalist no better than a monocrat and a Tory. The effect was denationalizing. Each lost confidence in the other's Americanism.

The Federalists [Liberals], in control of the Executive—and thus, in the common phrase, "in power"—were disposed to view the [Conservative] opposition as factious, if not treasonable. [George] Washington deprecated the spirit of party and thought it ought not to be tolerated in a popular government. Fisher Ames expressed a common Federalist [Liberal] conviction when he wrote in 1796: "It is a childish comfort that many enjoy, who say the minority aim at place only, not at the overthrow of government. They aim at setting mobs above law, not at the filling places which have known legal responsibility. The struggle against them is therefore *pro arts et focis* ["for God and country"]; it is for our rights and liberties." . . . Under these circumstances, when, in the minds of those in authority, party was identified with faction . . .[105]

These two factions or parties—the Liberal Federalists representing the privileged class, financial interests, and nationalism, and the Conservative Republicans representing the people, agrarian interests, and states' rights[106]—were by now "fast crystallizing into rival armies."[107] Wilson describes the political situation at the time:

Jefferson has said: "Men by their constitutions are naturally divided into two parties: those who fear and distrust the people, and wish to draw all power from them into the hands of the higher classes [that is, Liberals]; [and] those who identify themselves with the people, have confidence in them, cherish and consider them as the most honest and safe, although not the most wise depository of the public interests [that is, Conservatives]. In every country these two parties exist. In every one where they are free to speak and write they will declare themselves."

George Bancroft.

[Historian George] Bancroft has used similar language: "The one [party, the Conservative Republicans,] held to what was established, and made changes only from necessity, the other [party, the Liberal Federalists,] welcomed reform, and went out to meet it; the one [Federalists] anchored on men of property, the other [Republicans] on the mass of the people; the one [Federalist] loving liberty was ever anxious for order, the other [Republican] firmly attached to order, which it never doubted its power to maintain, was mainly anxious for freedom."

The two parties had now declared themselves: The one anchored on property, the other on the people. The one [Federalists] distrusted the people, and wished to draw power from them into the hands of the higher classes; the other [Republicans] confided in the people, and sought to keep all power in their control. Of the one Hamilton was the leader, of the other Jefferson was the leader. Behind the former were to be found the friends of strong [centralized big] government; behind the latter the friends of popular [limited small] government.[108]

As was to be expected, party rivalry "soon resulted in bitter personal hostility," each distrusting and fearing the other. Big government Liberal Hamilton began viciously attacking small government Conservative Jefferson in vindictive language. Jefferson responded to his arch nemesis this way:

Hamilton's system [of Liberal policies] flowed from principles adverse to liberty and was calculated to undermine and demolish the Republic by creating an influence of his department over the members of the legislature. If what was actually done begot uneasiness in those who wished for virtuous government, what was further proposed was not less threatening to the friends of the Constitution [the Conservatives]. From a report on the subject of manufactures (still to be acted upon) it was expressly assumed that the general government has a right to exercise all powers which may be for the general welfare; that is to say, all the legitimate powers of government; since no government has a legitimate right to do what is not for the welfare of the governed.

There was indeed a sham limitation of the universality of this power to cases where money is to be employed. But about what is it that money cannot be employed? Thus the object of these plans taken together is to draw all the powers of government into the hands of the general legislature, to establish means for corrupting a sufficient corps in that legislature to divide the honest votes and preponderate by their own the scale which suited, and to have the corps under the command of the Secretary of the Treasury for the purpose of subverting, step by step, the principles of the Constitution, which he has so often declared [by Liberals] to be "a thing of nothing, which must be changed."[109]

The house where Alexander Hamilton was born, Nevis Island, St. Croix.

In a 1792 letter to then U.S. President George Washington, Jefferson, the founder, inspirer, and counselor of the Republican Party,[110] described his organization as "that which seeks to preserve the government in its present form."[111] Some 75 years later, these exact words would be the rallying cry of the Southern Confederacy, the conservative Victorian descendants of Jefferson and the original Republican Party. Their enemy? The Northern Union, the liberal Victorian descendants of Alexander Hamilton and the Federalist Party.

Thus, by our second election in 1792, the year of Washington's second inauguration, America's two main parties—constructed around the personalities and beliefs of Jefferson and Hamilton—were well established. Pro-South Conservative John H. Moore writes:

> [Conservatives] Mr. Madison and Mr. Jefferson insisted upon a strict construction of the Constitution; [Liberal] Mr. Hamilton by his candid declaration, if you please, said he ignored it, and gave as his reason its weakness and worthlessness. By his industry and personal influence Hamilton rallied around him men who, infused with the same [left-wing] spirit, waged war with relentless fury upon the [Conservative] party [the Antifederalists or Republicans] which contended for the federal nature of the government of the union. They (Mr. Hamilton's party, known as the Federal Party) contended for a union, ignoring the Constitution in its meaning as the bond of true union. It was evidently his purpose to form a nation, though he well knew that purpose was repudiated by the convention that framed the Constitution. He acted and taught that the federal government was over the States, when

he knew, better than any man of his day, that the document which gave the federal government existence made it plain that it was a government between the States. The meaning given by usage and general acceptance to these two words—over and between—settles beyond any possible controversy the nature of the government of the United States. There is no national government at all by right, though there may be one by force. No such government can find existence in the Constitution of the United States. Here was the origin of the two parties in politics.

Mr. Hamilton by his example and political instructions opened in the history of our country the fountain of that vile stream known as politics, whose murky waters still flow with increasing volume and depth; whose baleful effects are felt in our day, or, changing the figure, he by his example and teaching summons from the realm of darkness that evil spirit who has corrupted public opinion until it has become fit for nothing but mischief; and too many, alas! like him, have also sworn to uphold and protect the Constitution and have not hesitated for partisan reasons to violate that oath.[112]

Our first president, Federalist George Washington, a Liberal.

Ironically, Washington himself, who had been against the very idea of political divisions, did not belong to either party and "had kept aloof from both and honestly endeavored to rise an impartial judge over their contests, the bitterness of which he always tried to moderate."[113] The politically neutral chief executive was actually instrumental in "preventing the formation of national parties" during his tenure,[114] retiring from office once party rivalry became too rancourous.[115] Nonetheless, though our first U.S. president embraced a number of conservative ideas, he and the Fourth Congress leaned more toward the liberal side of the spectrum, and with the policies of the Washington administration having been formulated by Hamilton,[116] Washington himself is commonly labeled a "Federalist" by historians.[117]

The 1914 edition of the *Cyclopedia of American Government* gives the following description of the beginnings of the Conservative or Republican Party in 1792. The Republican Party, it asserts, like the Anti-Federalist party [Conservative] with which it is often confounded, originated in opposition. Anti-Federalism meant opposition to the adoption of the Federal Constitution; Republicanism implied opposition to the policies of the new government under the Constitution. It was the financial programme of the first Federalist [Liberal] administration and the ulterior aims of [Liberal leader] Alexander Hamilton, first Secretary of the Treasury, which aroused the doubts of those who were later known as Republicans. It was one thing to restore the public credit; it was quite another to put money into the pockets of speculators and greedy capitalists. To provide for the payment of the public debt [by the Federal government] was a laudable aim [known as "Assumption"], but to ask states which had already paid their debts to assume also the obligations of their less provident sisters was a severe strain on public altruism. Moreover, to invite men of wealth to subscribe for the stock of a national bank whose incorporation was an act of doubtful constitutionality, was to encourage, said [James] Madison, "a mere scramble for so much public plunder." "Of all the shameful circumstances of this business," continued Madison in a letter to Jefferson, "it is among the greatest to see the [Liberal] members of the legislature who were most active in pushing this job openly grasping at its emoluments."

When the Secretary of the Treasury [Hamilton] intimated in his report on manufactures that Congress might promote the general welfare by appropriating money in any way it chose, Madison definitely parted company with his former collaborator, holding that by such an interpretation of the Constitution "the government is no longer a limited one, possessing enumerated powers, but an indefinite one, subject to particular restrictions."

Jefferson had already expressed himself in a similar way, when [George] Washington had asked his opinion on the constitutionality of the proposed national bank bill. The suspicions which the, Secretary of State entertained of his brilliant colleague were deep-seated. Hamilton's well-known preference for the British constitution and his disposition to convert his secretaryship of the Treasury into a sort of chief ministerial office, confirmed Jefferson's distrust. Had he and Madison been alone in their suspicions, their misgivings would not be worth recording; but they voiced the sentiments of an increasing number of men who disliked the aristocratic tone of the new [Liberalistic] government and who believed that the group which had the President's ear were monarchists at heart.

Before the first Congress adjourned, the nucleus of [the new Conservative Republican Party] . . . was at hand and its fundamental tenet roughly foreshadowed, namely: opposition to the increase of the powers of the Federal Government through the use of implied powers and at the expense of the state governments. The appearance of the first number of the national *Gazette* under the editorship of Philip Freneau was a sign that the further conduct of the [Liberal] administration would be subjected to searching criticism. The columns of the paper had much to say about "aristocratic juntos," "ministerial systems," and the [Liberal] control of the

Government by a wealthy body of capitalists and public creditors whose interests were in opposition to those of the people. When Hamilton's paper, the *United States Gazette*, attempted to stigmatize the [Conservative] opposition as essentially Anti-Federalist, Freneau replied that only those men were true friends of the Union who adhered to a limited and republican form of government and who were ready to resist the efforts which had been made "to substitute, in the room of our equal republic, a baneful monarchy." By posing as the only staunch supporters of republicanism [conservatism], the opposition [the Liberal Federalists] secured a great tactical advantage. To call one's self emphatically a Republican [a Conservative] was to cast aspersions upon the republicanism of one's opponents.

The decision of [George] Washington to serve a second term in the presidency averted a contest for which, indeed, the Republicans were hardly prepared; yet, as Jefferson put it, "the occasion of electing a Vice-President was seized as a proper one for expressing the public sense on the doctrines of the monocrats." The Republicans supported George Clinton of New York who had been a pronounced Anti-Federalist [Conservative]. Yet Jefferson was careful to distinguish between Republicans "who wish to preserve the government in its present form" [that is, true Conservatives] and those Anti-Federalists "who, though they dare not avow it, are opposed to any general government" [that is, anarchists]. The public sense, however, was more effectively expressed in the congressional elections which secured to the opposition the control of the next House. The [Liberal Federalist] party had not advanced beyond a negative program.[118]

The "Hamilton Float" in a parade in 1788 celebrating the ratification of the U.S. Constitution.

The year 1794 brought only an intensification of the massive political divide represented by the two great Founding Fathers, one conservative, one liberal:

> Jefferson and Hamilton, both members of Washington's Cabinet, had not agreed upon the form of government. Now that the Constitution had been adopted and was in full operation, they differed widely upon the proper construction of that instrument. [Conservative] Jefferson was for a strict construction, and for limiting the power of the Federal Government to that plainly conferred by the organic law. [Liberal] Hamilton wanted the general government to assume and exercise all powers which the most liberal construction would sanction. Hamilton advocated and Jefferson opposed, on the constitutional ground that it was the exercise of unwarranted powers, the incorporation of the Philadelphia Bank. Hamilton favored and Jefferson opposed any legislation which might tend to create or encourage monopolies. These two able and distinguished men were the founders of the two schools of thought which, to a great extent, divided the people in their day, and for many years thereafter, and in some degree even to the present.[119]

Our second president, Federalist John Adams, a Liberal.

In our third election in 1796, Washington's successor, John Adams, became our second chief executive. President Adams also veered to the left politically, and was a member of the Federalist Party,[120] or what we would now call the Democratic Party. He served one term, from 1797 to 1801, during which time the words "Democrat" and "Republican" came into common usage in everyday conversation, personal letters, and political speeches as organization names—revealing a thriving two-party system.[121]

That same year, on April 24, a troubled Jefferson wrote a letter to Philip Mazzei, noting the drastic swing toward liberalism in the U.S. government. The following excerpt provides a dramatic illustration of the partisanship already well developed at the time between the Antifederalists (Conservatives) and Federalists (Liberals):

> The aspect of our politics has wonderfully changed since you left us [said

sarcastically]. In place of that noble love of liberty and republican [Conservative] Government which carried us triumphantly through the [Revolutionary] war, an Anglican, Monarchical and Aristocritical party [the Liberal Federalists] has sprung up, whose avowed object is to draw over us the substance, as they have already done the forms, of the British government. The main body of our citizens, however, remain true to their republican [Conservative] principles. The whole landed interest is republican [Conservative], and so is a great mass of talent. Against us are the Executive, the Judiciary, two out of three branches of the legislature, all the officers of the government, all who want to be officers, all timid men [Liberals] who prefer the calm of despotism to the boisterous sea of liberty, British merchants, and Americans trading on British capitals, speculators, and holders in the banks and public funds,—a contrivance invented for the purpose of corruption, and for assimilating us in all things to the rotten as well as the sound parts of the [Liberal] British model.

It would give you a fever were I to name to you the apostates who have gone over to these heresies; men who were Samsons in the field, and Solomons in the council, but who have had their heads shorn by the harlot [monarchical] England. In short, we [Conservatives] are likely to preserve the liberty we have obtained only by unremitting labors and perils. But we shall preserve them; and our mass of weight and wealth on the good side is so great as to leave no danger that force will ever be attempted against us. We have only to awake and snap the Liliputian cords [of the Liberal Federalists] with which they have been entangling us during the first sleep which succeeded our labors.[122]

Our third president, Republican Thomas Jefferson, a Conservative.

In 1798, during the second year of President John Adams' tenure, he passed the first of a number of Alien and Sedition Acts, instigating the first organized states' rights movement under the U.S. Constitution. This stimulated sectionalism while helping our third president, Thomas Jefferson, win our fourth election in 1800. In the meantime, by the year 1801 the Liberals (Federalists), having been "gradually diminished by the force of public opinion,"[123] were now out of power in every branch of government except the judiciary. The remaining members, however, continued to use the name "Federalist Party."[124]

As we have seen, Jefferson—who served two terms, from 1801 to 1809—was not only a Republican and thus a Conservative at the time, he was the founder of that party, then officially known as the Democratic-Republican Party.[125] In stark contrast to the England-loving Federalists, who desired an all powerful, monarchy-style Federal government based on aristocracy (and who modeled their contributions to the U.S. Constitution on

"Classical Liberal" John Locke, a left-leaning Conservative.

the ideas of English philosopher John Locke),[126] the France-loving Republicans (who modeled their contributions to the U.S. Constitution on the ideas of French political scholar Baron de Montesquieu)[127] desired a government built on the Gallic notions of "liberty, equality, and fraternity,"[128] or what Jefferson referred to as "republican simplicity,"[129] with political power resting in the hands of the working class majority.[130] Accordingly, he humbly saw himself as nothing more than a private citizen who had become the "chief magistrate of a free country."[131]

As evidence, on March 4, 1801, an English tourist watched Jefferson arrive to deliver his First Inaugural Address at Washington, D.C., and described the momentous occasion like this:

> He came . . . without ostentation. His dress was of plain cloth, and he rode on horseback to the Capitol, without a single guard or even a servant in his train, dismounted without assistance, and hitched the bridle of his horse to the palisades.[132]

During his famous speech Jefferson tried to pacify the growing tensions between the two parties, while simultaneously discussing the form of government preferred by Conservatives, or as they were then known, Republicans:

> We have called by different names brethren of the same principle. We are all republicans—all federalists. If there be any among us who would wish

to dissolve this union, or to change its republican form, let them stand undisturbed as monuments of the safety with which error of opinion may be tolerated where reason is left free to combat it. I know, indeed, that some honest men fear that a republican [Conservative] government cannot be strong; that this government is not strong enough. But would the honest patriot, in the full tide of successful experiment, abandon a government which has so far kept us free and firm, on the theoretic and visionary fear that this government, the world's best hope, may, by possibility, want energy to preserve itself? I trust not; I believe this, on the contrary, [to be] the strongest government on earth. I believe it the only one where every man, at the call of the law, would fly to the standard of the law, and would meet invasions of the public order, as his own personal concern. Sometimes it is said that man cannot be trusted with the government of himself—Can he then be trusted with the government of others? Or have we found angels in the form of kings to govern him? Let history answer the question.

Let us then, with courage and confidence, pursue our own federal and republican principles; our attachment to union and representative

Baron de Montesquieu inspired the Conservative Founding Fathers to form the U.S. as a confederacy.

government. Kindly separated by nature, and a wide ocean, from the exterminating havoc of one quarter of the globe [that is, the overbearing monarchy, Great Britain]; too high-minded to endure the degradations of the others; possessing a chosen Country, with room enough for descendants to the thousandth and thousandth generation; entertaining a due sense of our equal right to the use of our own faculties, to the acquisition of our own industry, to honour and confidence from our fellow citizens, resulting not from birth, but from our actions, and their sense of them; enlightened by a benign religion, professed indeed and practised in various forms, yet all of them inculcating honesty, truth, temperance, gratitude, and the love of man; acknowledging and adoring an over-ruling Providence, which by all its dispensations proves that it delights in the happiness of man here, and his greater happiness hereafter; with all these blessings, what more is necessary to make us a happy and prosperous people?

Still one thing more, fellow citizens; a wise and frugal government, which restraining men from injuring one another, shall leave them otherwise free to regulate their own pursuits of industry and improvement, and shall not take from the mouth of labour the bread it has earned [promoted by Liberalism and Socialism]. This is the sum of good [Conservative] government; and this is necessary to close the circle of our felicities.

About to enter, fellow citizens, on the exercise of duties, which comprehend everything dear and valuable to you, it is proper you should understand what I deem the essential principles of our government, and consequently those which ought to shape its administration. I will compress them within the narrowest compass they will bear, stating the general principle, but not all its limitations: equal and exact justice to all men, of whatever state or persuasion, religious or political; peace, commerce, and honest friendship with all nations; entangling alliances with none; the support of the state governments in all their rights, as the most competent administration for our domestic concerns, and the surest bulwarks against anti-republican [that is, Liberal] tendencies: the preservation of the general government in its whole constitutional vigour, as the sheet-anchor of our peace at home, and safety abroad; a jealous care of the right of election by the people; a mild and safe corrective of abuses which are lopped by the sword of revolution, where peaceable remedies are unprovided; absolute acquiescence in the decisions of the majority, the vital principle of republics, from which is no appeal but to force, the vital principle and immediate parent of despotism; a well-disciplined militia, our best reliance in peace, and for the first moments of war, till regulars may relieve them; the supremacy of the civil over the military authority; economy in the public expense, that

Jefferson held that only conservative principles could lead to American "peace, liberty, and safety."

labour may be lightly burthened; the honest payment of our debts, and sacred preservation of the public faith; encouragement of agriculture, and of commerce, as its hand maid; the diffusion of information, and arraignment of all abuses at the bar of public reason; freedom of religion, freedom of the press, and freedom of the person, under protection of the *habeas corpus*; and trial by juries impartially selected.

These [Conservative] principles form the bright constellation which has gone before us, and guided our steps through an age of revolution and reformation. The wisdom of all our sages, and blood of our heroes, have been devoted to their attainment; they should be the creed of our political faith; the text of civic instruction, the touchstone by which to try the services of those we trust; and, should we wander from them in moments of error or of alarm, let us hasten to retrace our steps, and regain the road which alone leads to peace, liberty, and safety.[133]

Revealingly, after his inauguration, our informal third president, who vigorously shunned pomp and ceremony, walked back to his boarding house on foot and sat at the "common table" for dinner.[134]

As he did not capitalize the words, what Jefferson meant exactly by his famous statement, "we are all republicans—all federalists," has been the subject of much debate over the last two centuries, calling into question whether individual parties existed at the time. However, let us survey several letters he penned around the same period, the first which he wrote to John Dickinson on March 6, 1801, only two days afterward:

> The tough sides of our Argosie have been thoroughly tried. Her strength has stood the waves into which she was steered [by the Liberal Federalists], with a view to sink her. We shall now put her upon her Republican [Conservative] tack, and she will now show, by the beauty of her motion, the skill of her builders.[135]

A few weeks later, on March 21, Jefferson included the following comments in a letter to Dr. Joseph Priestley:

> I have been, above all things, solaced by the prospect which opened on us, in the event of a non-election of a President, in which case the federal government would have been in the situation of a clock or a watch run down. There was no idea of force, nor any occasion for it. A convention invited by the Republican [Conservative] members of Congress, with the virtual President and Vice-President, would have been on the ground in eight weeks, would have repaired the constitution where it was defective, and wound it up again.[136]

Early American "classical Liberal" or Conservative, Dr. Joseph Priestly, famed historian, chemist, philosopher, and Unitarian.

In another epistle addressed to John Dickinson, Jefferson makes obvious reference to the Federalists:

They retired into the judiciary as a stronghold. There the remains of Federalism [here, loosely Liberalism] are to be preserved and fed from the treasury; and from that battery all the works of Republicanism [Conservatism] are to be beaten down and erased.[137]

Our fourth president, Republican James Madison, a Conservative.

It is clear from these passages alone (and there are many others),[138] that from the beginning of his presidency on, Jefferson recognized two distinct political parties. As for his "we are all" Inaugural statement, he was merely commenting on the fact that, despite their differences, members of both the Republican Party and the Federalist Party generally supported the idea of a republican government—even if they had very different ideas on how it should be operated.

The 1804 election, our fifth, gave Jefferson his second term, and by 1806 some began calling the Republican Party the Democratic Party, but it was not official, and the original title remained.[139]

Our fourth president, James Madison, elected in 1808 (our sixth election) and again in 1812 (our seventh), was a Conservative, and so a confirmed Republican. During his two terms in office, 1809 to 1817, he was benefitted by a Republican majority in both Houses.[140]

James Monroe, our fifth president, was elected twice: once in 1816 (our eighth election) and again in 1820 (our ninth). It was during the former year that Rufus King of New York became the last presidential candidate presented by the Federalists.[141] Why? Let us pause to look at this significant event in U.S. history.

After the American victory at the Battle of New Orleans in January 1815, patriotism swept the land under the Madison administration, and the Federalist Party (Liberal)—which had refused to back the U.S. in the war, had given succor to the enemy, endorsed the unpopular Alien and Sedition Acts,[142] and had even threatened to split up the Union by supporting the secessionist Hartford Convention (1814-1815)—was discredited, mocked, and condemned.[143]   Charged with being "unpatriotic,"[144] and not understanding how to properly use the caucus system,[145] as a result, by 1820 the entire party had gone extinct,[146] a victim of its own liberal excesses.

Continuing, President Monroe, a Conservative, that is, a member of the Republican Party, served his two terms from 1817 to 1825. With "no divisions of parties in this administration," "nearly all citizens called themselves Republicans." Hence the popular nickname for Monroe's eight year tenure: "The Era of Good Feeling." Indeed, there were no candidates nominated in 1821, the start of Monroe's second term. Without opposition, Monroe simply received the unanimous vote of the electors.[147]

Our fifth president, Republican James Monroe, a Conservative, presided over a unique period in American history: "The Era of Good Feeling."

Nonetheless, Liberals were alive and well, pushing, as they always do, for more control of the people and for bigger and bigger government. One of these was the left-leaning Kentuckian Henry Clay, "a convert to theories and measures hostile to the earliest and most cherished principles of the old Republican party."[148] The progressive statesman (one of whose posthumous biographers was, revealingly, radical socialist Forty-Eighter Carl Schurz)[149] was now beginning to develop and refine his leftist "American System,"[150] along with his Tariff and Internal Improvements program,[151] the latter which today we refer to as the "corporate welfare system."[152] Of this Southern Liberal it has been truly said:

No one pleaded more eloquently for a larger conception of the functions of the National Government than Clay.[153]

Though it had been addressed earlier by Presidents Washington, Adams, and Jefferson, it was under President Monroe that the U.S. issued one of its most important principles: The Monroe Doctrine (actually part of a larger speech), which stated that the U.S. would no longer permit colonization, or even interference, by European countries anywhere in the Americas.[154]

The "good feeling" of party unification that permeated America during the Monroe administration was not to last, of course. With our upcoming tenth election in 1824, the battle over his successor began to split the Republican Party in two: one group supporting John Quincy Adams, and thus known as "the Adams men," the other siding with Andrew Jackson, and thus known as "the Jackson men." Both camps continued to call themselves Republicans. However, to distinguish themselves from one another, the more liberal branch, the Adams men (who revered Federalist Hamilton), took on the title the "National Republicans,"[155] while the more conservative branch, the Jackson men (who venerated Republican Jefferson),

Our sixth president, left-leaning John Quincy Adams, switched parties at least five times, four of them which were Liberal. During his one term in the White House, however, he belonged to the Republican or Conservative Party of Jefferson.

took on the title the "Democratic-Republicans,"[156] the original name of Jefferson's party.[157]

John Quincy Adams (the son of our third president, John Adams) won, becoming our sixth president, serving one term, from 1825 to 1829. A left-leaning National Republican—in reality, a Federalist Liberal of sorts, who changed parties numerous times—Adams had the misfortune of being in office when debate over the Tariff of 1828 arose. This sectional bill, which unfairly taxed the South, created additional friction between the North and Dixie, helping lay the groundwork for the coming "Civil War" in 1861.[158] It was rightfully nicknamed the "Tariff of Abominations."[159] But it was nowhere near as abominable as what was to come under the reign of our future Liberal presidents.

Z

FROM JACKSON TO BUCHANAN 1828 TO 1868

I T WAS DURING THE ELECTION of 1828, our eleventh quadrennial election, just prior to John Quincy Adams leaving office in early 1829, that one of the most significant events in the history of our two party system occurred. Regarding so-called "Southern slavery" that year, Thomas Hart Benton writes:

> There was no jealousy, or hostile, or aggressive spirit in the North at that time against the South![160]

Southern Conservative Thomas Hart Benton.

As we will see, Yankee "jealousy, hostility, and aggressiveness" would begin, however, in three short years with the publication of William Lloyd Garrison's biased, malefic, fictitious newspaper, *The Liberator*.

The National Republicans (Liberals) and the Democratic-Republicans (Conservatives) once again met on the political battlefield that year to fight over the upcoming presidential election. Adams was put back up for reelection by the former, Andrew Jackson was once again selected as the nominee by the latter; essentially a rematch between the two, carried over from the 1824 election.

Jackson, a strong states' rights Conservative who "professed the necessity of restoring the Republican principles" of Jefferson,[161] handily won both the popular vote and the electoral vote, and in 1829 he became America's seventh president. He repeated this triumph in the election of 1832 (our 12th election), ultimately serving two terms, from 1829 to 1837.[162]

For us, however, the most important result of the 1828 election, as well as the two-term Jackson administration, was that these events brought about yet another schism in the Republican Party: just as the Jeffersonian Republicans had dropped the

Our seventh president, Democrat Andrew Jackson, at that time a Conservative.

word "Democrat" from their name by the year 1799 (thus becoming the "Republican Party"), in 1828 their political descendants, Jackson's Conservative party, the Democratic-Republicans,[163] decided to drop the word "Republicans" from their name,[164] becoming simply the "Democratic Party."[165] And this is the name by which they were classified by Congress that year.[166] Of this event Curtis writes:

> Previous to the year 1828, the term "Democrat" had only been used in derision and contempt, as, for instance, when Mrs. [Martha] Washington said, finding a trace of dirt upon her wall after a reception: "It was no Federalist; none but a filthy Democrat would mark a place on the wall with his good-for nothing head in that manner."[167]

During the election of 1832, the Liberals' party, the National Republicans (originally the Federalist Party),[168] became known as the Anti-Masonic Party,[169] but by 1834 they began to go by the term "Whig."[170] The name Whig was intended to sharply contrast with what they considered to be the conservatism (or Toryism) of the Jacksonian camp,[171] to whom they gave "the offensive name of 'Tories.'"[172]

Macy gives a brief outline of the origin and development of the

American Whigs, and in so doing illustrates the complexity of the history of our two-party system, while attributing its birth to Thomas Jefferson:

> When Thomas Jefferson found himself in serious and protracted controversy with the administration of Washington [1789-1797], he encouraged the formation of Democratic [Conservative] Clubs to resist the encroachments of the central government upon local governments and upon personal liberties. These clubs were similar to the Jacobin Clubs in France and to the Patriot Societies in America. The supporters of the administration did not, to any considerable extent, organize local societies to strengthen their policy. The result was that the Republicans [Conservatives] or the party of Jefferson became locally organized throughout the land, while the Federal party [Liberals] never was thus locally organized. It was largely because of this local organization that the Republican party [Conservatives] endured and the Federal party [Liberals] became extinct.
>
> All permanent party organizations have arisen out of the [Conservative] party of Jefferson. When, during the administration of [Conservative] John Quincy Adams, a party began to be formed called National Republicans, its members were denounced as Federalists [Liberals] by their political enemies; and when, in 1834, the same party took the name Whig [Liberal], it was still denounced as Federal. This was because of the popular prejudice which was associated with the name Federalist. "To revive the ghost of Federalism" was the easiest method of bringing a party into reproach. But the Whig party [Liberal] was organized by men who had had long training in the [Conservative] party of Jefferson. The Whigs first called themselves Republicans [Liberals], and when the party went out in confusion, twenty years later, its members again found themselves enrolled either in a Republican [Liberal] or a Democratic [Conservative] party, and each of these parties claimed descent from the [Conservative] party of Jefferson. Jefferson was both a Democrat and a Republican.
>
> From the beginning of party organization he was stigmatized by his enemies as a Democrat. He called himself a Republican or a Democratic-Republican. As the term Democrat became a mark of honor rather than of reproach, it gradually superseded the earlier term. When Jefferson died, in 1826, that branch of his party which was crystallizing around the [Conservative] leadership of Andrew Jackson and Martin Van Buren commonly bore the name Democrat [Conservative]. The Whigs [Liberals] always stoutly maintained that this was not the party of Jefferson. It was in their eyes a new and dangerous party which had filched the name of the party of Jefferson. The Whigs [Liberals] themselves gloried in their alleged political descent from Jefferson. They repudiated with scorn the term Federal [a Liberal], which their enemies sought to fasten upon them. They looked with envious eyes upon the more popular name of their opponents.
>
> The first national Whig [Liberal] convention, in 1839, assumed the

official title of "Democratic Whig Convention." From this it would seem that the Whigs also wished to filch the name Democrat; but it was not long before the great body of the northern Whigs [Liberals] found themselves in full possession [in 1854] of the good old Jeffersonian name, Republican [then Liberal]. It would be a great mistake, however, to conclude that the [Conservative] party of Jefferson endured because it was more fortunate in the selection of names. It endured because it took organic form in harmony with its political environment. The Federal party [Liberals] died because it created no organs in touch with the people.[173]

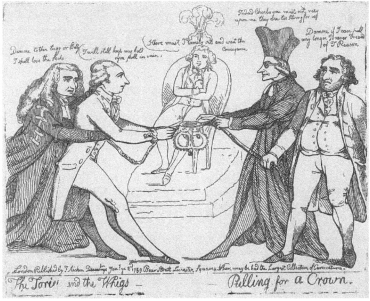

The American Whigs of 1834 took their name from the Whigs of Great Britain. In this 1789 political cartoon, titled "The Tories and the Whigs Pulling for a Crown," George, Prince of Wales, sits on his throne in the background awaiting the winner of a tug-of-war over the crown between the Tories (on the left) represented by politician Baron Edward Thurlow and politician William Pitt the Younger, and the Whigs (on the right) represented by philosopher Edmund Burke and statesman Charles James Fox.

How long can positive relations last? In politics, not very long! With two opposing parties back in the ring together in 1834, the newly emerging Whig Party officially put an end to the "Era of Good Feeling," replacing it with what one historian has well described as the "Era of Hard Feeling."[174]

The Liberals' selection of the name Whig in 1834 was no accident, as noted in the 1908 edition of the *Dictionary of the United States*:

> The name of Whigs was [first] taken by the [progressive] party in the [early American] colonies which furthered the Revolution [1775-1783], because their principles were but the application to America of those principles which the Whigs of England had advocated, and had secured through the Revolution of 1688. In [America in] 1834 the name was revived. The Federal [Federalist or Liberal] party had virtually come to an end about 1817. Henceforth all American politicians were simply Republicans. But, as will usually happen in such cases, a divergence of views developed itself within the party. [By this time, the now left-leaning John Quincy] Adams and [Henry] Clay and their [liberal] followers, on the one hand, advocated a policy of protection and Federal internal improvements [corporate welfare] and a broad or loose construction of the Constitution.

Whig Edward Everett, a Liberal.

> Others, [that is, Conservatives,] construing the Constitution strictly, opposed these things; these found a leader in [Andrew] Jackson. The former took the name of "National Republicans." Adams was their candidate in 1828. After his defeat their chief leader was Clay, whom they nominated for President in 1831. Their opposition to Jackson drew to them various elements and, as opponents of executive usurpation, the coalition took the old name of Whigs in 1834. The Whig body always formed rather a coalition than a party. They were united in opposition to Jackson, but the Northern Whigs favored the U.S. Bank, a protective tariff, etc., while the Southern Whigs were strict constructionists. In the election of 1836 these various elements supported various candidates. In that of 1840 they united upon the "available" [William Henry] Harrison, and triumphantly elected him and [John] Tyler in a campaign of unthinking enthusiasm. Harrison died, and the Whigs quarreled violently with Tyler. In 1844 they nominated their real leader, Clay, who narrowly missed election.
>
> The annexation of Texas and the Mexican War and the Wilmot Proviso now brought slavery to the front as the leading issue of politics. This was fatal to the Whigs, for it was sure to divide the Northern and Southern Whigs. In 1848 they preserved themselves temporarily by passing over Clay and [Daniel] Webster and nominating a military candidate, [Zachary] Taylor. He was elected. But when similar tactics were tried in 1852, with [Winfield] Scott, the party was decisively defeated. It was disintegrating because of the inability to maintain any opinion on slavery.

The Northern Whigs became Free-Soilers, and by 1856, Republicans [that is, Liberals]; the Southern [Whigs], Democrats [that is, Conservatives]. Many Whigs went temporarily into the American party. A small portion of them formed the Constitutional Union party, which nominated [John] Bell and [Edward] Everett in 1860. Parties became sectional, and the Whig party ceased to exist. Its chief leaders were, beside those mentioned, in the [Liberal] North: [Robert C.] Winthrop, [Rufus] Choate, [William H.] Seward, [Thurlow] Weed and [Horace] Greeley; in the [Conservative] South, [William P.] Mangum, [John M.] Berrien, [John] Forsyth, [Alexander H.] Stephens, [Robert A.] Toombs, [Seargent S.] Prentiss and [John J.] Crittenden; in the West, [John] McLean, [Joshua R.] Giddings, [Thomas] Ewing and [Thomas] Corwin.[175]

In 1854, some 25 years after Andrew Jackson's victory and the emergence of the Democrat/Whig two-party system, Conservative Southern Senator Thomas Hart Benton wrote:

The election of General Jackson was a triumph of Democratic [that is, Conservative] principle and an assertion of the people's right to govern themselves. That principle had been violated in the Presidential election in the House of Representatives in the session of 1824 and 1825, and the sanction or rebuke of that violation was a leading question in the whole canvass. It was also a triumph over the [Liberals']
protective policy, the federal internal improvement policy, the latitudinous construction of the Constitution, and of the Democracy over the Federalists [Liberals], then called National Republicans, and was the re-establishment of parties on principle, according to the landmarks of the early ages of the government. For although Mr. [John Quincy] Adams had received confidence and office from Mr. [James] Madison and Mr. [James] Monroe, and had classed with the democratic [Conservative] party during the fusion of parties in the "era of good feeling," yet he had previously been federal [Liberal]; and in the re-establishment of old party lines which began to take place after the election of Mr. Adams in the House of Representatives, his affinities, and policy, became those

Whig Robert Charles Winthrop, a Liberal.

of his former party; and as a party, with many individual exceptions, they became his supporters and his strength. General Jackson, on the contrary, had always been democratic [Conservative], so classing when he was a senator in Congress under the administration of the first Mr. Adams [John], and when party lines were most straightly drawn, and upon principle: and as such now receiving the support of men and States which took their political position at that time, and had maintained it ever since.[176]

An anti-Whig political cartoon from 1838, attacking
and abasing Whig icon Henry Clay, a Liberal.

The 1914 *Cyclopedia of American Government* makes these comments
on the Jackson administration and "the split in the Democratic-
Republican Party":

> The surprising fact revealed by the presidential vote of 1824 was the
> strength of the Jackson following, particularly in the democratic West.
> Jackson, indeed, received the highest number of electoral votes, though not
> the majority necessary for an election. The subsequent election by the House,
> of [John Quincy] Adams who stood second on the list, had momentous
> consequences. The disappointed followers of Jackson declared that the will
> of the people had been defeated. When [Henry] Clay, whose influence had
> been exerted in behalf of Adams, was given the chief post in the new Cabinet,
> Jackson himself joined in the cry of "corrupt-bargain." Jackson was at once
> renominated by his own state, and the administration of Adams became
> virtually a prolonged campaign for the presidency. In Congress every
> opportunity was seized to unite the Jackson, [William H.] Crawford and
> [John C.] Calhoun forces into a party. Though President Adams avowed bold
> doctrines of loose construction, the opposition was too little united on

principle to take issue with him on this ground. The election of 1828 involved men rather than measures. The Jackson following demanded his vindication and that of the sovereign people whose will had been defeated four years before.

Against the gathering forces of the new democracy Adams made no headway. The triumphant election of Jackson and his subsequent policy opened wide the breach in the ranks of the Democratic-Republican party. Out of the welter of factional conflict emerged eventually two parties—the National Republican [Liberal], which accepted Clay's leadership, and the Democratic party [Conservative], whose purposes and aspirations were embodied in Andrew Jackson.[177]

This 1831 engraving entitled the "AntiMasonic Apron," contrasts the Anti-Mason Party with the Masons, who assail the former's evils, including "ignorance, tyranny, anarchy, and intolerance." The Masons list their virtues, "honour, sincerity, charity, patriotism, law, order, equal rights, and fortitude," on the right.

Wilson writes of the complex makeup of the various wings and branches of the Liberal Whig Party:

According to the *Whig Almanac* for 1838 . . . the new [Whig] party was composed: (1) "Most of those, who under the name of National Republicans had previously been known as [the left-leaning] supporters of Adams and Clay, and advocates of the American system"; (2) "Most of those

[Conservatives], who acting in the defence of what they deemed or assumed the threatened rights of the States had been stigmatized as nullifiers, or the less virulent States' rights men, who were thrown into a position of armed neutrality towards the administration by the doctrines of the proclamation of 1832 against South Carolina"; (3) "A majority of those before known as Anti-Masons" [an anti-Masonic party formed in 1828 and led by Thurlow Weed and William H. Seward; in 1832 their presidential candidate William Wirt was vainly run against Jackson]; (4) "Many, who up to that time had been known as Jackson men, but who united in condemning the high-handed conduct of the executive, the immolation of [William J.] Duane and the subserviency of [Roger B.] Taney"; (5) "Numbers who had not before taken any part in politics, but who were now awakened from their apathy by the palpable usurpations of the executive and the imminent peril of our whole fabric of constitutional liberty and national prosperity."[178]

Here, under right-leaning U.S. President Andrew Jackson, we see that the Democratic Party was originally founded as a *conservative* organization in 1828, with the name becoming official by 1832. As we will discover, decades later it was this same right-wing party to which Conservative Confederate President Jefferson Davis, as well as most of the Southern population, belonged.[179]

An 1828 campaign poster of Conservative General Andrew Jackson, emphasizing his valor during the War of 1812 and his victory at New Orleans. The words at the top read: "Protector & Defender of Beauty and Booty."

The Whigs, as we shall also discuss, persisted into the 1850s, but dissolved prior to the Civil War, after which its left-wing members joined the Liberals' newly formed Republican Party (1854), the party of big government progressive Abraham Lincoln (1860). Let us bear these vital facts in mind as we continue with our study.

Our eighth president, Martin Van Buren, elected in 1836 (our 13th election), and the first president born under the U.S. Flag, was a Democrat, and thus, at the time, a Conservative. Serving one term, from 1837 to 1841, he pledged to "follow in the footsteps of his illustrious predecessor," and according to the doctrines of the democratic [Conservative] school as existing in the original formation of parties; close observance to the Federal Constitution as written; no latitudinarian [loose] construction permitted; or doubtful powers assumed; faithful adherence to all its compromises, economy in the administration of the government, peace, friendship and fair dealing with all foreign nations, entangling alliances with none.[180]

Thanks to interfering Yankees and self-righteous South-hating Liberals, during the last years of the Jackson administration an aggressive Northern abolition movement had sprung up,[181] mainly under the nefarious influence of New England busybody, ultra-left-winger, and anti-South proponent William Lloyd Garrison.[182] In reality the Northern abolition movement had nothing to do with true abolitionary sentiment: many of its white members not only abhorred their own race (a mental

Our eighth president, Democrat Martin Van Buren, at the time a Conservative.

disorder known as "ethnomasochism")[183] while pretending to worship the black one, but they also belonged to the white racist, Yankee-founded organization known as the American Colonization Society, whose primary mission was to deport all blacks in order to make America "white from coast to coast."[184] Garrison's protest against *Southern* slavery then was simply a protest against white Southerners, whom, like many Liberals (of all races) today, detested anyone of European descent, and in particular *Southerners* of European descent.

Further proof comes from the fact that the American Abolition Movement itself had begun a century earlier in the *South*—in Virginia, to be exact, where the first voluntary emancipation had taken place in 1655.[185] It was here, in Dixie, that thousands of well-known Southerners, from George Washington, James Madison, and Thomas Jefferson, to Benjamin S. Hedrick, Daniel Reaves Goodlow, and the Grimké Sisters, Sarah and Angelina, had struggled long and mightily to rid the South of the hated "peculiar institution."[186]

Despite the fact that during President Jackson's tenure the South was moving ever closer to complete abolition, in 1831 Garrison began issuing his highly antagonistic anti-South newspaper, *The Liberator*, calling

Southern slave owners "criminals"[187] and *Southern* slavery a "moral evil."[188] It did not matter to him that slavery was still legal in every state under the Constitution, that there were also thousands of *black* slave owners across America, that both the American slave trade and American slavery had gotten their start in his own home state (Massachusetts), or that his own region still possessed somewhere between 500,000 and 1 million slaves under the ownership of some 315,000 white Northern slaveholders.[189]

It was due to these very facts that Conservative Constitution-abiding President Van Buren, a Democrat, promised not to allow government interference "with slavery in the States where it existed, or in the District

New England busybody, meddler, and South-hating Liberal, William Lloyd Garrison, whose malicious and false attacks on the South paved the way for the American Civil War.

of Columbia, without the consent of those States."[190] This conservative tradition, of non-interference with constitutionally approved slavery, would carry on into the 1860s, where it was continued by the Southern Confederacy and its Democratic leader, Conservative President Jefferson Davis. Not for love of slavery, a Liberal myth, but for love of the Constitution.

By this period, the late 1830s, America had finally established a full-fledged party system, which was based on ideas formulated by the Democrats (Conservatives).[191] With national, state, county, and town parties now linked together nationwide by congressional districts, and with appointed delegates being sent to state and national conventions, the two parties were fairly well counterbalanced against one another.[192] This achievement did nothing to improve relations between Conservatives and Liberals, however, nor could our now more proportional party system prevent national disasters.

Only a year after Conservative Democratic President Van Buren's victory at the polls, the Panic of 1837 struck, a financial crisis that caused depreciation of currency, the suspension of banks, widespread unemployment, lack of consumer confidence, and a massive recession.

The masthead of Garrison's unpopular newspaper, *The Liberator*, disingenuously showing Jesus castigating a Southern slave owner. Jesus never spoke of slavery and the Bible itself condones it in countless scriptures. Additionally, slavery was still being practiced in the North by over 300,000 Yankee slaverholders.

This catastrophe gave hope to the Whigs (Liberals) that they could win the upcoming 1840 election.

In an attempt to assure Van Buren of a second term, the Democrats (Conservatives) formulated a nine-resolution platform outlining their policies, which I have provided below. This platform demonstrates the traditional conservatism of the Democratic Party in 1840:

1. That the federal government is one of limited powers, derived solely from the Constitution, and the grants of power shown therein ought to be strictly construed by all the departments and agents of the government, and that it is inexpedient and dangerous to exercise doubtful constitutional powers.

2. That the Constitution does not confer upon the general government the power to commence or carry on a general system of internal improvement [in modern terms, "corporate welfare"].

3. That the Constitution does not confer authority upon the federal government, directly or indirectly, to assume the debts of the several States [a consolidating Liberal concept known as "Assumption"], contracted for local internal improvements or other State purposes; nor would such assumption be just or expedient.

4. That justice and sound policy forbid the federal government to foster one branch of industry to the detriment of another, or to cherish the interest of one portion to the injury of another portion of our common country—that every citizen and every section of the country has a right to demand and insist upon an equality of rights and privileges, and to complete and ample protection of persons and property from domestic violence or foreign aggression.

5. That it is the duty of every branch of the government to enforce and practice the most rigid economy in conducting our public affairs, and that no

more revenue ought to be raised than is required to defray the necessary expenses of the government.

6. That Congress has no power to charter a United States Bank; that we believe such an institution one of deadly hostility to the best interests of the country, dangerous to our republican institutions and the liberties of the people, and calculated to place the business of the country within the control of a concentrated money power, and above the laws and the will of the people.

7. That Congress has no power, under the Constitution, to interfere with or control the domestic institutions of the several States; and that such States are the sole and proper judges of everything pertaining to their own affairs, not prohibited by the Constitution; that all efforts, by abolitionists or others, made to induce Congress to interfere with questions of slavery, or take incipient steps in relation thereto, are calculated to lead to the most alarming and dangerous consequences, and that all such efforts have an inevitable tendency to diminish the happiness of the people and endanger the stability and permanency of the Union, and ought not to be countenanced by any friend to our political institutions.

8. That the separation of the moneys of the government from banking institutions is indispensable for the safety of the funds of the government and the rights of the people.

9. That the liberal [which we now call "conservative"] principles embodied by Jefferson in the Declaration of Independence, and sanctioned in the Constitution, which makes ours the land of liberty and the asylum of the oppressed of every nation, have ever been cardinal principles in the Democratic faith; and every attempt to abridge the present privilege of becoming citizens, and the owners of soil among us, ought to be resisted with the same spirit which swept the Alien and Sedition Laws from our statute-book.[193]

Our ninth president, Whig William Henry Harrison, a Liberal.

Despite the successes of the conservative Van Buren administration, the Whigs used scare tactics, the Panic of 1837, and, some say, fraud, to frighten the public, and the Liberal Whig Party won our 14th election in 1840. Whig candidate William Henry Harrison became our ninth president, and was inaugurated on March 4, 1841.[194]

Tragically, Harrison was only in office for a single month before passing away, and on April 4, 1841, Whig John Tyler became the first vice president to ascend to the presidency due to the death of the chief executive.

Our tenth U.S. president, though belonging to the Whig Party (Liberal), was, unbeknownst to his fellow Whigs, not a Liberal through and through. Being a traditional Southerner, Tyler held a number of conservative views, and his constant vetoes of progressive Congressional Whig proposals (such as tariff issues and the Fiscal Bank) engendered not only hisses and boos,

Our tenth president, Whig John Tyler, a right-leaning Liberal.

but ultimately his complete rejection by party members.[195]

The now severely weakened Liberal Whig Party left the door open for a Conservative Democratic Party win in the 1844 election, and Democrat James Knox Polk was put forth as the presidential nominee—in large part because he supported the annexation of Texas. The Democratic Party platform reaffirmed the 1840 resolutions, with one more added, one specifically directed at the left-wing policies of the Whigs:

> Resolved: That the American Democracy [that is, Republic] place their trust, not in factitious symbols, not in displays and appeals insulting to the judgment and subversive of the intellect of the people, but in a clear reliance on the intelligence, patriotism and discriminating justice of the American people.[196]

Our eleventh president, Democrat John Knox Polk, a Conservative.

With the Liberal vote split between the Whigs (their presidential nominee was Henry Clay) and the Liberty Party (their presidential nominee was abolitionist James G. Birney), the Democratic Party won the 1844 election (our 15th), and Conservative Democrat Polk became our eleventh chief executive, serving one term, from 1845 to 1849.

Though begun under Tyler, the annexation of Texas was completed under Polk in 1845, precipitating the Mexican-

Mexican War heroes, Winfield Scott (left) and Zachary Taylor (right).

American War (1846-1848). Due in great part to the military expertise of Generals Zachary Taylor and Winfield Scott, the United States won the conflict, extending its territory from the Atlantic to the Pacific Oceans.

The election of 1848, our 16th, was greatly impacted by the "slavery question," which was growing more acute with each passing year. Both the Liberal Whigs and the Conservative Democrats found increasing division within their parties over the issue, the former between the antislavery Northern Whigs and the pro-choice-slavery Southern Whigs, the latter between the "Hunkers"[197] and the "Barnburners."[198] We will note here that the Barnburners were an antislavery faction who became known as the "Free Soil Democrats."[199]

The Whigs decided on Zachary Taylor of Mexican War fame as their presidential candidate, while the Democrats put up Van Buren. Taylor got 1,360,099 popular votes and 163 electoral votes; Van Buren received only 291,265 popular votes and zero electoral votes, making Zachary Taylor our 12th president.[200]

Interestingly, Taylor, a Louisiana plantation owner and slaveholder, had no party affiliation prior to his becoming president. According to one historian "he was taken up by the Whigs solely because of his availability." Despite his lack of political experience, President Taylor presided over a largely positive and productive era. The only snag was the ever present slavery agitation, which a handful of loud and aggressive radical Northern Leftists wanted to keep before the public for purely political reasons.[201] This, of course, continued to drive a sectional wedge between the South and the North. Not because the South wanted to "preserve

Our 12th president, Whig Zachary Taylor, a Liberal.

slavery," as anti-South writers still dishonestly preach, but because Dixie—the birthplace of the American Abolition Movement—wanted to end slavery in its own region, not according to a prescribed plan laid out by those who hated them, but in its own time and way, for its own benefit, and for the benefit of the millions of whites and blacks who would be affected.[202]

With his sudden death in July 1850, Taylor was relieved of this problem, which passed over to his successor, Liberal Whig Vice President Millard Fillmore, who became our 13th president, serving one term, from 1850 to 1853.

Our 13th president, Whig Millard Fillmore, a Liberal.

Before long our 17th election, the 1852 election, loomed, and the Whigs and the Democrats once again began to vie for executive power. The former picked Fillmore as their presidential nominee, the latter put forth Conservative Democrat Franklin Pierce. Meanwhile the politically mixed Free Soil Democrats chose party-switching, left-leaning John P. Hale of New Hampshire as their nominee.

Pierce, who "leaned visibly toward the South,"[203] won handily with 1,601,274 popular votes and 254 electoral votes, becoming our 14th president, serving one term, from 1853 to 1857.[204]

A significant event occurred after the 1852 election: due to a lack of national elements,[205] guiding principles, and a solid long-term platform that backed established candidates with known views, the Whig Party (Liberal) now began to rapidly break up and disappear.[206] Only once in its history had it nominated a true Whig with an authentic Whig platform, and that it was in 1844 with the candidacy of left-leaning Henry Clay—who lost.[207]

What then became of the Liberal members of the Whig Party? Its right-

Our 14th president, Democrat Franklin Pierce, a Conservative.

leaning Southern members joined the Conservative Democratic Party, while its left-leaning Northern members divided themselves between the Conservative Democrats and the newly emerging Liberal party, which would be given the name the "Republican Party," in 1854.[208] Harvey comments on what he appropriately calls the "Whig wreck":

> The Whig wreck became complete when, in 1854, the Kansas-Nebraska act made slavery extension the Democratic [Conservative] programme, and the Whigs became the larger element of the new party [Liberals] which adopted the Republican name.[209]

A Whig campaign poster from 1848, showing presidential nominee Zachary Taylor on the left, and vice presidential nominee Millard Fillmore on the right. The banner at the bottom reads: "The people's choice for president & vice president from 1849 to 1853."

Let us emphatically state here that the Democrats (Conservatives) in 1854 were not trying to "extend" slavery, as Harvey claims. They were states' righters seeking to have a law put in place that would leave the decision up to each individual state. For example, under the Pierce administration the government's policy toward the states and slavery remained not pro-slavery, but pro-choice.[210] The Kansas-Nebraska Act, which passed on May 30, 1854, admitted these territories as states *with or without slavery,*

> as their constitutions might prescribe, at the time of admission, and repealed the Missouri Compromise of 1850, by declaring it:
>
> > "inconsistent with the principle of non-intervention by Congress with slavery in the States and Territories, as recognized by the legislation of 1850, commonly called The Compromise Measures, it being the true intent and meaning of this act, not to legislate slavery into any State or Territory nor to exclude it therefrom, but to leave the people thereof perfectly free to form and regulate their domestic institutions in their own way, subject only to the Constitution of the United States."[211]

This clause in the Kansas-Nebraska Bill was deeply offensive to the Free Soil Democrats and the antislavery Northern Whigs, the latter who were now temporarily calling themselves "Anti-Nebraska Men," but who by 1852 had begun to refer to themselves as the "American Party." Their opponents, however, called them the "Know-Nothing Party," due to their refusal to share the secret workings of their organization with the public, and this was the name that stuck, momentarily.[212]

As this drawing from the late 1860s shows, the original Ku Klux Klan, which I call the Reconstruction KKK, had nothing to do with racism. It was directed at carpetbaggers: unscrupulous Yankees coming south to prey on the weak, the disenfranchised, and the homeless. Violent racists posing as KKK members later infiltrated the organization and began using it to commit crimes against African-Americans, at which time Nathan Bedford Forrest—neither the group's founder or leader, but rather the South's most influential former Confederate officer at the time—closed it down in 1869. Despite claims to the contrary, the modern KKK has no connection to the Reconstruction KKK, which was designed to be temporary, and thus lasted only three years.

Like many Liberals today, the Know-Nothings, a Protestant splinter group of the Whigs[213] and thus also a direct descendant of Hamilton's Liberal Federalist Party,[214] were vehemently anti-Catholic.[215] Earlier, in

Boston in 1849, they had formed an anti-papal, anti-foreigner group known as the "Order of the Star-Spangled Banner."[216] Many of the Order's secret grips, passwords, signals, rituals, and symbols were later adopted by the Southern Ku Klux Klan of the late 1860s, a group which I more accurately call the Reconstruction Ku Klux Klan.[217] Let us note here that the unfairly defamed Reconstruction KKK was actually a conservative, nonracist, anti-carpetbag, pro-Constitution organization, with thousands of African-American members, aides, and supporters. Founded as a temporary group to help maintain law and order in the South during Reconstruction, it lasted only from 1865 to 1869, and has *absolutely no connection whatsoever to today's KKK.*[218]

A mid 19th-Century Know-Nothing poster. The Caption reads: "Uncle Sam's Youngest Son, Citizen Know Nothing."

The un-American views, particularly the religious intolerance, of the Know-Nothing Party or American Party made it obvious that it was anything but "American."[219] Yet it seems to be due to these very policies that the party soon caught the interest and attention of the "Forty-Eighters." Who were the Forty-Eighters?

Some 4,000 European atheists, freethinkers, socialists, Marxists, and communists, who were now flocking to the United States[220] after their failed socialist revolution in Europe in 1848.[221] Like 18th-Century French extremists, who abhorred Christianity so completely that they threw out the Christian calendar, renamed the days and months of the year, declared a new "year one" in 1792, and substituted the Christian Faith with a "Cult of Reason,"[222] Forty-Eighters had no use for religion—except, as with their Leninist counterparts in Russia,[223] to be used as an opiate to intellectually medicate and manipulate the masses.[224]

An 1852 lithograph paying tribute to European Forty-Eighter Louis Kossuth, a Hungarian radical who led an 1848 revolt against the Austrian government, symbolized by the three-headed monster on the right. American sympathy for the Forty-Eighters is represented by the man, no doubt a socialist, on the left holding a U.S. flag.

With the ongoing disintegration of the Whig Party, as well as the frailty of the new Know-Nothing Party, these anti-Christian, anti-American European radicals saw a golden opportunity to resuscitate and renew their revolution in the U.S.[225] How? By infiltrating the broken and thus weakened Left-wing of American politics, as well as the U.S.

military, and infusing them with their big government socialist ideas, policies, and principles.[226] With no official major Liberal party, and only a group of fragmenting minor Liberal parties trying to fill the void, there was no better time for them to act.

Why would thousands of European immigrants be interested in an anti-immigrant organization, and why would it be interested in them?

There is no simple answer to this question other than to state that during the early 1850s, Liberals, socialists, revolutionaries, communists, radicals, collectivists, and progressives of every kind were desperate to take back the White House. This made them willing to ignore petty differences in exchange for the enormous political advantages they could accrue by joining forces against the Democrats (Conservatives).

The French Revolution of 1848 was supported by a majority of European radicals and socialists, thousands who fled to the U.S. after it failed—where they hoped to resuscitate the revolt by combining with the members of Lincoln's Republican Party, the Liberal party at the time. This 1848 hand-colored lithograph is entitled: "Burning the royal carriages at the Chateau d'Eu, February 24, 1848."

The state of Connecticut offers an excellent example of the political situation at the time, with parties coming and going almost weekly, confusingly changing names, platforms, and candidates as it suited their purposes at the moment. Writes Curtis:

Connecticut was a State controlled by the Federalists [Liberals] during the early part of the Nineteenth Century. The Charter of King Charles, which was the Constitution of the State until 1818, and the laws passed under it, gave the established Congregationalist order and its ministry certain privileges, and the Federal Party sustained them and objected to any new Constitution. Members of other denominations of Christians who had been Federalists [Liberals], began to leave the Federal Party on this account, and the so-called Toleration Party grew up between 1812 and 1818. This made parties more evenly balanced in the State, and so the Tolerationists and anti-Federalists [Conservatives] naturally became Democrats [Conservatives], and the Federalists became Whigs [Liberals].

In the eastern part of the State, and in the northwestern part of the State the Baptists and Methodists were inclined to be Democrats [Conservatives]. The Protection issue, which came to the front in the 1830s and 1840s, however, tended to make the State Whig [Liberal] on account of the theories of Protection laid down by Henry Clay and others. Yet, in the campaigns of 1844 and 1848 the parties were very evenly divided. Henry Clay [a Whig] carried the State in 1844, as did [William Henry] Harrison [a Whig] in 1840.

An 1852 Conservative political cartoon denigrating the presidential aspirations of U.S. war hero and Whig Winfield Scott (far left), a Liberal. Miss Liberty blocks his entrance to the Capitol Building. The caption reads: "The poor soldier and his ticket for soup."

The Democratic Party [Conservative] was growing stronger, however, on account of the Mexican War feeling [that is, patriotism], and might have carried the State in 1848, but the Baptists and the Methodist Democrats, especially in the country towns of the State, became Free-Soilers [Liberals] when the anti-slavery issue was worked up in the 1840s, and enough Free-Soil Democrats voted for [Martin] Van Buren [Conservative] in 1848 to give the electoral vote to [left-leaning Zachary] Taylor rather than [Conservative Lewis] Cass. The Democrats [Conservatives] elected their Governor in 1850, 1851, 1852 and 1853. The Democrats carried the State for [Franklin] Pierce [Conservative] in 1852.

In 1853 a few Free-Soilers, so-called, were elected to the Legislature and they were generally men who had been Democrats [in this case, antislavery Conservatives]. The Kansas-Nebraska Act carried the State against the Democrats [Conservatives] in 1854, and the State officials called themselves Whigs [Liberals]. In 1855 the American Party [Liberal] came to the front, and while the Whig Party renominated their old ticket of 1854, which had then been successful, the American or Know-Nothing Party candidates [Liberals] were victorious. Men called themselves "Democrats," "Americans," "American Whigs," and "American Democrats," and a few "Free-Soilers" were elected.

An 1856 election cartoon entitled, "The great presidential sweepstakes of 1856," showing Whig Millard Fillmore (a Liberal) in a carriage, leading the race for the White House. Behind him Franklin Pierce carries fellow Democrat James Buchanan (both Conservatives) on his shoulders. In the rear Left-wing abolitionists Horace Greeley, John C. Frémont, and Henry Ward Beecher wade through the "abolition cess pool."

In 1856 the State officers elected, in April, were the nominees of the American Party [Liberals]. The Republican Party [Liberal] had candidates at this election, however, who polled 6700 votes. The Democratic candidates [Conservatives] polled about 32,000 votes, and the American or Know-Nothing candidates [Liberals] polled over 26,000. Under the Constitution of Connecticut at that time the candidates were not elected who failed to receive a majority of all the votes cast, and the General Assembly elected the State officers, and when the General Assembly met in May, in 1856, they elected the American candidates [Liberals].

The men elected to the Legislature that year called themselves "Americans" or "Democrats," but there were a few men who called themselves either "Republicans" or "American Republicans." In 1857 the American Republicans [Liberals] carried the State, but a large proportion of the men who were not Democrats called themselves "Union," which meant a union of the opposition to the Democratic party [Conservative].

In the spring election of 1858, when William A. Buckingham [Liberal] was elected, the successful candidates labelled themselves "Republicans" [Liberals]. The successful candidates for State officers in 1854 in Connecticut called themselves "Whigs" [Liberals]. In 1855 and 1856, "Americans." In 1857 "American Republicans" and "Union Republicans" and "Union." In 1858 they called themselves, with very few exceptions, "Republicans" [all Liberal].[227]

Significantly, it was amidst this chaotic, jumbled, swiftly changing political scene that the Republican Party (Liberal) of Abraham Lincoln and his socialist and communist followers was formed in 1854.

While the facts are not completely clear (no two historians agree on precisely what took place, or when, why, and where), for our purpose we can piece together enough to get an accurate picture of the foundations of the 1854 Republican Party and the role it played in the American "Civil War."

The schoolhouse at Ripon, Wisconsin, where some claim the Republican Party was born on March 20, 1854. This was not the Conservative Republican Party of Ronald Reagan, however, but the Liberal party of progressive Abraham Lincoln, the equivalent of today's Democratic Party.

Gathering together the many now partyless members of the old progressive parties (mainly Whigs, Free-Soilers, and anti-slavery Democrats),[228] as well as anti-South, anti-states' rights Liberals, this group of discontented American left-wingers and anti-religious European communists put their entire focus on forming a faction that could beat the Democrats (Conservatives) in the 1856 election.[229]

Hoping to pick up support from the now burgeoning antislavery movement in the North, on February 28, 1854, representatives met at Ripon, Wisconsin, where they resolved to establish a new party based on, not the abolition of slavery, but "resistance to the *extension* of slavery" outside the South,[230] as well as noninterference with slavery where it already existed legally.[231]

This was not the Republican Party of today, but quite another kind of group altogether; one completely dissimilar, disconnected, and even opposite in purpose and function from the Conservative 21st-Century Republican Party, as we are about to see.

The radical left-wing underpinnings of the 1854 Republican Party were evident from the start. It was certainly no accident that they met at the Wisconsin Phalanx "Ceresco," a former socialist commune based on the ideas of French socialist Charles Fourier;[232] that their Whig leader, Alvan Earle Bovay, was a former secretary of the National Reform Association or NRA (a group that had been enthusiastically embraced by the Communist League of America); that NRA veterans helped publish the first American edition of Karl Marx and Friedrich Engels' *The Communist Manifesto*;[233] or that labor advocate Bovay

Left-winger Alvan Earle Bovay, who had close ties to socialists and communists, was the founder of the Victorian Era Republican Party, America's Liberal party from 1854 to 1896.

himself was a disciple of radical English-American reformer George Henry Evans,[234] an early 19th-Century socialist.[235]

For the name of the new party Bovay suggested using the one that had been discarded by the Democratic-Republicans (Conservatives) in 1828: "Republicans."[236] On May 23, 1854, just one day after the passage of the Kansas-Nebraska Act, the Republican Party, then the *Liberal* party, got its unofficial start,[237] and on July 6, at Jackson, Michigan,[238] where the first state officers were nominated, the party was made official.[239] Tellingly, Galusha A. Grow, "the Father of the Republican Party,"[240] was in attendance at the "Convention Under the Oaks," as the Jackson meeting is called.[241] A progressive, anti-South, radical Republican from Connecticut—who later served as Speaker of the House under Lincoln (who Grow viewed as too lenient toward the South)[242]—Grow's conservative critics often correctly referred to him as a "socialist,"[243] and he was widely viewed as the chief representative of the "workingman's idealism."[244]

Yankee socialist Galusha A. Grow, known as "the Father of the Republican Party."

Impatient with the Conservative policies of President Pierce (who had signed the Kansas-Nebraska Bill into law on May 30),[245] the new Republican Party (Liberals) condemned the spread of slavery, helped disseminate anti-South propaganda, pushed for the issuance of an Emancipation Proclamation, and urged a "civil war" against the South.[246]

In 1856 the scattered remnants of the several Liberal parties held conventions in preparation for the presidential election that November: the Know-Nothings in Philadelphia on February 22 nominated Millard Fillmore; the Whigs in Baltimore on September 17 supported Fillmore as well; the Republicans (Liberals), in their first convention, met at Philadelphia on June 17, nominating "the Great Pathfinder," John C. Frémont, for president.[247]

Since the formation of the 1854 Republican Party was, in great part, influenced by socialists and communists, it is not surprising to learn that Frémont too was heavily supported by political radicals, and that four years later, as a Union general during the "Civil War," socialists readily joined his army, occupying every rank from private all the way up to general.[248]

The Democratic Convention (Conservatives) was held at Cincinnati on June 7, where staunch Conservative James Buchanan was nominated unanimously. According to Wilson:

> The [Conservative] platform adopted reaffirmed the resolutions of 1840 and 1844, denounced the organization of a [Liberal] party with secret and religious tests [the Know-Nothings], declared in favor of the strict and faithful execution of the compromise measures of 1850, and denounced all attempts of renewing in Congress or out of it the agitation of the slavery question; recognized and adopted the principles contained in the organic laws organizing the Territories of Kansas and Nebraska as the only sound and safe solution of the slavery question; non-interference of Congress with slavery in the States or in the District of Columbia.[249]

With its purposefully overt Liberal anti-South policies, the conservative South had no interest in the newly formed, Yankee-founded, ultra liberal Republican Party, and so it was virtually ignored in Dixie during our 18th election in 1856. Liberal Republican Frémont, of course, won most of the Northern states, while Conservative Democrat Buchanan won most of the Southern states. When all was said and done Frémont came away with 1,341264 popular votes and 114 electoral votes; Buchanan received 1,838,169 popular votes and 174 electoral votes, making him our 15th chief executive.[250] "The Bachelor President" served only one term, from 1857 to 1861.

Liberal John C. Frémont, the first nominee of the new Republican Party in 1856. Later a Union general, his army would be filled with socialists, radicals, and revolutionaries, many of them Forty-Eighters.

Despite Buchanan's win, the enormous groundswell of support for Frémont in the North revealed a danger that the Founding Fathers had warned of generations earlier: the formation of a party based not on politics, but on sectionalism;[251] or more specifically, on a burning hatred for the South, her independent-minded people, her unswerving conservatism, her strong religiosity, her steadfast patriotism, her love of

Our 15th president, Democrat James Buchanan, a Conservative.

the Constitution, her humble agrarian culture, her proud military heritage, and her Old European traditions. This nefarious South-hating faction was none other that the new Liberal party, the first purely sectional political party in American history. And it had given itself the name, the "Republican Party." As I have noted, this was *not* the Republican Party of Thomas Jefferson (early 19th Century), nor the Republican Party of Ronald Reagan (late 20th Century). It was the American Liberal-Socialist-

A map of the election of 1856, the first Republican campaign, showing the popular and electoral votes of the candidates.

Communist Party of the mid 19th Century, dressed up in sheep's clothing, using a name that its members hoped would disguise their true agenda and help them attract voters.

It was thus that in 1856 the Buchanan administration emerged during what we Southerners consider the beginning of truly "evil times." For it was while he was in the White House that the "Bloody Kansas" border war broke out between antislavery and pro-choice slavery forces, the infamous Dred Scott case arose, and sinister Yankee psychopath-abolitionist John Brown—another Yankee Liberal avidly supported by socialists[252]—launched his attack at Harpers Ferry. These events brought the slavery question into even sharper focus and increased sectional hostilities, making slavery virtually the sole issue between the Conservative Democrats (who rightfully argued that slavery was then still legal under the Constitution in every state and territory in the U.S.) and the Liberal Republicans (who wrongly held that slavery was "unconstitutional").[253] The latter's view—based on emotion and opinion rather than on law and fact—was only natural, for Liberals then, as today, do not like the Constitution and its many conservative restrictions on governmental reach and power.

As mentioned, Buchanan served only one term, and in 1860 he handed over the Democratic presidential nomination to Conservative Illinois Senator Stephen A. Douglas for the upcoming November election. Their slogan was the epitome of conservative thinking: "The Constitution as it is and the Union as it was."[254]

Democrat Stephen A. Douglas, the "Little Giant," a Conservative.

Our 16th president, Republican Abraham Lincoln, a Liberal.

Unfortunately, Buchanan's Conservative party, that is, the Democratic Party, split into three different factions before the election: the Northern Democrats, the Southern Democrats, and the Constitutional Union Party—the latter being the left-leaning remnants of the old Whig Party and the Know-Nothings.[255] This diluted the Conservative, largely Southern vote, allowing big government Liberal Abraham Lincoln to score a victory.[256]

Lincoln, of course, was a lifelong Liberal, and had been a member of the Whig Party since the 1840s[257] (he had campaigned, for instance, for Whig candidate William Henry Harrison in 1840),[258] and had only recently became a member of the 1854 Republican Party (Liberals). Though elected with only 39.8 percent of the total popular vote, "The Rail-Splitter" won the Electoral College with 180 votes, becoming our 16th president in our 19th election.[259]

In all, Lincoln received nearly one million popular votes less than his opponents combined,[260] making him a minority president.[261] More shocking is the fact that out of the total population of the U.S. that November 6, only one out of every seventeen eligible whites voted for him.[262] In 1911 Dodd summed up Lincoln's 1860 win this way:

> The count showed that the Republicans polled in these states 387,603 votes, or a majority over all other candidates of only 30,000, while in the whole Northwest Lincoln's majority was only 6600 over all other candidates. A change of one vote in 27 would have given these states to [Conservative Democrat Stephen A.] Douglas, and a change of one vote in 20 would have given him the whole Northwest, and the contest would have been transferred to the national House of Representatives where the South would almost certainly have won.
>
> It seems, therefore, fair to conclude that the flood-tide of Republican [Liberal] idealism was reached in 1856-1858; that the able and well organized aristocracy of the South came near to winning their point—an election in the House; that the property and religious influences of the Northwest compelled Lincoln and his advisers to recede from the high ground of 1856-1858; and finally that the contest was won only on a narrow margin by the votes of the foreigners whom the railroads poured in great numbers into the contested

region. The election of Lincoln and, as it turned out, the fate of the Union were thus determined not by native Americans [natural-born citizens] but by voters who knew least of American history and institutions.[263]

Though the Southern Confederacy had not yet been formed, ten of the Southern states did not even bother putting Lincoln on their ballots, considering him too perfidious to run the nation. (Lincoln himself had admitted he was not qualified to be president, but this did not stop his Liberal followers from voting for him.)[264] In fact, that year all of his popular votes and all of his electoral ones, came from Northern or Western states: he did not receive a single popular vote in the South.[265] Thus the only people who voted in his first election were those most likely to cast their ballot for Lincoln to begin with. And *all* of these were white, taxpaying males (at the time non-taxpaying males, women, free blacks, black slaves, and Native-Americans were not allowed to vote).[266]

An 1860 Republican campaign banner, with an illustration of a beardless Lincoln surrounded by 33 stars. His name is misspelled. Lincoln's running mate, Yankee Liberal Hannibal Hamlin of Maine, is also promoted.

Those white taxpaying *Northern* males who did vote in 1860 sided in great numbers with Lincoln. The most important segment of this group was his Wall Street Boys: Yankee financiers, merchants, and industrialists,[267] all keen to put anyone into the Oval Office who would not interfere with slavery, but instead would maintain the lucrative Northern slave trade—which had been in operation since 1636, and was still going strong.[268] The candidate who promised to do just this was Abraham Lincoln.[269] For, as we have seen, his new party, the Republican Party, had been formed solely to stop the spread of slavery, not slavery itself,[270] which is why he promised not to interfere with slavery in his First Inaugural Speech.[271] Later, these same backers rewarded Liberal Lincoln by donating millions of dollars from their slave profits to fund his war against the Conservative South.[272] Not to crush slavery (which was not the reason for the War),[273] but to force the Southern states back into the Union so that Lincoln and his Wall Street Boys could continue collecting their "revenue" from Dixie.[274]

Furthermore, there can be little question that bribery, lying, horse-trading, and cheating took place on Lincoln's behalf during the 1860 election, and that prime administrative positions and other political favors were swapped for votes. In May, at the National Republican Convention, Lincoln's campaign manager, David Davis, interrupted the printing presses so that a ballot could not be taken, had fake tickets made in order to fill seats, then pledged other nominees their choice of governmental posts if they would support Lincoln.[275]

Lincoln's secretary of war, Simon Cameron, only endorsed "Honest Abe" because he was pledged a cabinet position (Cameron would go on to allow administration-wide corruption regarding the approval of military contracts).[276] Then there was Lincoln's secretary of the interior, Caleb B. Smith, also promised a post; this time in exchange for delivering the Indiana delegation.[277] Lincoln also appointed countless numbers of political backers to high-ranking military posts, many of them, to the chagrin of Yankee soldiers, who had no military experience.[278] The list goes on and on.

Lincoln's secretary of war, Simon Cameron.

This all occurred, obviously, under Lincoln's supervision,[279] for his convention managers later admitted that they had been allowed to promise "anything and everything" to anyone who would vote for him.[280] (Lincoln would pay for this double-dealing: his sordid campaign promises necessitated appointing a myriad of individuals with opposing viewpoints, creating a split cabinet that he was forced to do battle with throughout his entire first term.)[281]

Of the 1860 presidential election, Judge George L. Christian of Richmond, Virginia, writes that Lincoln

> was only nominated by means of a corrupt bargain entered into between his representatives and those of Simon Cameron, of Pennsylvania, and Caleb B. Smith, of Indiana, by which Cabinet positions were pledged both to Cameron and to Smith in consideration for the votes controlled by them, in the [1860 Chicago] convention, and which pledges Lincoln fulfilled, and, in that way made himself a party to these corrupt bargains.
>
> He was nominated purely as the sectional candidate of a sectional party, and not only received no votes in several of the Southern States, but he failed to get a popular majority of the section which nominated and elected him, and received nearly one million votes less than a popular majority of the vote of the country.[282]

Fort Sumter, South Carolina, April 9, 1863, the scene of one of Lincoln's earliest crimes as president. The Second National Confederate Flag flies proudly over the garrison.

Only days after his election the Southern states were meeting to discuss their future, and within weeks they began to secede, starting with South Carolina.[283] Lincoln boiled over with indignation at the formation of the Confederate States of America (named after one of early 19th-Century nicknames for the U.S.),[284] and in revenge tricked the South into firing the first shot at the Battle of Fort Sumter.[285] This launched the war that he so craved and needed in order to create his socialistic dream of an "indivisible nation" based on liberal policies and an all-white, black-free America.[286]

3

LINCOLN AND THE ELECTION OF 1860

I T IS NOW 1860, "THE most fateful year in our history."[287] We have arrived at that momentous point in American politics where a unique newly formed Republican Party first arises as a *Liberal* party out of the ashes of the progressive Whig Party, which was a descendant of the Federalist Party—the Liberal party of leftist U.S. Founding Fathers Alexander Hamilton and John Adams.[288]

Federalist Alexander Hamilton, the Liberal big government progenitor of Lincoln's Republican Party.

The Republican Party's first opponents in 1860 were the Democrats, or Conservatives, the descendants of Conservative Thomas Jefferson and James Madison's right-wing faction, the Democratic-Republican Party, which dates back to the Washington administration (1789-1797). In mere months the American "Civil War" would begin. Of this period Wilson writes:

> The election of [Liberal Republican] Abraham Lincoln made the first serious break in the control of the federal government by the Democratic [Conservative] party since the inauguration of Mr. Jefferson; the election of

[William H.] Harrison by the Whigs in 1840 having proved a barren victory by reason of his early death, and the administration of [Zachary] Taylor and [Millard] Fillmore having been almost immediately followed by the dissolution of the Whig party. The closing days of Mr. [James] Buchanan's administration were devoted to an earnest effort on the part of some of the most patriotic men of the country to avert the dissolution of the Union; among which were the compromise measures proposed by Mr. [John J.] Crittenden, of Kentucky, virtually restoring the line of the Missouri Compromise as a permanent division between the free and the slave territory of the country. Although earnestly supported by the President [Buchanan], Mr. Crittenden's propositions were defeated in the Senate. A Peace Convention also assembled in Washington on the invitation of the State of Virginia, but its proceedings were fruitless, and with the secession of the Southern States and the withdrawal of their representatives from both Houses of Congress, the war began.[289]

Party-changing Whig and Constitutional Unionist John J. Crittenden, a Liberal.

The Republicans (Liberals) of 1860, our country's first sectional party, were now under the control of Lincoln, the "right makes might" president,[290] and one of the most ardent South-haters, anti-states' rights advocates, and big government progressives to have ever sprung from American soil. It is little wonder that it was his election that launched the secession of the Southern states, for he was well-known to the Southern people as being "hostile to our institutions and fatally bent upon our ruin."[291] And by "institutions" they did not just mean slavery—which the South had been trying to get rid of for centuries.[292] They were also referring to Dixie's many conservative traditions, customs, practices, and beliefs, which had long been under threat of "Northernization" by self-righteous, South-loathing Yankee Liberals.[293] In the eyes of Southerners,

a purely sectional party had got control of the government,—a party whose members, in spite of the disavowal in its platform, had condoned the behavior of [anti-South Yankee psychotic] John Brown,—a party whose leader had predicted that the country would become all slave or all free.[294]

Meanwhile, Democrats (Conservatives) in the seceded Southern states unanimously selected Conservative American patriot Jefferson Davis to serve as president of their new legally formed Republic, the C.S.A. With a sociopathic, warmongering, criminal-minded, Constitution-hating, Liberal agnostic in the U.S. White House, and an honest, peacemaking, law-abiding, Constitution-loving, Conservative Christian in the C.S. White House, from the outset the South had little chance of winning the War. Those who refuse to play by the rules always have an advantage over those who do, and so it was with the bloody, illicit, and unnecessary conflict of 1861.[295] In 1889 Wilson described the situation this way:

The Confederacy's first and, thus far, only president, Democrat Jefferson Davis, a Conservative.

The close of Mr. Buchanan's administration left the Republicans [Liberals] in control of both branches of Congress, and the tariff of 1846, as reduced in 1857, was superseded by the Act of March 2, 1861, known as the Morrill tariff, framed on the protective theory, with increase of rates and the substitution of specific for *ad valorem* ["according to value"] duties. The Republican party [of 1860] was in its origin a sectional party, and such it has chosen to remain throughout its entire history [that is, up until 1896, which arrived after Wilson's book was written]. It came into power [in 1854] upon the doctrine of restricting slavery to the States in which it then existed, and excluding it from the Territories belonging to the Union.

But it was largely in its [Liberal] composition and [Liberal] controlling elements a loose construction party, and its accession to power being followed immediately by the secession of the Southern States and four years of civil war, in which every power of the national government was strained to restore its authority over the seceded States and compel their return to the Union, it naturally grew more accustomed to absolute power and military rule than to the careful observance of the Constitution, of the rights of the States, or the great safeguards of personal liberty. Military necessity was often appealed to as temporarily superseding the Constitution and the laws.

The Democratic party [Conservative], trained for more than sixty years in the school of strict construction; of equal rights; of the supremacy of the civil over the military power; of reverence for the Constitution and for those fundamental principles of liberty out of which free government springs, and by whose observance alone free government can be maintained and perpetuated, challenged these violations of the great rights which government was ordained to secure—the suspension of the writ of *habeas corpus*; the denial of the right of trial by jury; the trial of citizens by military tribunals in time of peace or in States where civil courts were open; the interference with liberty of the press, with the right of popular assemblage and the like. Its general position on these questions was vindicated by the decision of the United States Supreme Court in the celebrated case of Lambdin Milligan, who was arrested by order of the general commanding the military district of Indiana; tried by a military commission, and sentenced to be hung. Milligan petitioned the Circuit Court of the United States for the district of Indiana to be discharged, on the ground that the military commission had no jurisdiction to try him; and that the right of trial by jury was guaranteed to him by the Constitution. In deciding this case the court declared, "That no graver question was ever considered by this court, or one that more nearly concerns the rights of the whole people; for it is the birthright of every citizen, when charged with crime, to be tried and punished according to law," and used these memorable words: "The Constitution of the United States is a law for rulers and people, equally in war and in peace, and covers with the shield of its protection all classes of men, at all times and under all circumstances."[296]

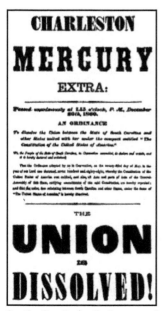

South Carolina's Ordinance of Secession, issued December 20, 1860, only weeks after Lincoln's election.

To increase our understanding of Lincolnian Liberalism and the activities of his left-wing administration between 1861 and 1865, let us take a closer look at the sociopolitical background of both "Honest Abe" and the Republican Party (Liberal) which he headed for the four darkest years in American history.

As is clear from tracing his political lineage, Abraham Lincoln was a political descendant of Hamilton and the early American Federalists, monarchists, and consolidationists, which is why, like modern day Liberals, he did not like the Constitution.[297] His own liberal compatriots called it a "scrap of paper," a "covenant with death and a league with hell,"[298] and "a thing of nothing, which must be changed."[299] Hamilton himself referred to it as "weak,"[300] "a frail and

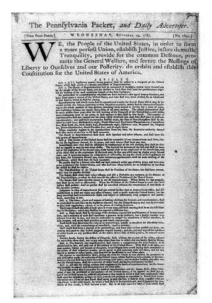

The first page of the U.S. Constitution, printed in *The Pennsylvania Packer and Daily Advertiser*, September 19, 1787. Ever since its ratification Liberals, like Lincoln, have shown disregard and disdain for America's most important document, referring to it as everything from a "scrap of paper" to a "worthless fabric."

worthless fabric,"[301] while John Adams had such a low opinion of it that he assumed it would disappear within a generation.[302] A half century later radical William Lloyd Garrison burned the Constitution in the public square.[303] In our own time big government Liberal Barack Hussein Obama followed in Lincoln's footsteps, referring to the Constitution as "an imperfect document," while his anti-American followers eagerly campaigned to throw out the entire document, calling it "old, outdated, and useless."[304]

As a leftist, Lincoln, who began his political life as a Whig (Liberal),[305] was no different than Obama and every other progressive on this particular score. In February 1861, while meeting with a Southern peace commission at Willard's Hotel in Washington, D.C., the president-elect was asked by New York businessman William E. Dodge what he was going to do to prevent war with the South. Lincoln's response is chilling:

> When I get to the Oval Office, I shall take an oath to the best of my ability to preserve, protect, and defend the Constitution. This is a great and solemn duty. With the support of the people and the assistance of the Almighty I shall undertake to perform it. I have full faith that I shall perform it. It is not the Constitution as I would like to have it, but as it is that is to be defended.[306]

Reading between the lines, it is obvious that even prior to becoming president, Lincoln was plotting to alter, and even destroy, the carefully constructed government of Jefferson, Madison, Monroe, Paine, Gerry, Mason, Henry, and the other *conservative* Founders.

American Founding Father Benjamin Franklin at the Court of France in 1778.

This crime was to be just the most recent of untold hundreds that Liberals (mainly in the North) had been perpetuating against Conservatives (mainly in the South) since the turn of the 19th-Century, violating both the Constitution and the decisions of the Supreme Court.[307] These leftist outrages against the conservative, traditional, Christian South stretched forward into the Civil War period (1861-1865) and went on long after, through Reconstruction (1865-1877) and the Grant administration (1869-1877)—a period known even to North-leaning historians as one of the most corrupt and "deplorable" Liberal presidencies in U.S. history; the "nadir of national disgrace," one writer called it.[308] A partial list of unconstitutional acts committed by Victorian American Liberals includes:

"1. The Missouri Compromise, 1820. Slave territory restricted and no Constitutional authority for it.
"2. The Tariff Acts of 1828 and 1833. The Constitution says the tariff must be uniform—one section must not be discriminated against in favor of another.
"3. Violation of the Fugitive Slave Law. Article 4, Section 2, Clause 3.
"4. Coercion in 1861. Article 4, Section 4.
"5. Laws of neutrality, Trent Affair. Article 6, Clause 2—Violation of International Law.

"6. Writ of *Habeas Corpus* suspended. Article 1, Section 9, Clause 2.

"7. War was declared without the consent of Congress, 1861. Article 1, Section 8, Clauses 11, 12.

"8. Emancipation Proclamation. Article 4, Section 3, Clause 2.

"9. West Virginia made a State. Article 4, Section 3, Clause 1.

"10. The Hanging of Mrs. [Mary] Surratt. Amendments—Article 5.

"11. The Execution of [Confederate Captain] Henry Wirz. Amendments—Article 6.

"12. [Issuance of] the Fourteenth and Fifteenth Amendments. Article 5. [Note: These two "Civil War Amendments" were anti-Conservative in character and intention.]

"13. The Seizure without compensation of property after surrender. Amendments—Articles 4 and 6.

"14. Squatter Sovereignty. It allowed a territorial government to exclude slavery.

"15. The liberty of the press taken away. Amendments—Article 1. [Note: For example, during his administration Lincoln illegally shut down between 300 and 400 Conservative and pro-South newspapers in the North.]

"16. The Freedom of Speech Denied. [Clement L.] Vallandigham imprisoned in Ohio. Amendments—Article 1.

"17. Blockading ports of States that were held by the Federal Government to be still in the Union."[309]

Under such circumstances it is little wonder that the conservative, Constitution-loving Southern states wanted to secede, that they did secede, and that they fought back so forcefully during Reconstruction (the second phase of the Liberals' war on the conservative South) forming such nonracist Conservative groups as the

Yankee Democrat Clement L. Vallandigham was only one of thousands of Conservatives who had his constitutional rights violated by Liberal Lincoln.

pro-Constitution, anti-carpetbag Ku Klux Klan.[310]

One of the questions I am asked most often, and one which helped inspire this very book, is what proof I have that Republican Lincoln was a Liberal with leftist tendencies. In light of our modern definition of Republicans as "Conservatives" and Democrats as "Liberals," this question is entirely understandable. Besides the copious evidence already discussed, let us look at some additional facts and in doing so shed greater light on the Liberalism of the "Civil War" Republican Party and the Conservatism of the "Civil War" Democratic Party.

Though pro-North, pro-Lincoln partisans will never discuss it or even acknowledge it, our anti-Confederacy sixteenth president surrounded himself with political revolutionaries,[311] was collaborating

with them as early as 1856[312]—long before he was even nominated for president,[313] was supported by thousands of radical European socialists called the "Forty-Eighters,"[314] was adored by socialists and communists alike, and has always been honored by nationalists, dictators, revolutionaries, humanists, freethinkers, and communists from around the world.[315] These would include national socialists like Adolf Hitler,[316] Marxist socialists like Karl Marx,[317] European socialists like George Julian Harney,[318] American socialists like Horace Greeley,[319] radical socialists like Alexander Ivanovich Herzen,[320] and Christian socialists like Francis Bellamy (author of America's socialistic Pledge of Allegiance).[321] Lincoln has even been supported by anarchists like Mikhail Bakunin.[322] Marx, the founder of modern

Socialists, communists, Marxists, radicals, free thinkers, leftists, subversives, atheists, anarchists, revolutionaries, and later Nazis, were all drawn to Abraham Lincoln, not Jefferson Davis. Why? The answer is obvious.

communism, was so enamored with "Honest Abe" that he wrote him a personal letter supporting his election[323]—something the South-hating communist would have never done for Conservative Confederate President Jefferson Davis.

Lincoln was not just supported by radicals, he went out of his way to court them. To boost his support among left-wing Europeans, and in particular progressive Germans, for example, on May 30, 1859, he secretly purchased a German-American newspaper, the Springfield *Illinois Staats-Anzeiger*, if it promised to promote his party's policies.[324] This was not a problem, of course, since the paper, like many of the other German-American journals, was already left-leaning.[325] Lincoln then contracted its editor, Dr. Theodore Canisius—a German-born progressive with an affinity for Italian socialist,[326] fascist,[327] and revolutionary Giuseppe Garibaldi[328]—to campaign for him in German-speaking communities throughout Illinois.[329] This liberalist propaganda tool helped Lincoln secure a large number of German-American votes in the 1860 election.[330] For Canisius' hard work in the name of Liberalism Lincoln later awarded him the position of Consulate in Vienna.[331]

Lincoln referred to the conservative Confederate Cause as a "revolution," the same word that Karl Marx and thousands of other socialists and communists used to describe it. The only real "revolution" was Lincoln's attempt to overturn the U.S. Constitution.

Lincoln's progressiveness is also the reason that, in the 1930s, American communists formed a military organization called "The Abraham Lincoln Battalion," and it is why the 1939 Communist Party Convention in Chicago, Illinois, affectionately displayed an enormous image of Lincoln over the center of its stage, flanked by pictures of Russian communist dictators Vladimir Lenin on one side and Joseph Stalin on the other.[332]

In the Summer of 1861 Lincoln asked Italian socialist revolutionary Giuseppe Garibaldi to lead the U.S. military against the conservative Confederacy. The position eventually went to Liberal slave owner Ulysses S. Grant, soon to become our 18th president.

Lincoln's deep-seated liberalism is why he himself was an enthusiastic supporter of revolutions, revolutionary ideas, and revolutionary leaders, such as those who headed the 1848 socialist revolts in

Naturally, dictatorial Liberal Lincoln has always been revered by dictators, one of the more famous being Nazi leader Adolf Hitler, who wrote fondly of Lincoln's anti-states' rights policies in his biography *Mein Kampf* ("My Struggle").

Europe;[333] it is why, in July 1861, he specifically asked the European socialist military leader Giuseppe Garibaldi to head the Union army;[334] it is why he gave well-known Forty-Eighter Reinhold Solger a post in the U.S. Treasury Department;[335] it is why he selected socialists for his administration, men such as the notorious radical Charles A. Dana[336] (managing editor of socialist Horace Greeley's New York *Tribune*[337]—both who were personal friends of Karl Marx),[338] a revolutionary who served as Lincoln's Assistant Secretary of War (under Edwin M. Stanton);[339] it is why he employed socialists to aid in his election campaigns, men like Forty-Eighter Casper Butz (who helped draft the Republican platform),[340] Friedrich Kapp (a presidential elector for Lincoln), and Friedrich Karl Franz Hecker, a Union officer who assisted in founding the Republican Party and later promoted the election of Lincoln in 1860.[341]

It is also why Lincoln was worshiped by socialistic radicals in the Republican Party, "enemies of the Constitution"[342] like Wendell Phillips, James A. Garfield, and Thaddeus Stevens—the same men who called for the execution of Southern slave owners (Conservatives), seizure of Southern plantations, and the redistribution of their wealth and property to other Liberals, progressives, and socialists.[343]

Lincoln's entrenched progressive views are also why he enlisted so many left-wing officers in his armies, men such as socialist-communist Union General Joseph Wedemeyer[344] (a personal friend of Marx and Engels),[345] communist Union General August Willich, communist Union Lieutenant Fritz Jacobi, communist Union Major Robert Rosa,[346] socialist Union General Max Weber,[347] socialist Union General Francis Channing Barlow,[348] communist Union Colonel Fritz Anneke,[349] communist Union Adjutant Anselm Albert,[350] socialist Union Colonel Charles Zagonyi,[351] socialist Union General (under General John C. Frémont) Alexander Sandor Asboth,[352] socialist Union Colonel George

Duncan Wells,[353] socialist Union General Alexander Schimmelfennig,[354] socialist Union Captain Isidor Bush,[355] socialist Union General Franz Sigel,[356] socialist Union Captain Gustav Von Struve,[357] socialist Union Chief Topographical Engineer (under Frémont) Johan Fiala,[358] socialist Union General Albin Francisco Schoepf,[359] socialist Union Colonel Henry Ramming,[360] socialist Union General Peter Joseph Osterhaus,[361] socialist Chief of the Ohio Army's Secret Service (under Union General George B. McClellan) Allan Pinkerton,[362] and

German socialist Karl Marx followed President Lincoln's career with great interest, personally congratulating him on his 1860 victory at the polls.

socialist Union General Friedrich Salomon,[363] among countless others.

A number of these anti-American European progressives were instrumental in organizing Union regiments, such as Yankee Generals Julius Stahel and Ludwig Blenker (who together set up the First German Rifles or Eighth New York Infantry).[364] No doubt the most famous socialist in Lincoln's army was the German-American revolutionary Carl Schurz,[365] a Forty-Eighter who arrived in America in 1852.[366] During the War Schurz not only rose to the rank of general,[367] but earlier, in 1860, he had campaigned for Lincoln and given speeches on his behalf,[368] later in his career serving as a Missouri Senator, U.S. Minister to Spain,[369] and U.S. Secretary of the Interior.[370] Naturally big government Liberal Lincoln and big government socialist Schurz considered themselves "good friends."[371]

Radical German socialist Friedrich Engels cowrote The Communist Manifesto with Marx. The two were friends with many of Lincoln's left-wing associates, administrators, and military officials.

The depth of passion socialists have always had for big government progressive Lincoln can be seen in the following May 1869 letter from the General Council of the

International Labor-Union to the National Labor Union. Among the many statements it contained were the following:

> In our address of felicitation to Mr. Lincoln on the occasion of his reelection to the presidency of the United States [in 1864], we expressed our conviction that the civil war would prove as important to the progress of the working class as the War of the Revolution had been for the progress of the bourgeoisie.
>
> And actually the victorious termination of the antislavery war has inaugurated a new epoch in the annals of the working class. In the United States an independent labor movement has since sprung into life, which is not being viewed with much favor by the old [Conservative] parties and the professional politicians.[372]

Forty-Eighter, Union General Carl Schurz, one of Lincoln's most ardent socialist admirers, played a major role in the Republican campaign of 1860, the Liberal party of that era.

Here we have confirmation from the Left that the American "Civil War" was indeed a contest between Conservatives or capitalists (which, generally speaking, Victorian socialists referred to as the "bourgeoisie") and Liberals (which they called the "proletariat" or laborers), and that these same socialists viewed the conflict as an "antislavery war"—even though Lincoln and Davis repeatedly and vigorously denied this throughout the bloody contest.[373]

While today's Liberals and uneducated Conservatives are fond of repeating the tired old yarn about the Civil War being "a battle over slavery," one must always bear in mind that it was 19th-Century socialists and communists—men and women who hated both the South and the concept of states' rights, and who would stop at nothing to destroy both—who most enthusiastically promoted this egregious lie. And why did they detest states' rights? Because they could not turn the U.S. into one large "indissoluble Union" or "indivisible nation" if the individual states were considered little "nations" unto themselves, with the power to ignore or overturn the decisions and activities of the central government.[374] This, in turn, is why early American Liberals, socialists, collectivists, and communists loathed the conservative South—and still do.

Was Lincoln himself a socialist? Not technically speaking. He owned private property (for example, his Greek Revival house in Springfield, Illinois) and businesses (for example, the German newspaper, the *Illinois Staats-Anzeiger*),[375] and as a lawyer often represented railroad corporations,[376] all three which are considered "sins" in the Church of Socialism.

Lincoln signing his fake and illegal Emancipation Proclamation. The President never referred to it as an "abolitionary measure" or a "civil rights emancipation." Instead he called it what it actually was: a "temporary war measure" and a "military emancipation." Hence, his radical left-wing friends and associates viewed the Emancipation Proclamation as a continuation of the violent socialist revolution that had failed in Europe in 1848.

However, his left-wing followers correctly saw his overall big government politics as progressive, and, as such, in harmony with many of their socialistic aims and causes. Thus, for them the "Civil War" was seen as a class struggle between the bourgeoisie (the middle class "oppressors") and the proletariat (the "oppressed" working class),[377] with even the Emancipation Proclamation counting as a socialist program—one not for the benefit of black civil rights, but for the benefit of the socialists' agenda, which needed free men to help advance the communist revolution and build its utopian democratic society.[378]

It was for these reasons that in 1863 British statesman Benjamin Disraeli could say that the conflict in the U.S. was a "great revolution" that would completely alter America,[379] while the *Springfield Republican* (of Massachusetts) championed the emancipatory edict as "the greatest social and political revolution of the age."[380] In 1892 socialists went as far as to boast that "socialism triumphed over statecraft [that is, states' rights] within a month, when Abraham Lincoln signed the Emancipation Proclamation."[381] Furthermore, they bragged, New England socialist Wendell Phillips went about

> the land telling his fellow-citizens that the chattel slaves having been freed, next in order was the emancipation of the wage slaves—as had been demanded over thirty years before by the originators of the [socialist] movement.[382]

Indeed, it was under our 16th president that the socialistic term "New Deal" arose, a phrase later borrowed by our 32nd president,[383] the same Liberal who launched the modern welfare state,[384] Franklin D. Roosevelt—who patterned his social legislation after Lincoln.[385]

New England socialist Margaret Fuller, faithful Lincoln devotee.

Lincoln and his socialist devotees worked closely together during his entire presidency. One of them was the tireless and obsessive socialist campaigner Carl Schurz, who even his own party members considered "irregular."[386] Schurz contributed to the writing of the 1860 Republican platform (successfully injecting a number of his anti-American ideas into the program),[387] while another socialist, Robert Dale Owen (son of famed Welsh-American utopian socialist Robert Owen),[388] helped inspire Lincoln's illegal and fake Emancipation Proclamation. According to socialist writer Morris Hillquit:

> [Owen's] letter to President Lincoln is said to have been a potent factor in bringing about the President's proclamation abolishing chattel slavery.[389]

In plain English, Lincoln's War and his Emancipation Proclamation were both, in great part, inspired by socialists, promoted by revolutionaries,

Socialist Ralph Waldo Emerson, one of many South-hating Yankee Liberals who adored Lincoln.

and encouraged by radical left-wingers in his party.

Other socialists—as well as those who "were favorably disposed toward Fourierism"[390]—who admired or even loved Lincoln, were Ralph Waldo Emerson, Nathaniel Hawthorne, Parke Godwin, Theodore Parker, George Ripley, William Ellery Channing, Margaret Fuller, George W. Curtis, Henry David Thoreau, and Amos Bronson Alcott, father of famed Concordian Louisa May Alcott (author of *Little Women*).[391] Why would such esteemed American reformers idolize and support Lincoln if he was not, in one way or another, in sympathy with their progressive goals, beliefs, and ideologies?

Scores of other socialists, radicals, and freethinkers, many of them foreign, either aided Lincoln in his 1860 campaign or actually worked in his administration; in many cases, both. Some began assisting him as early as 1854, the year the Republican (Liberal) Party was founded to limit, not abolish, slavery.[392] Individuals from these groups included: Frederick Hassaurek (Lincoln's minister to Ecuador);[393] Nicholas J. Rusch (a Union captain, Lieutenant Governor of Iowa, and Commissioner of German Emigration);[394] George Schneider (a supporter of Lincoln since 1856,[395] he was known as the "voice of the Forty-Eighters" and served as Lincoln's consul at Elsinore, Denmark);[396] Herman Kreismann (Secretary of the Legation at Berlin, Germany); Gustav Körner (Union colonel of volunteers and, after Schurz, Minister to Spain);[397] Johann Bernhard Stallo (like Lincoln, an anti-Bible, anti-Christian);[398] Heinrich Börnstein (Union military

Socialist Henry David Thoreau of Concord, Massachusetts, famed author of the American classic, *Walden*. Thoreau hated "Southern" slavery and loved Yankee Lincoln, but conveniently ignored the long history of slavery in his own New England town.

commander and consul to Bremen, Germany);[399] Carl Rotteck (a prominent Forty-Eighter);[400] Wilhelm Hoffbauer (another conspicuous Forty-Eighter);[401] and the aforementioned Theodore Canisius (one of Lincoln's business partners and also consul to Vienna, Austria).[402]

At least 42 of Lincoln's delegates at the 1860 Chicago Republican Convention were native Germans, many, if not most, who were socialists and were involved in some form of radical leftist politics. Lincoln's pre-convention group was also packed with Forty-Eighters, European ultra-liberals who supported his progressive ideas; men such as: Adolf Douai, Johannes Gambs, Elias Peissner, Heinrich Vortriede, Adolph Wiesner, Karl Dänzer, August Becker, Jakob Müller, Hermann Kiefer, Bernhard Domschke, Johannes Georg Günther, Robert Blum, and Karl Röser.[403]

LINCOLN
and the
COMMUNISTS
By Earl Browder

The cover of Earl Browder's 1936 book, Lincoln and the Communists, put out by the Workers Library Publishers. Another volume illustrating the overt link between our sixteenth president and the Far-Left.

Like moths to a flame, left-wingers, revolutionaries, humanists, Marxists, anarchists, radicals of all sorts, even fascists, have long been drawn to Lincoln, resulting in numerous books on the president's innate "socialism" and "communism." In 1936, communist Earl Browder came out with his book *Lincoln and the Communists*, writing admiringly:

> If the [communist] tradition of Lincoln is to survive, if his words shall play a role in political life today, this will be due not to the Republicans nor the Democrats, but to the modern representatives of historical progress, the Communists. Today, it is left to the Communist Party to revive the words of Lincoln.[404]

Twenty-six years earlier, in 1910, socialist Burke McCarty penned *Little Sermons in Socialism by Abraham Lincoln*. In it McCarty writes:

> We do not claim that Abraham Lincoln was a Socialist, for the word had not been coined in his day.[405] We do not claim that he would, if he had lived, been a Socialist to-day, for we do not know this.
> We do claim, and know, however, that Abraham Lincoln was in spirit

to the hour of his death, a class conscious working man, that his sympathies were with that class, that he voiced the great principles of the modern constructive Socialism of to-day, and that had he lived and been loyal and consistent with these principles which he always professed, he would be found within the ranks of the Socialist Party.[406]

As an example, McCarty notes that one of the socialist's credos is the unification of workers worldwide, and records the following words by Lincoln, uttered November 21, 1864, before a working men's association:

The strongest bond of human sympathy outside the family relation should be one uniting all working people of all nations, tongues and kindreds.[407]

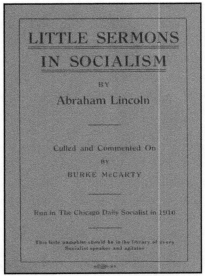

The cover of Burke McCarty's 1910 book, *Little Sermons in Socialism by Abraham Lincoln*, which appeared in *The Chicago Daily Socialist* that year. While the facts it contains have been suppressed today, early 20th-Century Americans were fully aware of who and what Lincoln was.

Lincoln's socialistic dislike of capitalism was evident early on, as McCarty points out, citing one of the future U.S. president's political speeches from 1837:

> These capitalists generally act harmoniously and in concert, to fleece the people, and now that they have got into a quarrel with themselves, we are called upon to appropriate the people's money to settle the quarrel.[408]

In November 1864, again, as McCarty shows, Lincoln toed the socialist party line by speaking out against corporations and the wealthy class who owned them:

> As a result of the war, corporations have been enthroned and an ear of corruption in high places will follow, and the money power of the country will endeavor to prolong its reign by working upon the prejudices of the people, until all wealth is aggregated in a few hands, and the Republic is destroyed!
>
> I feel at this moment more anxiety for the safety of my country than ever before, even in the midst of war. God grant that my suspicions may prove groundless![409]

Socialist Louisa May Alcott, noted Concordian and author of *Little Women*, supported Lincoln and the abolition of black slavery in the South. But she neglected to write about the inhumane treatment of freed Yankee slaves who had been banished by their owners to fetid squatter's camps around Walden Pond after the issuance of the Thirteenth Amendment.

President Lincoln even brought up his socialistic views in his First Annual Message to Congress on December 3, 1861. "Fellow-citizens of the Senate and House of Representatives," he declared that day:

> Labor is prior to, and independent of, capital. Capital is only the fruit of labor, and could never have existed if labor had not first existed. Labor is the superior of capital, and deserves much the higher consideration. Capital has its rights, which are as worthy of protection as any other rights. Nor is it denied that there is, and probably always will be, a relation between labor and capital, producing mutual benefits. The error is in assuming that the whole labor of community exists within that relation. A few men own capital, and that few avoid labor themselves, and with their capital hire or buy another few to labor for them.[410]

In 1863, after being made an honorary member of the socialist group, The Republican Workingmen's Association, President Lincoln invited its members to the White House and gave a lengthy and appreciative speech that began with these words:

> Gentlemen of the Committee: The honorary membership in your association, as generously tendered, is gratefully accepted.[411]

Obviously, at the very least, Lincoln possessed what I call "socialistic tendencies." Otherwise he would not have "gratefully accepted" an invitation to become a member of a socialist organization. Birds of a feather do flock together.

The thrust of his address to The Republican Workingmen's Association concerned the "Civil War." It was not abolitionary in tone, however, for Lincoln was no abolitionist.[412] Rather it was socialistic through and through. The "existing rebellion," he noted, is not about the "perpetuation of African slavery . . . it is, in fact, a war upon the rights of all working people."[413]

In 1913, German-American socialist and historian Herman Schlüter—who represented the American Socialist Party at its Second International Congress in 1904—published his book, *Lincoln,*

Lincoln eagerly selected socialists to serve in both his administration and his military, "gratefully accepted" an honorary membership in a socialist organization, and implemented dozens of socialist-style acts and policies during his presidency. I call these "socialistic tendencies."

Labor and Slavery: A Chapter from the Social History of America. Entirely devoted to our sixteenth president, Schlüter, while admitting that "Abraham Lincoln was not a Socialist, nor was he particularly friendly to workingmen,"[414] gives numerous examples of "Honest Abe's" socialist proclivities. One of these comes from the year 1847, at which time "Lincoln's approach to socialism"[415] emerged in his comments on labor issues:

> In the early days of our race the Almighty said to the first of our race, "In the sweat of thy face shalt thou eat bread," and since then, if we except the light and the air of heaven, no good thing has been or can be enjoyed by us without having first cost labor. And inasmuch as most good things are produced by labor, it follows that all such things of right belong to those whose labor has produced them. But it has so happened, in all ages of the world, that some have labored, and others have without labor enjoyed a large proportion of the fruits. This is wrong, and should not continue. To secure to each laborer the whole product of his labor, or as nearly as possible, is a worthy object of any good government.[416]

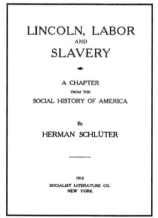

LINCOLN, LABOR
AND
SLAVERY
◆
A CHAPTER
FROM THE
SOCIAL HISTORY OF AMERICA

By
HERMAN SCHLÜTER

———

1913
SOCIALIST LITERATURE CO.
NEW YORK

The title page of Herman Schlüter's 1913 book, *Lincoln, Labor and Slavery*, published by the Socialist Literature Company. Another work filled with facts that most Americans are completely unaware of due to suppression, our faulty education system, and the widespread ignorance of the history of our two party system.

Admittedly Lincoln was not a pure socialist. Many Victorian socialists themselves viewed him as a "representative of the lower middle class, known in Europe as the *petit bourgeoisie.*"[417] Thus, we must not take his words out of context. However, it is clear that not only was he a publically avowed Liberal (he was, after all, the highest leader of the Republican Party, *the* Liberal party of that era, for nearly five years), but he held leftist views on countless issues. No doubt this is one of the reasons he was an avid reader of the New York *Tribune*, a left-wing newspaper owned by socialist Horace Greeley,[418] who was, as mentioned, closely associated with New Hampshire radical Charles A. Dana.[419] Who was Dana? A revolutionary who served as Lincoln's Assistant Secretary of War,[420] a Union assistant adjutant

Ultra socialist Charles A. Dana, friend of Karl Marx and Lincoln's assistant secretary of war.

general,[421] and managing editor of Greeley's *Tribune*. Dana was also an eyewitness to the socialist European revolution in 1848[422] and a mutual friend of the veritable founder of modern communism, Karl Marx[423]—who Greeley hired to write for his progressive newspaper.[424]

Seen through the lens of the "x number of degrees of separation" theory, Lincoln's connections to revolutionaries and socialists are seemingly endless. Dana alone, for example, just one of the president's radical administrators, was a member of and teacher,[425] as well as a director, at Brook Farm,[426] the famous socialist commune[427] founded in 1841 by the pre-Marxist utopian socialist George Ripley,[428] where Dana also worked as the manager of the group's periodical the *Harbinger*. The *Harbinger* had strong ties to the defunct Transcendental publication, the *Dial*, owned by socialist Margaret Fuller (and later Emerson),[429] which published "reform" articles on such topics as Fourierism and socialism.[430] Dana was also a member of "The Saturday Night Club," a Boston intellectual group whose members included other socialists, like Emerson and Hawthorne,[431] who were in turn friends with socialists Thoreau, Parker, Channing, and Alcott.[432] Such connections between Lincoln and the Far-Left could be drawn out almost indefinitely.

Without question the ultimate proof of Lincoln's progressive and even sometimes radical leftist political views comes from the fact that not only did he have much in common with Hitler (including a burning hatred of states' rights),[433] but the U.S. president actually borrowed (or assimilated) many of his wartime ideas from *The Communist Manifesto*, written by Marx and Engels in 1848. From my own study and

Utopian socialist George Ripley, founder of the socialist commune Brook Farm, and an associate of Charles A. Dana.

research into this issue I would include the following in this list:

1. The Communist Manifesto: "A heavy progressive or graduated income tax."[434] Lincoln was the founder of what would become the IRS.[435]

2. The Communist Manifesto: "Confiscation of the property of all rebels."[436] Lincoln ordered the seizure of the property of Southerners (especially wealthy ones), and after the War this property was given away, redistributed, or sold to carpetbaggers, Northern radicals, and industrialists.[437]

3. The Communist Manifesto: "Centralization of credit in the hands of the State, by means of a national bank with State capital and an exclusive monopoly."[438] Lincoln was instrumental in pushing for the establishment of a national banking system,[439] which began on February 25, 1863, under the new National Bank Act.[440]

4. The Communist Manifesto: "Centralization of the means of communication and transport in the hands of the State."[441] Lincoln was associated with enlarging the postal service, granting railroad contracts, and setting up the Bureau of Printing and Engraving.[442] The conservative South

Liberal Lincoln once told a government official: "The entire South needs to be obliterated and replaced with new businessmen and new ideas," a view that came straight from the South-hating, South-shaming socialist playbook.

was, of course, opposed to this kind of "government liberality," but the U.S. Congress under Lincoln forged ahead regardless.[443]

5. The Communist Manifesto: "The bringing into cultivation of wastelands, and the improvement of the soil generally in accordance with a common plan."[444] The Department of Agriculture was founded during the Lincoln Administration.[445]

6. The Communist Manifesto: "Gradual abolition of the distinction between town and country, by a more equable distribution of the population over the country."[446] One of Lincoln's chief goals was the Northernization of the South, to be remade into the industrial likeness of the Northeast. As Lincoln once coldly said to Interior Department official T. J. Barnett: "The entire South needs to be obliterated and replaced with new businessmen and new ideas."[447]

7. The Communist Manifesto: "Free [that is, tax-payer/government-sponsored] education for all children in public schools."[448] Lincoln's Morrill Act, passed by Congress in 1862, gave 20,000 acres of public lands to each representative in Congress. The proceeds from the sale of these lands were used to establish the first land-grant colleges, which focused on agricultural, mechanical, scientific, military, and classical arts and subjects.[449]

Lincoln also opposed organized religion and was a self-admitted anti-Bible, anti-Christian "infidel,"[450] which aligns him with anti-religious liberals, socialists, and communists, like Marx and Engels, the world over.[451]

Marx (shown here) and Lincoln had much in common and shared similar views on a number of issues.

We must also consider the fact that leftists who came after Lincoln imitated *him* specifically, not Conservative Jefferson Davis. In 1867, for instance, under the auspices of Democrat (a Conservative at the time) President Andrew Johnson (a rare Southerner who remained loyal to the Union during Lincoln's War), the intrusive, expensive, cumbersome, unnecessary, and unconstitutional Department of Education was begun. Strengthened from the 1950s onward and officially launched and expanded in 1980 by ultra Liberal President Jimmy Carter, today it has grown into a massive propaganda machine, one of whose main purposes is to inculcate our youth with socialist, progressive, communist, anti-American ideas and doctrines. This, of course, perfectly accords with the motivations of the early American socialists and communists who promoted both Lincoln and documents like *The Communist Manifesto*.[452]

Proof that Lincoln's Republican Party was a liberal body hell bent on destroying not slavery but the Constitution, and that Davis' Democratic Party was a conservative body fighting to save not slavery but the Constitution, can be seen in the remarks made by those living in the mid 1800s.

Confederate icon and Democrat Robert E. Lee, like Jefferson Davis, a Southern Conservative who hated slavery and loved the Constitution, significant facts that have been left out of our history books.

We will look at a few of these now. But before we do, we must correctly define the word "democracy." Why? Because in the Victorian Era this word meant something different than it does today. Add to this the problem created by uneducated modern day Liberals, who continue to insist that "the U.S. is a democracy."

It cannot be strongly emphasized enough that the U.S. is not now and never has been a democracy. The Founders were very much against the idea of forming a democracy, which is why the word does not appear in any of our country's most important documents. These would include: the Declaration of Independence, the Articles of Confederation,[453] the U.S. Constitution,[454] and the constitutions of the 50 states.[455] In 1770, Scotsman Alexander Fraser Tytler explained why enlightened early Americans and Europeans were so against the concept of democracy:

A democracy cannot exist as a permanent form of government. It can only exist until the voters discover that they can vote themselves largesse from the public treasury. From that moment on, the majority always votes for the candidates promising the most benefits from the public treasury, with the result that a democracy always collapses over loose fiscal policy, always followed by a dictatorship. The average age of the world's greatest civilizations has been 200 years. These nations have progressed through this sequence: From bondage to spiritual faith; From spiritual faith to great courage; From courage to liberty; From liberty to abundance; From abundance to selfishness; From selfishness to apathy; From apathy to dependence; From dependence back into bondage.[456]

Even many 18th-Century American Liberals understood the perils of living under a pure democracy. In 1788 big government Federalist Alexander Hamilton uttered the following words at a convention in Poughkeepsie, New York:

> It has been observed, that a pure democracy, if it were practicable, would be the most perfect government. Experience has proved, that no position in politics is more false than this. The ancient democracies, in which the people themselves deliberated, never possessed one feature of good government. Their very character was tyranny; their figure deformity.[457]

Even early American Liberals, like Federalist Alexander Hamilton, understood the dangers of pure democracy.

In 1922 noted historian David S. Muzzey made these comments on the concept of democracy:

> Democracy is a relative term. A literal rule of the people [that is, a "pure democracy"] is possible only in small communities like a New England town or a Swiss canton. In large political units, like state or nation, a pure democracy yields to a representative democracy [known today as a "republic"]. [Here,] instead of "government of the people by the people" there is government of the people by their chosen agents—with a great variety of qualifications for both the agents and the choosers.
>
> The fathers of the American republic were not concerned to strengthen democracy on these shores. They made no provision in the Constitution for

enlarging the suffrage, accepting as qualified to vote for national representatives and presidential electors those whom the various states allowed to vote for "the most numerous branch" of their legislatures. And the suffrage in the various states, in turn, was quite generally the same as in the old colonial governments, which were anything but "democratic." It is estimated that in Washington's administration not more than one male adult in seven was a voter, while the actual direction of politics was in the hands of a small group of "the rich, the well born, and the able," who regarded any disposition of the people at large to interfere with their prerogative as a kind of ungrateful impertinence.

Even Jefferson, who was looked on as a dangerous innovator for his devotion to the "French doctrine" of the rights of man, confined his "democracy" in practice to furthering the interests of the common people through the authorities already established instead of overthrowing those authorities. He made no campaign for the extension of the suffrage or the principles of "direct government" [that is, direct democracy]. In fact, the social soil of the old states, with their colonial traditions, was not favorable to the growth of a real democracy. [458]

In 1788, in *The Federalist*, James Madison discusses the confusion between a republic (that is, a *representative democracy*), and a democracy (that is, a *direct democracy*):

> The error which limits republican government to a narrow district, has been unfolded and refuted in preceding papers. I remark here only, that it seems to owe its rise and prevalence chiefly to the confounding of a republic with a democracy; and applying to the former, reasonings drawn from the nature of the latter.
>
> The true distinction between these forms, was also adverted to on a former occasion. It is, that in a democracy, the people meet and exercise the government in person: in a republic, they assemble and administer it by their representatives and agents. A democracy, consequently, must be confined to a small spot. A republic may be extended over a large region.
>
> To this accidental source of the error, may be added the artifice of some celebrated authors, whose writings have had a great share in forming the modern standard of political opinions. Being subjects, either of an absolute, or limited monarchy, they have endeavored to heighten the advantages, or palliate the evils, of those forms by placing in comparison with them the vices and defects of the republican, and by citing, as specimens of the latter, turbulent democracies of ancient Greece and modern Italy. Under the confusion of names, it has been an easy task to transfer to a republic, observations applicable to a democracy only; and, among others, the observation that it can never be established but among a small number of people, living within a small compass of territory. [459]

In essence, a democracy is a political body that is *ruled by majority*. The Founding Fathers, however, intentionally set up the U.S. as a republic: a political body that is *ruled by law*.[460]

More technically, the U.S. began as a Confederate Constitutional Republic, "Confederate" meaning a group of all powerful sovereign nation-states operating under the auspices of a small limited central government; "Constitutional" meaning that the states are bound by an official constitution that can only be changed by their citizens; and "Republic" meaning a government run by representatives elected by its citizens rather than by direct vote (which would be a pure democracy).[461]

Some important Conservative U.S. statesmen and politicians from the Victorian Era. From the top going clockwise: Lucius Q. Lamar, Thomas F. Bayard, Benjamin H. Hill, Augustus H. Garland, James B. Beck, Samuel J. Randall. Center: Alexander H. Stephens.

Now that we have established the meaning of "democracy," as well as the intent of the Founders, let us look at some early American views on both the liberal origins and core principles of Lincoln and the Republican Party, and the conservative origins and core principles of Jefferson Davis and the Democratic Party. We will begin with Southern author Elizabeth Avery Meriwether, who wrote under the pseudonym "George Edmonds." In the following excerpts from 1904 she uses the word "monarchy" for what we now call *liberalism*, and the word "democracy" for "republicanism" or "Americanism"—or what we now call *conservatism* (the Democrats had, up until recently, been Conservatives before, as we will see, switching party platforms in 1896).[462] Meriwether writes:

The underlying cause of every conflict between man and man, tribe and tribe, country and country, has been on the one side a craving for power, on the other side an effort to escape that power. The nascent spirit of one is Monarchy [liberalism], of the other Democracy [conservatism]. These two principles are inherently and eternally antagonistic, and underlie nearly, if not every, war fought on earth. Stratas of superficial causes usually overlay and cover up the real causes of war, as they did in the war on the South [1861-1865].

The seven years' war which severed the seceded Colonies from British rule was an open, undisguised fight between Monarchy [liberalism] and Democracy [conservatism]. The four years' war between the Southern and Northern States was a fight between the same old enemies. Monarchy and Democracy, though the astute Republican party [then Liberal], while heart and soul Imperialistic [left-wing], concealed and covered up that principle under loud declarations of Freedom and blatant professions of humanitarianism. Under these hypocritical cloaks, the Monarchic [Liberal] principles had full swing for four years, and committed every species of crime and outrage peculiar to enraged Monarchists [Liberals]. When the [British] soldiers of Monarchy [Liberalism] in 1783 took ships and sailed Eastward to their kingly country [England], the soldiers of Democracy [conservatism] fondly hoped they had driven their ancient enemy forever from this New Continent. The snake was scotched, but not killed. Nor was it banished. It remained here in our midst with veiled features and softened voice, biding its chance to up and regain its former power.

Federalist Gouverneur Morris of New York, an early American Liberal.

Alexander Hamilton was the head and front of American Monarchists [Liberals]. He wanted to make this Government a pure Monarchy [defined here in our modern terms as a federalized socialist nation]. Hamilton advocated a "strong centralized Government," of imperial policy. Gouverneur Morris, a contemporary and friend of Hamilton, said:

"Hamilton hated Republican [then Conservative] Government, and never failed on every occasion to advocate the excellence of and avow his attachment to a Monarchic [Liberal] form of Government."

From the formation of the Union, the Federalists [Liberals] of New England hated and feared Democratic [Conservative] principles. Their great leader, Hamilton, made no secret of this feeling. In his speech at a New York banquet Hamilton, in high opposition to [Thomas] Jefferson's Democracy [conservatism], cried out: "The People! Gentlemen, I tell you the people are a great Beast!" In 1796 [Liberal] Gov. [Oliver] Walcott, of Connecticut, said: "I sincerely declare that I wish the [Liberal] Northern States would separate from the [Conservative] Southern the moment that event (the election of [Conservative] Jefferson) shall take place."

Federalist William Plumer, one of scores of early Yankee Liberals who campaigned for the secession of the Northern states a half century before the South began seceding in 1860.

Congressman [William] Plumer [of New Hampshire], a Federalist [big government Liberal] and an ardent Secessionist, in 1804 declared that "All dissatisfied with the measures of the Government looked to a separation of the States as a remedy for grievances."

As early as 1796 men of Massachusetts began to talk of New England seceding from the Union. It was declared that if [Liberal John] Jay's negotiation closing the Mississippi for twenty years could not be adopted, it was high time for the New England States to secede from the Union and form a Confederation by themselves.

The Monarchic [liberal/dictatorial] principles did not thrive under Hamilton's lead. Hamilton was too plain spoken. The Republican [Liberal] party [formed in 1854] became more astute. In 1861, while making loud professions of desiring the largest freedom for the people, that party was making ready to rob them of every liberty they possessed. "At the formation of this Union," says [Liberal journalist] E. P. [Edward Payson] Powell, "Hamilton laid before the Constitutional Convention of 1787 eleven propositions, which he wished to make the basis of the Union, but they were so Monarchistic [liberalistic] in tone they received no support whatever."

The Republican [Liberal] war on the South stood solidly on Monarchic [Liberal] principles. The [Conservative] principles of 1776 were set aside in the 1860s, but not for years after the [conservative] South was conquered did Republicans [then Liberals] openly admit they were inspired by the spirit of Monarchy [socialism, centralization, and empire building]. During [Conservative U.S. President William] McKinley's last campaign, Hamilton was loudly lauded and Jefferson decried as a visionary, a French anarchist. Hamilton Clubs were organized and Republican [Liberal] novelists set to writing romances with [left-wing] Hamilton as the hero. During [Liberal James A.] Garfield's campaign, a Republican [liberal] paper, the Lemars, Iowa, *Sentinel*, said:

Republican President James A. Garfield, a Liberal, sought to destroy states' rights and establish an all powerful national government.

"Garfield's rule will be the transitory period between State Sovereignty [conservatism and traditionalism] and National Sovereignty [liberalism and socialism]. The United States Senate will give way to a National Senate. State Constitutions and the United States Senate are relics of State Sovereignty [states' rights] and implements of treason. Garfield's Presidency will be the Regency of Stalwartism [partisan devotion]; after that—Rex [that is, King]."

Fate used the hand of an insane "Stalwart" [Charles J. Guiteau of Illinois] to impede, if not estop, the Monarchic plans of that time [by assassinating Garfield]. The New York *Sun*, July 3rd, 1881, quoted President Garfield as saying:

"The influence of [Thomas] Jefferson's Democratic [conservative] principles is rapidly waning, while the principles of Hamilton [liberalism] are rapidly increasing. Power has been gravitating toward the Central Government."

Power did not gravitate, it was wrenched at one jerk to the Central Government by Lincoln's hand. Not until after Hamilton and Jefferson had passed away did the followers of Jefferson drop the name "Republican" which they had borne during his life, and [in 1828] assume the name "Democrat."

[Representative] Democracy—the rule of the people—is more expressive of Jefferson's doctrines. Not until 1854 did the men of the Federal and Whig persuasion [Liberals all] unite and organize a party and take the name "Republican." The Republican party of the 1860s was the legitimate offspring of the old New England Federalists [early American Liberals], and inherited all its progenitor's faiths, hopes, hates and purposes, viz: Passion for power, fear and hate of Democracy, hate of the Union, belief in States' Rights, in States' Sovereignty, in Secession, and the strong persistent determination to break the Union asunder and form of the Northeast section a Northeastern Confederacy. All these ideas belonged to the old Federalists of New England, and were handed down to the [newly formed] Republican [Liberal] party in 1854.

Wendell Phillips, New England's tongue of fire, speaking of the inherent purposes of his party, said: "The Republican [Liberal] party is in no sense a national party. It is a party of the North, organized against the [Conservative] South."

Even Yankee Liberal Wendell Phillips admitted that the Republican Party, the Liberal party of Abraham Lincoln, was formed as an anti-South faction.

The Republican [Liberal] party was organized against the South, organized to fight the [Conservative] South in every possible way; to fight as its progenitors, the Federalists [early American Liberals], had fought from 1796 to 1854, with calumnies, vituperations, false charges, every word and phrase hate could use, until the time came to use guns, bayonets, bullets, cannon balls and shells; and faithfully did that party carry out the ignoble and cruel purpose of its organization.

The war on the South was begun by the Federalists [Liberals] of New England in 1796. In 1814 a work of some four hundred and fifty pages, called *The Olive Branch*, was published in Boston, which throws electric light on certain almost forgotten events in New England's history.[463] *The Olive Branch* contains extracts from a series of remarkable productions called the "Pelham Papers," which appeared in the Connecticut *Courant* in the year 1796. The

Courant was published by Hudson and Goodwin, men of Revolutionary standing. The Pelham Papers were said to have been the joint production of men of the first talent and influence in the State. Commenting on these papers of 1796, *The Olive Branch* of 1814 says:

"A Northeastern Confederacy has been the object for a number of years. They (the [Liberal] politicians of New England) have repeatedly advocated in public print, separation of the States. The project of separation was formed shortly after the adoption of the Federal [U.S.] Constitution. The promulgation of the project first appeared in the year 1796, in these Pelham Papers. At that time there was none of that catalogue of grievances which since that period, have been fabricated to justify the recent attempt to dissolve the Union."[464]

This refers to the efforts made in 1804 and 1814 to get the New England States to secede from the Union, so they might be separated from the Democratic [conservative] Southern and Western States. *The Olive Branch* continues:

"At that time there was no 'Virginia Dynasty,' no 'Democratic [conservative] Madness,' no 'war with Great Britain.' The affairs of the country seemed to be precisely according to New England's [Liberals'] fondest wishes. Yet at that favorable time (1796) New England was dissatisfied with the Union and begun to plot to get out of it. The common people, however, were not then ready to break up the Union. The common people at that time had no dislike of the [conservative] Southern States.

Then [liberal] New England writers, preachers and politicians deliberately began the wicked work of poisoning their minds against the [conservative] Southern States. To sow hostility, discord and jealousy between the different sections of the Union was the first step New England took to accomplish her favorite object, a separation of the States. Without this efficient instrument, all New England's efforts would have been utterly unavailing. Had the honest yeomanry of the Eastern States continued to respect and regard their Southern fellow-citizens as friends and brothers, having one common interest in the promotion of the general welfare, it would be impossible to have made them instruments in the unholy work of destroying the noble, the splendid Union."[465]

But for the unholy work of having taught the common people of [liberal] New England to hate the [conservative] people of the South, the cruel war of the 1860s would never have been fought. "For eighteen years," continues *The*

Olive Branch (the eighteen years from 1796 to 1814),

> "the most unceasing endeavors have been used to poison the minds of the people of the [liberal] Eastern States toward, and to alienate them from, their fellow-citizens of the [conservative] Southern States. The people of the South have been portrayed as 'demons incarnate,' as destitute of all the 'good qualities which dignify and adorn human nature.' Nothing can exceed the virulence drawn [by Yankee Liberals] of the [conservative] South's people, their descriptions of whom would more have suited the ferocious inhabitants of New Zealand than a polished, civilized people."[466]

Victorian historians correctly considered Lincoln a mid 19th-Century version of Liberal monarchist Alexander Hamilton.

. . . Mr. A. K. Fiske, a distinguished Republican [Liberal], throws some light on the relationship of the two parties, Hamilton's and Jefferson's; in other words, the party favoring Monarchy [liberalism] and the party favoring Democracy [conservatism], the rule of the people. "Hamilton and Jefferson," says Fiske in April 1879,

> "represent the two opposing ideas which prevailed at the time our Government was formed, and which, with some variations, have been the basis of our political divisions into parties ever since, and have been involved in all the contests and controversies in our constitutional career. [Liberal] Hamilton embodied the tendency to a centralization of power in the national Government. There is no doubt that he would have preferred a monarchy. [Conservative] Jefferson, on the other hand, represented the demand for a complete diffusion of sovereignty among the people, and its

exercise locally and in the States, and the confining of national functions as closely as possible under the most restrictive interpretation of the Constitution."

Mr. Fiske admits that Hamilton, the monarchist, represented the [Liberal] party which opposed the sovereignty of the people. A writer in the St. Louis *Globe-Democrat*, a staunch [liberal] advocate of Hamilton's strong government doctrines, in that paper, March 6, 1898, made this significant comment:

> "The resemblance between [Liberal] Hamilton and [Liberal] Lincoln is so close no one can resist it. Hamilton is dwarfed by no man. A just parallel of Hamilton and Lincoln will show them alike in many ways. They were alike almost to the point of identity. Hamilton's work made Lincoln's possible."

Hamilton's tomb, Trinity Churchyard, New York City. Hamilton's desire to transform the U.S. into a European-style monarchy was later refurbished as "big government" politics by Liberals like Lincoln and Obama.

Hamilton's monarchic principles certainly made Lincoln's work possible. Lincoln put in practice what Hamilton had advocated. Hamilton made no concealment of his monarchic principles; he preferred a monarchy such as England has, but failing that he wanted a President for life and the Governors of States appointed by the President. Until seated in the White House, Lincoln talked Democracy [conservatism] and affected great esteem for Jefferson's Democratic [conservative] principles.

As soon as he held in his grip the machinery of government, he schemed for absolute power, and as soon as he was commander in chief of nearly 3,000,000 armed men, no imperial despot in pagan time ever wielded more autocratic power than did Abraham Lincoln, and Republican [Liberal] writers of today [1904, the year of this writing] are so imbued with imperialism they laud and glorify Lincoln for his usurpation of power.

Slave owning Liberal, Union General Ulysses S. Grant, was a member of Lincoln's anti-South party, whose goal was to overthrow the Constitution and enlarge the powers of the central government.

Although [today, 1904,] well informed Republicans [Liberals] know that the war on the South was waged neither to save the Union nor to free slaves, it does not suit that party to be candid on this subject. Now and then, however, some Republican [Liberal] forgets the party's policy of secrecy and tells the truth. That boldly imperialistic Republican [Liberal] journal, the *Globe-Democrat*, of St. Louis, in its issue of April 9, 1900, had an article which uncovers facts, even to the foundation stones, on which rested the war of the 1860's. Consider the following:

> "Lincoln, Grant and the Union armies gave a victory to Hamiltonism (Monarchy) [liberalism] when it subjugated the Confederates (Democrats) [Conservatives] in the South. (This is strictly true; it was a victory over Democracy [conservatism] by Monarchy [liberalism].) The cardinal doctrines of Democracy [conservatism] are the enlargement of the power of the States [that is, states' rights]. All the prodigious energies of the war could not extinguish these. The lesson of the war was extreme and

extraordinary, and yet in a sense ineffective."

Ineffective, because it did not crush out the very life of Democracy [conservatism]. Monarchists [Liberals] always appear to be ignorant of the fact that there is a streak of divinity in Democracy [conservatism] which cannot be killed. Monarchy [liberalism] a thousand and ten thousand times has fancied it has forever put an end to Democracy [conservatism], but sooner or later it rises up, fronts and fights for the rights of humanity with all its power.

"The Democrats [Conservatives]," continues the *Globe-Democrat*, "have been since the war more strenuous than before in insisting on the preservation of the power of the States."

The cardinal doctrine of the Democratic [Conservative] party has not been, since the formation of the Union, the enlargement of State power, but has been the preservation of the power reserved to the States by the Constitution [states' rights]. The cardinal power of the Republican [Liberal] party, since the day Mr. Lincoln assumed the Presidency, has been the enlargement of executive power. No well-informed man can deny this.[467]

Washington (left) and Hamilton (right) meeting for the first time.

Here are some more samples from those who lived in the Victorian Era, eyewitnesses to the right-wing policies of the American Conservative Party, the Democrats, and the left-wing policies of the American Liberal Party, the Republicans, during and after Lincoln's War. Again, let us bear in mind that the word "democracy" was defined differently in the 1800s, a fact that I will note in brackets where appropriate:

The Republican [Liberal] party [of Lincoln] is in no sense a National party; it is a party pledged to work for the downfall of Democracy [conservatism], the downfall of the [Founding Father's voluntary] Union, and the destruction of the United States Constitution. The religious creed of the party was hate of Democracy [conservatism], hate of the [original] Union, hate of the Constitution, and hate of the Southern people. . . . The Republican [Liberal] party is the first sectional party ever organized in this country. It does not know its own face and calls itself National, but it is not National, it is sectional. It is the party of the North pledged against the South. It was organized with hatred of the Constitution.

The Republican [Liberal] party that elected Abraham Lincoln is pledged to the downfall of the [Founders'] Union and the destruction of the United States Constitution. William Lloyd Garrison believed in the Constitutional right to hold slaves, and said the Union must be dissolved to free them. He believed in the Constitutional right of secession, so was willing to publicly burn the Constitution to destroy that right and called it 'a compact with death and a league with hell." — Wendell Phillips of Massachusetts.[468]

South-loathing Yankee Liberal Benjamin F. Wade sympathized with the South for seceding.

"Mr. Lincoln assumed the dictatorship, overthrew the government as it was formed by issuing a military edict or decree which changed the fundamental law of the land, and declared that he would maintain this by all the military and naval power of the United States."—R. G. Horton, Northern author.[469]

"Mr. Lincoln, finding a geographical party in the process of formation, allowed himself to be placed at its head, and encouraged its action by that sectional declaration, 'I believe this government cannot permanently endure half slave and half free.' That expression gave hope to the abolitionists [Radicals], and defeated [Conservative] Stephen Douglas."—George Lunt of Massachusetts.[470]

"I do not blame the [conservative] people of the South for seceding, for the men of that [Liberal Republican] party about to take the reins of government in their hands are her mortal foes, and stand ready to trample her institutions under feet." — Benjamin F. Wade from Ohio, a confirmed South-loather.[471]

"The Republican [Liberal] party is a conspiracy under the form, but in violation of the [conservative] spirit of the Constitution of the United States to exclude the [conservative] citizens of slaveholding States from all sharing in the government of the country, and to compel them to adapt their institutions to the opinions of the [liberal] citizens of the free [Northern] States." — Judge William A. Duer of New York.[472]

New Yorker William A. Duer said that Lincoln's Liberal Republican Party was nothing but a "conspiracy" to Northernize the Conservative South.

"The nomination of Mr. Lincoln was purely accidental, and that he was a sectional candidate upon merely sectional grounds none can deny and for the first time in the history of the republic, a candidate was thus presented for the suffrages of its citizens." — George Lunt of Massachusetts.[473]

"Many Republicans [at the time Liberals] desire a dissolution of the Union and urge war as a means of accomplishing dissolution. . . . The leaders of the Republican party are striving to break up the Union under pretense of unbounded devotion to it. Hostility to slavery on the part of the [left-wing] disunionists is stronger than fidelity to the Constitution." — Stephen A. Douglas of Illinois.[474]

Yankee Democrat Stephen A. Douglas, a Conservative, declared what was and still is obvious to all thinking people: Lincoln's Republican Party (Liberal) was trying to destroy the Union through warfare while pretending to "preserve" it.

"I shall stress that this war was not waged by the [liberal] North to preserve the Union, or to maintain Republican [here meaning conservative] institutions, but to destroy both. It will be seen that the war changed the entire character and system of our government, overthrew the rights of States, and forced amendments against the action of the people. . . . At the very time the abolitionists [Liberals] were preaching a mad crusade against the Union, and *educating a generation to hate the government of our fathers*, Southern men, the great [Conservative] leaders of the South, were begging and imploring that the Union might be preserved." — R. G. Horton, Northern author.[475]

"Republican [Liberal] hate has blasted the fair heritage of our fathers. The prediction made two years before Daniel Webster's death has literally come true. He said: 'If these [left-wing] fanatics (abolitionists) ever get the power in their own hands they will override the Constitution, set the Supreme Court at defiance, change and make laws to suit themselves, lay violent hands on them who differ in opinion, or who dare question their fidelity, and finally deluge the country with blood.'" — The *Cincinnati Enquirer*, January 15, 1881.[476]

If this sounds exactly like the Liberal Party of today, that is because it is! They are one and the same, the Liberal 21st-Century Democratic party being the direct descendant of the Liberal 19th-Century Republicans.

How few are aware of this reality is readily demonstrated by the fact that today's Liberals routinely and ignorantly compare the Conservative Confederates to the Socialist Nazis—despite the obvious fact that they were on opposite ends of the political spectrum and had not a single thing in common. Uneducated early 20th-Century Liberals engaged in a similar and equally absurd ploy by comparing the isolationistic Confederates of the American "Civil War" (1861-1865) to the imperialistic Germans of World War I (1914-1918).

Comparing the Germans of World War I, shown here, with the Confederates of the Civil War reveals an appalling ignorance of both the history of international politics and America's two-party system.

Happily, many early Yankees refused to accept or believe the anti-South propaganda put out by progressives regarding the Confederacy, Lincoln's War, and World War I. Matthew Page Andrews of Baltimore, Maryland, cites one of these intelligent, well-informed Northerners, Reverend A. W. Littlefield, in the following relevant article from 1918, entitled, "Fighting For the Same Principle." It was written in the final year of "the War to End All Wars":

> In view of the fact that every newspaper and periodical in the North has in one way or another made some comparison between the Germany of to-day and the Southern Confederacy, I feel sure that your readers will be particularly interested in seeing some extracts from a remarkable letter I received from Rev. A. W. Littlefield, of Needham, a loyal and liberal [here meaning "generous"] son of Massachusetts. He writes:
>
> > "Now, as evolution and growth are always likely to develop too far in any given direction unless restrained by opposing and complementary forces, the [liberal] North was sure to so

overdevelop the issue of 'a perfect Union, one and inseparable,' that the States holding to 'consent of the governed, local self-government, and self-determination of sovereign States,' in this case the [conservative] Southern States, were sure to array themselves against the [liberal] Northern States, which were the sponsors of Lincoln's view and that of the North generally.

In reality, the Civil War equivalent of these World War I German machine gunners was Lincoln and his Republican Party (Liberals), not the Southern Democratic Confederates (Conservatives), who were fighting to preserve states' rights, the Constitution, and the government of the U.S. Founding Fathers.

"Not only did the tendency of a principle to overdevelop itself show itself on our continent, but in Europe Germany has done this very thing to the fullest extent—viz, carried federation to the complete extreme of imperialism. And nothing but Allied success in this war can prevent the evolutionary process, unrestrained, from completely Romanizing (Prussianizing in this case) the whole world. And nothing but the taking up of arms in 1861 by the South has prevented the imperializing of America, in my judgment. I am not quite sure that Charles Francis Adams [Jr.] saw this fact. Certainly most Americans are not in the least aware of it, if one may judge from history and current comment. The mere A B C of evolutionary processes ought to teach people its tendency and its danger if restraining elements are not brought to bear. The [conservative] South furnished such restraint in America, and the [conservative] Allies are doing likewise in this world war.

"If the South and the Allies occupy the same status in principle, why did not the South win? Not only because superior forces were arrayed against her, but because the North succeeded in convincing her people that the South was abjectly immoral, in that she 'held human beings in bondage.' This issue completely obscured the great politico-economic morality of the Southern people, the really true Americans. That feeling, that the South should be crushed because of her 'iniquitous immorality,' was dominant in 1861 and still persists to-day.

"I surely believe that had the North and England really understood that the South was fighting for precisely such principles as the Allies are fighting for to-day, there would have been no war against the South; and had that been the case, I also am of the opinion that the Anglo-Southern American principles would have so affected the world that Germany would never have gotten her start in her attempt to imperialize mankind. But the evolutionary process was developing so fast in Europe and the seeming immorality of the South in holding human beings in bondage was brought so to the fore that the coalition of real Englishmen in the Old and the New World could not at that time be consummated. That union is now at hand, and there can be but one result.

The 1861 First National Confederate Flag (above left), with its red and white stripes and circle of 13 white stars on a blue field, was purposefully designed to imitate the Betsy Ross Flag (above right), with its red and white stripes and circle of 13 stars on a blue field, and which was one of the first national flags used by the U.S. in the 1790s. Here we have yet more evidence that the Conservative South was not trying to "destroy the Union of our Fathers," as Liberal Lincoln was fond of saying, but rather was trying to preserve it. It was the Victorian Liberals, then known as the Republican Party, who were trying to destroy it.

"I verily believe that in principle the new federation of the English-speaking peoples and their Latin allies could do no better when they come to draw up the constitution for world federation than to take for their model the Constitution of the Confederate States with but very slight modifications. For unless such principles become the basis of this coming world federation, evolutionary processes, just because they constantly tend to over-development, will irresistibly carry world federation, even under Allied auspices, over the line into world imperialism, precisely as the Germans most desire and are so savagely fighting for."

Mr. Littlefield goes further to say that the North was wrong in her contention and that might [physical force] triumphed because of the struggle of the South against undue centralization, great crushing combinations of business and provincialism, and commerce-killing high tariffs. He adds "that the so-called 'Lost Cause' is not dead, but has become the herald of the patriot dawn": that historically these things should be "settled right"; and that "the coming generation needs to realize these truths so that legislation may be modified away from imperialism back to true federalism [that is, confederalism or republicanism] resting upon the true principles of consent of the governed, local self-government, and the self-determination of sovereign States."[477]

Having thoroughly examined Lincoln's first term in office as a big government Leftist heading the socialistic Liberal Republican Party of 1860, we now pass onto his reelection by Liberals in 1864. From there it would be a mere 32 years until the two main parties switched platforms, making the election of 1896 one of the most important yet seldom discussed chapters in American history—and which thus necessitated the writing of this very book.

The Battle of Hampton Roads, March 8-9, 1862, where two ironclads, the CSS *Virginia* (left) and the USS *Monitor* (right), fought off the coast of Norfolk, Virginia. The Confederate States of America was a constitutionally formed republic at the time. Why then were there U.S. warships in C.S. waters? It was just another case of self-righteous Northern Liberals seeking to control the lives of Southern Conservatives, the same battle that rages on today.

4

FROM LINCOLN TO CLEVELAND 1864 TO 1896

OPERATING UNDER THE REPUBLICANS' NEW temporary name, the National Union Party (made up of old-time Whigs and antislavery Republicans from 1860),[478] Liberal Lincoln won the 1864 election, our 20th, employing many of the same diabolical tactics he used to get elected in 1860. Helped along considerably that year by Confederate General John Bell Hood's disastrous loss at the Battle of Atlanta (July 22, 1864),[479] Lincoln pulled out all the stops in an effort to get reelected, lowering himself to criminal behavior unheard of by any American president before or since. Unfortunately for Dixie, his reelection illegalities succeeded and he was handed a second term.[480]

Though Lincoln won both the popular and the electoral votes in 1864, this, his second victory, was nothing to brag about. Not only did he use countless tricks and

Confederate General John Bell Hood inadvertently helped Lincoln win the 1864 election.

crimes to insure the outcome, but none of the Southern states voted in the U.S. elections that year (for Lincoln a loss of 80 potential electoral votes). They were now part of a separate, sovereign, and foreign republic: the Confederate States of America, named after an early nickname for the U.S.A.,[481] and which President Jefferson Davis correctly called "the last best hope of liberty."[482]

Of the Northerners and Westerners who voted in the 1864 U.S. election, only 55 percent (2,218,388 individuals of 4,031,887) thought Lincoln deserved a second chance. A full 45 percent (1,813,499 individuals), nearly half, voted for Lincoln's main opposition, George B. McClellan, whose party platform and vice presidential running mate, George Hunt Pendleton, were antiwar and openly condemned Lincoln for flagrantly curbing civil liberties. Lincoln won then by only 400,000 votes,[483] and many of these were illicitly obtained, as we will see.

Conservative Confederate President Jefferson Davis referred to the U.S.A. of the Founding Generation as "the last best hope of liberty," a concept completely foreign to Liberals.

In 1864, as in 1860, all of Lincoln's electoral votes came from non-Southern states (except for West Virginia, which, as we will see, Lincoln had illegally created for this very purpose).[484] Yet, if only 38,111 people, a mere 1 percent of Northerners and Westerners, had changed their votes in specific regions, Lincoln would have forfeited even the electoral vote, and McClellan's peace party would have won.[485] If the South had also voted, it is, of course, a dead certainty that Lincoln would have lost that year,[486] which is undoubtedly one of the reasons he illegally banned the eleven states of the Confederacy from participating in the 1864 election.[487] This was unlawful because, according to Lincoln himself, the Confederacy was not a legitimate foreign country, it was still part of the Union.

Indeed, for the rest of his life he never publicly recognized the Confederacy as anything other than eleven states "in rebellion" against the U.S.A.—even though, as President Davis pointed out privately, Lincoln was obviously fully aware that the C.S.A. was a separate country, otherwise he would not have called up troops, enacted the Anaconda Plan, and blockaded the South (all which would have been unlawful otherwise).[488] Yet Lincoln must have desperately wanted Dixie's 80 electoral votes. Why then did he block the Southern states from the 1864 U.S. election?

For the same reason he did everything: political expediency. Why risk the embarrassment of allowing states to participate in the North's political process that he knew would never vote for him? The overt hypocrisy of his position never seemed to bother him.

Lincoln need not have taken time to bar the South from the 1864 U.S. election, however. She would not have accepted an invitation from him anyway. For since February 8, 1861, the eleven states of the Confederacy (and provisional Confederate governments in Missouri and Kentucky) had been operating as a legitimate, independent republic, one preoccupied with setting up her own government.[489]

We have now looked at just some of the crimes Lincoln committed in order to secure the *popular* votes he needed to get reelected. His attempts to specifically insure extra *electoral* votes for the 1864 election were no less underhanded.

On June 20, 1863, for example, he generated five additional electoral votes for himself by illegally creating the thirty-fifth state, West Virginia[490] (a clear violation of the U.S. Constitution's Article 4, Section 3, Clause 1).[491] This he did by encouraging the region that would become West Virginia, to secede from Virginia at a time when he had pronounced the secession of the Southern states unlawful.[492] Again, his double standard did not concern him.[493]

Liberal Union President Abraham Lincoln would have lost in 1864 by a landslide if the Southern states had voted in the U.S. election that year.

Shortly thereafter, Lincoln insidiously admitted the thirty-sixth state, Nevada, on October 31, a mere week before election day, November 8,

An 1864 Republican Party (Liberal) campaign banner featuring Lincoln and his running mate Andrew Johnson.

1864. Like West Virginia, a "Union" state, the hurried, last minute admission of Nevada raised Lincoln's electoral votes even higher, in this case by two (it would have been three, but one Nevada elector did not vote). While this latter action was not unlawful, it was not exactly proper,[494] for he and his party had tampered with the government's Electoral College. We will note here that along with West Virginia and Nevada, the state of Kansas had been created under Lincoln's auspices for the same reason as well.[495]

In light of such facts, could any sane person consider either Lincoln's 1860 or his 1864 victories fair and ethical? Some would say that this was just Liberal politics as usual.

Newspapers of the day spoke out against Lincoln's deviltries. He had "defrauded the American public in the most heinous ways," they cried, particularly in his use of armed Federal soldiers, who he posted ominously at polling stations to intimidate voters.[496] In 1920, Virginia Conservative, Judge George L. Christian, made note of Lincoln's

> standing with the Northern people at the election in November, 1864, when nearly one-half of these people voted against him, and when, but for the improper use of the army in controlling the election, it is believed he would have been defeated by McClellan, since in many of the States carried by Lincoln the popular vote was very close.[497]

Even before the 1864 votes were cast, dire predictions were made as to how "the Ape," as he was politely called across the South, would guarantee his victory. On November 7, for example, one day before the election, the *Richmond Dispatch* warned that Lincoln would use any means in his power, including his cabinet, his military officers, his spies, and fraud and bribery, to insure his election over McClellan. Lincoln's craftiness and guile were on display for all to see, with dishonesty and "the foulest corruptions" obvious at every level of his party. "This is the most glorious prank ever committed by the Ape," the paper cried angrily.[498]

The day after his reelection the *Richmond Dispatch* was, if anything, even more biting in its criticisms of the Liberal Republican from Illinois. On November 9, 1864, it ran another piece about "the vulgar tyrant" and "low buffoon," a "despicable animal who had already wasted millions of lives without the slightest remorse," and who "continued to demand more blood and more money in order to fulfill his direful schemes."[499] After having stripped the North of her liberties by stationing soldiers at the polls, throwing out her legislatures, illegally arresting Yankee politicians, silencing his critics through false arrest and imprisonment, and cunningly forcing his armies to vote for him, it is clear that Lincoln had only one agenda, the newspaper reported

Democrat and Union General George B. McClellan, a Yankee Conservative, referred to Liberal Lincoln variously as an "idiot," "the original gorilla," and "a well meaning baboon," sentiments with which the Conservative South could certainly relate. McClellan ran for president as a "peace Democrat" against war-hawk Republican Lincoln in the 1864 election, but lost, in part, due to Lincoln's overt dishonesty. Here is the *real* reason he was called "Honest Abe": sarcasm.

bitterly: "to crush and defeat all opponents in an attempt to rule the entire nation from Washington."[500]

It was under this ominous cloud of liberalistic corruption, graft, and vice that big government Liberal Lincoln entered his second term, overseeing a left-wing American thugocracy the likes which have never been seen before or since;[501] one with neither a plan for the slaves he was allegedly "freeing," or for the "reconstruction" of the seceded Southern states he was busy turning to rubble.[502]

Even left-leaning, Lincoln-admiring historians have had to acknowledge the war crimes of their idol. One of these, David S. Muzzey, wrote the following in 1922:

> From the fall of Fort Sumter to the meeting of the extra session of Congress nearly three months later, Abraham Lincoln was virtually a "dictator." By executive proclamation he increased the regular army and navy of the United States by some 40,000 men, although he had no constitutional right to add a single man to a regiment or a ship. He proclaimed a blockade of the ports of the cotton states and threatened with the fate of pirates anyone who should molest the commerce of the United States, although a blockade is an incident of war and war had been neither declared nor recognized. He authorized General [Winfield] Scott to suspend the writ of Habeas Corpus and make military arrests anywhere on the line between Philadelphia and Washington, although the right to suspend the writ is enumerated among the powers of Congress in the Constitution (Art. I, sect. 9, par. 2), and a decision of Chief Justice [John] Marshall at the time of the [Aaron] Burr conspiracy had denied it to the executive.
>
> When Congress met on July 4, Lincoln confessed the unconstitutionally of his proclamations, which, he said, "were ventured upon under what appeared to be a popular demand and a public necessity." Congress promptly and enthusiastically ratified his actions. A "higher law" had superseded the Constitution—the [Liberals'] law of self-preservation. Throughout the war Congress cooperated with the President, conferring on him the power to suspend the writ of Habeas Corpus whenever and wherever he deemed it necessary and allowing him great freedom in the interpretation and execution of its acts.[503]

For such actions Lincoln was routinely excoriated by both parties, particularly his own, the Republicans, the Liberal party of the day. Many of his more radically left constituents, for example, could not understand his refusal to issue an emancipation proclamation until halfway through the War, as Muzzey notes:

> Lincoln's deliberation [in stalling abolition] was interpreted as vacillation, his poise as baffled confusion, and his silence as a confession of political and military bankruptcy. In the same breath he was ridiculed as a "Simple Susan" and denounced as a "tyrant." The strict constitutionalist [that is, the Conservative] was offended by his assumption of "despotic" power in

suspending the writ of Habeas Corpus and making military arrests. The men who were more concerned for the preservation of their personal liberty than for the preservation of the Union resented the arbitrary proclamations interfering with the freedom of speech and action. [For starters, during the War Lincoln had interfered with elections in the Border States, as well as censoring or closing down between 300 and 400 newspapers for printing pro-peace or pro-South articles].[504]

President Lincoln canceled the emancipation proclamations of many of his military and government officials, such as Union General David Hunter. Why, if he was "against slavery"? Liberals would rather you not know the answer.

The extreme abolitionists thought that the South, cursed with slavery, was not worth keeping in the Union—especially at the cost of rivers of blood and unlimited treasure. The more moderate abolitionists scolded Lincoln for repudiating the [emancipation] proclamations of [John C.] Frémont and [David] Hunter and for not making the war from the beginning a crusade against slavery. The Copperheads [Yankee Southern-sympathizers], like the secessionists, protested against the "coercion" and "subjugation" of "sovereign states."[505]

In contrast, Confederate President Jefferson Davis was far

> more observant of constitutional limitations than was the [U.S.] Federal government [under Lincoln]. Lincoln was authorized by the act of March 3, 1863, to suspend the writ of Habeas Corpus whenever and wherever he pleased; but the Confederate Congress, in spite of the fact that the invading armies were encamped on the soil of the South, never gave President Davis this blanket authority. The writ was suspended in the South only for limited periods between the spring of 1862 and the summer of 1864, and military arrests were allowed only for "treason, conspiracy, desertion, and communicating intelligence to or trading unlawfully with the enemy."
>
> The Confederate Congress never made its paper money (Treasury notes) legal tender, as the North did the "greenbacks"; it never created a national banking-system to float and support its bonds, as Secretary [Salmon P.] Chase did; it never organized a Supreme Court, as it was directed to do by the Constitution, "in view . . . of the particularistic feeling which such an enlargement of the central authority would have necessarily stimulated."[506]

On April 14, 1865, however, early America's most progressive and Mephistophelean administration came to an end with the bullet of discontented Northerner John Wilkes Booth. Mortally wounded, Lincoln died the next day and the reigns of power were passed onto his vice president, Andrew Johnson, traditionally a centrist Southern Democrat (that is, a middle-of-the-road Conservative).

As Davis and Lincoln declared from the beginning to the end of the conflict (and Davis long after), the abolition of slavery was not the purpose of the War.[507] This is why, after all, the Emancipation Proclamation did not free a single slave,[508] it is why the War continued for two more years after it was issued,[509] and it is why full, complete, and official abolition did not come until eight months after Lincoln's death and the end of the War,[510] with the passage of the Thirteenth Amendment in December 1865.[511] Added to this was the beginning of so-called "Reconstruction," which

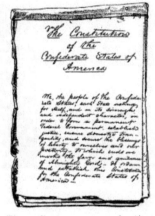

The first page of the Constitution of the Confederate States of America. During the Civil War Democratic President Jefferson Davis, a Conservative, followed the law more closely than Liberal Lincoln, which gave the Union a major advantage.

Our 17th president, National Unionist (Republican) Andrew Johnson, a right-leaning Liberal.

turned out to be nothing more than the second phase of the Liberals' vengeful war on the South, her conservative people and European traditions, and the U.S. Constitution.[512] All of this occurred within months after Johnson was sworn in as our 17th president, adding tremendous stress to a situation already nearing the breaking point: the tension between Southern loyalist Johnson and Lincoln's Republican (Liberal) Congress.

Regarded by Republican leaders as "a mere trustee of a power which belonged to them,"[513] rather than a popularly elected chief executive, Liberal forces at once set out to destroy Johnson and remove him from office. Though even Northern icons such as Liberal Union General Ulysses S. Grant looked forward to the promise of a speedy reunification as well as an improvement in North-South relations, ruling Republicans (Liberals) would not have it. Instead,

> "those [Liberals] entrusted with the law-making power" deliberately set themselves to the work of undoing it, of postponing for many years the reconciliation of the two sections; of embroiling the two races; of preparing the way for that era of carpet-bag government and military rule at the [conservative] South which will ever condemn at the bar of history—that bar where the voice of magnanimity is always heard and always honored—the reconstruction policy of the Republican party [Liberal], and the spirit of sectionalism and of intolerant partisanship by which it was dictated.[514]

As our 21st election approached in 1868, Liberal and Conservative forces chose their presidential candidates, the former selecting Grant, the latter putting up Copperhead Horatio Seymour of New York. While right up to the election the Republicans (Liberals) continued to issue one vindictive Reconstruction act after another against what they insultingly referred to as the "conquered provinces" of the South,[515] Democrats (Conservatives) formulated a commonsense platform in favor of amnesty for all past political offences and for the regulation of the elective franchise in the States by their citizens; all obligations of the government not expressly stating on their face, or in the law which authorized their issue, that they should be paid in coin to be paid in the lawful money of the United States; equal taxation of every species of property according to its real value, including government bonds and other public securities; a tariff for revenue upon foreign imports and such equal taxation under the internal revenue laws as will afford incidental protection to domestic manufactures and as will, without impairing the revenue, impose the least burden upon, and best promote and encourage, the great industrial interests of the country. It arraigned the Republican [Liberal] party for its reconstruction legislation and its extravagance, and declared the reconstruction acts of Congress usurpations, unconstitutional, revolutionary and void.[516]

A Liberal campaign poster, or "Republican Chart," for the presidential election of 1868. Presidential candidate Ulysses S. Grant and his running mate Schuyler Colfax are highlighted near the center. Around the border are portraits of various U.S. presidents, beginning with George Washington at the top, and ending with Andrew Johnson at the bottom right.

After the final tallies for the 1868 election were in, it was shown that Seymour received 2,703,249 popular votes and 80 electoral votes, while Grant got 3,012,833 popular votes and 214 electoral votes, making the Union military hero our 18th president.[517] His inauguration took place on March 4, 1869.

Despite the fact that by January 30, 1871, all of the former Confederate states had been coerced into returning to the Union, under President Grant the Liberals' harsh "Reconstruction" of the South continued unabated, if anything with more criminality and malevolence than before. Grant and his

Our 18th president, Republican Ulysses S. Grant, a Liberal.

Liberal Republican constituents were rightly taken to task by their more conservative critics "for their partisan control of the administration; for keeping alive the passions and resentments of the war to use to their own advantage, and for making the Civil Service the instrument of partisan tyranny, personal ambition and an object of selfish greed."[518] Of this period Wilson writes that

> for the next five or six years there was a saturnalia of profligacy and corruption combined with a perfect travesty of free government in those States of the South where negro suffrage controlled and where the "carpet-bagger" who, with very rare exceptions was a political adventurer without character and bent only on plunder, directed the legislation of the States, and where the army of the United States was used by the President to prop up this worthless and corrupt pretence to State government.[519]

As our 22nd election in 1872 drew closer, a faction of the Republican Party split off, calling themselves the "Liberal Republicans" (a stupendous oxymoron since the Republican Party at the time was *already* extremely Liberal, comprised as it was of thousands of socialists, communists, collectivists, and various types of revolutionaries). Though critical of the left-wing policies of the Grant administration, the Liberal Republicans nominated an extreme progressive for their presidential candidate: arch socialist Horace Greeley of New York—a personal friend of the founder of modern communism, Karl Marx.[520]

Just as bizarre, the Democratic Party, the Conservative party at the time, adopted the socialist platform of the Liberal Republican Party (whose founding was led by staunch Forty-Eighter,[521] German socialist Carl Schurz),[522] and cast their support for Greeley. A small segment of rational Democrats who could not abide Greeley nominated their own candidate: Conservative Democrat Charles O'Connor of New York. This was the first and only time in the history of the mainstream Democratic Party (Conservatives) that it did not nominate a candidate of its own, and what a mistake it was. Acknowledging that it could not win against the popular Liberal incumbent Grant, in an effort to contest him the Democratic Party simply endorsed its "lifelong enemy," ultra leftist radical Horace Greeley, a man

Socialist Horace Greeley, the presidential nominee of the Liberal Republican Party in the election of 1872—a reformist spinoff of the Republican Party, founded that year by socialist revolutionary Carl Schurz.

with whom it had no bond of sympathy at present, except that of opposition to the continued unfriendly legislation of the Republican party [Liberal] toward the [Conservative] South; to its succession of force bills, and its use of the army to uphold the plundering carpet-bag governments, whose misrule and almost unbearable wrongs had naturally aroused some unlawful resistance, which was in turn greedily seized upon to justify military interference and to inflame the [Liberal] people of the North against the [Conservative] South.[523]

On November 29, 1872, however, Greeley passed away suddenly, even before the final votes were cast, sealing Grant's reelection. The results were as follows: Grant received 3,597,132 popular votes, Greeley 2,834,125 popular votes, and O'Connor 29,489 popular votes.[524]

Grant's second term, filled with countless frauds and outrages (from the Whiskey Ring to the Crédit Mobilier), brought only more doom and gloom to both the country as a whole and to the Conservative South, which was still recovering from 16 years of Liberal violence, illegalities, and atrocities of every kind; from unlawful arrest, imprisonment, and deportation, to the torture, rape, and murder of Southern civilians—of all races and ages.[525]

A "Republican Chart" for the election of 1876, highlighting Liberal presidential candidate Rutherford B. Hayes and his running mate Liberal William A. Wheeler, the winners.

A "Democratic Chart" for the election of 1876, highlighting Conservative presidential candidate Samuel J. Tilden and his running mate Conservative Thomas A. Hendricks.

By the time of our 23rd election in 1876, Grant's scandal-ridden, two-term Republican (Liberal) tenure had helped considerably dampen enthusiasm for this left-wing, South-despising Party. But it was not enough to prevent it from retaking the White House in what many consider the most controversial presidential contest in American history. By overt sham, trickery, and partisanship, the Republicans' (Liberals') presidential nominee, Liberal Rutherford B. Hayes of Ohio, was able to steal away the legitimate win of the Democrats' (Conservatives') candidate, right-wing Governor Samuel J. Tilden of New York, who received the majority of both popular votes and electoral votes. We need not go into detail here, other than to say that this flagitious crime must rank alongside the outrageous criminal behavior of Lincoln and the Republican Party (Liberals) during the 1860 and 1864 elections.

Though President Hayes, our 19th chief executive, rose to power by illegitimate means, his presence in Washington benefitted the South in one way. It was under his administration, in the year 1877, that the last Yankee troops were withdrawn from Dixie and the vengeful Reconstruction Era was finally closed. The conservative South began the long road of healing and recovery that it had been denied under Liberals Lincoln and Grant.[526]

Our 24th election, the election of 1880, now loomed. The Republicans (Liberals) put forth South-loathing leftist James A. Garfield of Ohio as their presidential nominee, while the

Our 19th president, Republican Rutherford B. Hayes, a Liberal.

Democrats (Conservatives) selected Winfield Scott Hancock of Pennsylvania. In one of the tightest races in our history, Garfield won the popular vote by less than 10,000 votes: 4,454,416 to Hancock's 4,444,952. Garfield's real win came from the Electoral College, which gave him 214 votes to Hancock's 155.[527]

Garfield, our 20th president, was in office for only a few months when he was killed by an insane fellow Liberal from Illinois, Charles J. Guiteau. Garfield's vice president, Republican (Liberal) Chester A. Arthur, became our 21st president, serving out the remaining three years of the term, then retiring from politics.

Our 25th election, the election of 1884, pitted South-hating Republican (Liberal) presidential candidate James G. Blaine of Pennsylvania against South-respecting Democratic (Conservative) presidential candidate Grover Cleveland of New Jersey. In a narrow victory the Conservatives were able to retake the White House with Cleveland's 4,874,986 popular votes and 219

Our 20th president, Republican James A. Garfield, a Liberal.

electoral votes, to Blaine's 4,851,981 popular votes and 182 electoral votes.[528]

Our 21st president, Republican Chester A. Arthur, a Liberal.

Cleveland, our 22nd president, should be honored with every patriotic award possible for his respect toward not only conservative principles, but also toward the South and her people. Under his presidency sectionalism finally began to fade and Dixie once again began to fully share in the political power of the country. Wilson writes glowingly of the Cleveland administration:

> For the first time since 1861 representative men from the South appeared in the cabinet and shared in the honors and responsibilities of the administration. The position of the new President was one of unusual burden and beset with difficulties which the people have not yet fully comprehended and appreciated. He was himself a stranger, not only to his position but to all his surroundings and to the leaders and prominent men of his party [the Democratic Party, that is, Conservatives]. That party for nearly a quarter of a century had been the party of criticism and the party of opposition, too weak at times to interpose serious obstruction to the measures and policies of the dominant party [the Republican Party, that is, Liberals]. It had been returned to power not so much for the ideas and policies it represented, as because the people were weary of sectionalism, alarmed at the usurpations, and resentful of the centralization and rank Federalism [liberalism] of the Republican party [Liberal] and its subservience to special interests, and those

the interests of consolidated capital as against the people.

The shameless jugglery by which, in 1883, it had pretended to reduce taxes, while really making the masses more tributary to the protected interests, and labor more tributary to capital, had also alienated many from its ranks. It was natural, therefore, that upon its first return to power the Democratic party [Conservatives], made up of all the elements of opposition to the practices and policies of the past twenty years, should lack something of the homogeneousness and organic unity of a party organized upon clear and definite lines of public policy. The great majority of the party was undoubtedly true to Democratic [that is, conservative] principles, but there were co-operating with it many who were rather anti-Republicans [anti-Liberals] than real Democrats [Conservatives]. It is to the credit of the President [Cleveland] that, while he has steadily and faithfully administered the government upon those plain, rigid, business principles that had marked his official career as Governor of New York and are of the essence of practical Democracy, he has also shown himself a party leader, not in the machine [that is, mechanical] sense of the term, but as the

Our 22nd president, Democrat Grover Cleveland, a Conservative.

exponent of [conservative] ideas and policies, and that the Democratic party [Conservative] in 1888 is no longer a combination of loosely-tied forces of opposition to the Republicans [Liberals], but a great living organism, instinct with life, with enthusiasm, and rallied upon great principles which it understands, believes in, and is eager to champion.

. . . Impartial history will record that a Democratic [Conservative] President coming into power at the head of a party which had been offensively excluded from all political positions under the government for twenty-four years; which in every campaign had been fought and harried by the Pretorian band of federal office-holders [Liberals], and had been the victim of every conceivable wrong of the spoils system, by his moderation in removals, his painstaking care in appointments, and his enforcement of thorough business ideas in every department of the public service, has given to Civil Service Reform a far deeper root and a far more permanent and healthy growth than any of his predecessors, whose inaugurations only marked the transfer of the chief magistracy from one to another member of the same party. No one who contrasts the Presidential campaigns of 1884 and 1888 can fail to note how far the hand has moved forward on the dial, and whatever the result of the election may be, he cannot believe that it will ever move backward again. This has been the work of Grover Cleveland.[529]

During our 26th U.S. presidential election in 1888, Cleveland was once more nominated by the Democrats (Conservatives), while the Republicans (Liberals) nominated Benjamin Harrison of Ohio (a grandson of our ninth president, William Henry Harrison). Of this battle Liberal Pennsylvania historian Alexander K. McClure, himself a politician living at the time, wrote:

> I cannot recall another presidential contest that was conducted on both sides with greater dignity and decency than that between Cleveland and Harrison in 1888.[530]

Our 23rd president, Republican Benjamin Harrison, a Liberal.

Though, since he had won a public opinion poll, many assumed incumbent Cleveland would win, his half-hearted attitude, the loss of his home state, the withdrawal of support by Tammany Hall, and his views on the tariff all worked against him, costing him the election.[531] The vote had been close, however, with Conservative Cleveland receiving 5,540,329 popular votes and 168 electoral votes, Liberal Harrison receiving 5,439,853 popular votes and 233 electoral votes,[532] making the latter our 23rd president. McClure commented on the loss:

> Cleveland lost his election in 1888 by his message to Congress, delivered a year before, making the tariff and revenue question the sole issue before the country. His message referred to no other question than the issue of reduced revenues and taxes. I saw him on Saturday night before the meeting of Congress, and with Speaker [John Griffin] Carlisle, who was to be re-elected to the Speakership on the following Monday, earnestly urged him to modify his message. Carlisle was quite as positive as I was in assuring him that it would result in disaster to himself and his administration.
>
> His answer was that possibly we were right, but that it was a duty that should be performed, and while he might fall, he believed the country would vindicate him at an early day. He was a man who gave very serious thought to his official duties, performed them with great fidelity, and when convinced as to his duty none could dissuade him from his purpose. But for that message he would certainly have been re-elected President in 1888.[533]

In preparation for our 27th election in 1892, the Democrats (Conservatives) met at Chicago, Illinois, in June, where they renominated Cleveland. The party platform called for lowering the tariff, enactment of antitrust laws, home rule for Ireland, the building of a canal through Central America, and statehood for Arizona and New Mexico.[534]

Meanwhile the Republicans (Liberals) met at Minneapolis, Minnesota, also in June, renominating Benjamin Harrison with these words:

> We commend the able, patriotic, and thoroughly American administration of President Harrison. Under it the country has enjoyed remarkable prosperity, and the dignity and honor of the nation, at home and abroad, have been faithfully maintained, and we offer the record of pledges kept as a guarantee of faithful performance in the future.[535]

Though six states—North Dakota (1889), South Dakota (1889), Montana (1889), Washington (1889), Idaho (1890), and Wyoming (1890)—were admitted to the Union during Harrison's tenure (adding some 17 additional electoral votes),[536] he presided over a disjointed administration, and was never able to fully bring his party together. This, combined with his "cold" personality, for which he was known as the "human iceberg,"[537] and the fact that of the six new states only North Dakota voted for him, precluded a second term.

Our 24th president, Democrat Grover Cleveland, Conservative.

The results of the 1892 election were as follows: Cleveland with 5,556,918 popular votes and 277 electoral votes; Harrison with 5,176,108 popular votes and 145 electoral votes.[538] Cleveland was now our 24th president, and, as he had also been our 22nd president, he became the first and only U.S. chief executive in American history to hold two terms non-consecutively.

Concerning the topic of this book, we come now to the most important election in American history: the presidential election of 1896, one known as a "realigning election." For it was at this juncture that the two main parties switched platforms, becoming the parties we are so familiar with today. Since the emergence of the Republican Party during the Pierce administration (1853-1857), it had been a liberally oriented party; from the birth of the Democratic Party at the election of Andrew Jackson (1828), it had been a conservatively oriented party.

Our 28th election in 1896, the year of "political reversal,"[539] changed all of this: for the first time in its history the Republican Party (the one founded in 1854 by Liberals and European socialists, and which is in no way connected to the Republican Party of Thomas Jefferson) put up a Conservative candidate: politically moderate Republican William McKinley of Ohio. And for the first time in their history the Democratic Party (founded in 1828 by Conservatives and American traditionalists) put up a Liberal candidate: politically progressive Democrat William Jennings Bryan of Illinois.

By doing this, in essence the Republican Party (which was Liberal from 1854 to 1896) became the Republican (that is, Conservative) Party we know today, while the Democratic Party (which was Conservative from 1828 to 1896) became the Democratic (that is, Liberal) Party we know today.

A Democratic poster for the election of 1896, showing the dramatic change that overtook the two main parties that year. Though the Democratic Party began the 1896 campaign as the Conservative party (which it had been since 1828 and the presidency of Democrat Andrew Jackson, a Conservative), its 1896 nominee for president, William Jennings Bryan (above left), was a political Liberal. This forced the Republican Party, then Liberal, to choose a Conservative nominee, William McKinley. A vestige of the Democratic Party's conservative history can be seen in the nomination that year of Bryan's running mate, vice presidential candidate Arthur Sewall (above right), a longtime Democrat, that is, a Conservative.

What most often confuses people is that the names of the parties did not actually change. Only the platforms and the members of the parties changed. In other words, in 1896 the Democratic Party, which had been conservative in 1895, took on a liberal platform, after which its original conservative members fled to the Republican Party. And this was only possible because in 1896 the Republican Party, which had been liberal in 1895, had no choice but to take on a conservative platform, after which its original liberal members jumped ship to the Democratic Party.[540]

There are two questions we must now answer: why did this momentous change occur, and why in this particular year, 1896?

The answers are not always clear and no two historians agree as to why or which influences had what effect. We must content ourselves then with a cursory look at the main sociopolitical factors leading up to the election of 1896, and how they impacted the Democratic and Republican choices of candidates and platforms that year. In doing so the American "Civil War," Lincoln's War, the War for Southern Independence, will finally become comprehensible in a factual and historically accurate way.

Liberalism has been a part of American politics from June 21, 1788, the day the U.S. Constitution was ratified and the original Confederation of 13 colonies became the United States of America, a republic also known as "The Confederate States of America."[541] The most famous of the group we would now think of as early American Liberals was Founding Father Alexander Hamilton. A member of the leftist Federalist Party, he espoused an "aristocratic constitution" that would establish an all-powerful consolidated central government overseen by "the rich, the well-born, and the able." Why? Because like nearly all Liberals then as now, Hamilton had little respect for "the people," whom he derogatorily called "turbulent and changing," "a great beast," an "uncontrollable" mass who

Alexander Hamilton's statue in Washington, D.C.

"seldom judge or determine right,"[542] and whom he believed, as John Adams asserted, were "the worst conceivable keepers of their own liberty," since they could "neither judge, nor think, nor will as a political body."[543] As for his preference for big government and his detestation for small government, Liberal Hamilton wrote:

> There is something noble and magnificent in the perspective of a great, Federal Republic [a Liberal concept], closely linked in the pursuit of a common interest, tranquil and prosperous at home, respectable abroad, but there is something proportionately diminutive and contemptible in the prospect of a number of petty states [a Conservative concept], with the appearance only of Union, jarring, jealous, and perverse, without any determined direction, fluctuating and unhappy at home, weak and insignificant by their dissensions in the eyes of other nations. . . . Happy America [will be] if those to whom thou hast intrusted the guardianship of thy infancy know how to provide for thy future repose [that is, run by Liberals], but [she will be] miserable and undone if their negligence or ignorance permits the spirit of discord to erect her banners on the ruins of thy tranquillity [that is, run by Conservatives]![544]

Today we refer to these types of Liberals as "elitists": self-righteous, highly emotional, strongly opinionated individuals schooled in radical (usually failed 19th-Century European) left-wing theories and ideologies, who maintain that a national government (federal rights and mass enslavement) is superior to self-government (states' rights and personal freedom). Of Hamiltonian Federalism Muzzey writes:

> Otto, the secretary of the French legation at New York, wrote home to Vergennes in October, 1786, "Although there are no nobles in America, there is a class of men [Liberals], denominated gentlemen, who by reason of their wealth, their talents, and their education, their families or the offices which they hold, aspire to a preeminence which the common people refuses to grant them . . . and moreover, they are creditors, and therefore interested in strengthening the government and watching over the execution of the laws."
>
> Hamilton himself, in the speech in which he recommended to the [1787] convention at Philadelphia his plan for an "aristocratic" constitution, said: "All communities divide themselves into the few and the many. The few are the rich and well born, the other, the mass of the populace. . . . The people are turbulent and changing; they seldom judge or determine right. Give, therefore, to the first class [that is, Liberal elites] a distinct, permanent share in the government. They will check the boisterousness of the second."

> It was this "first class"—the solid men of wealth, birth, and position, the large merchants, manufacturers, and capitalists, the holders of the public securities, the clergy and the lawyers, the advocates of energy and full competency in the national government—who rallied to the support of Hamilton's program. They were called Federalists [Liberals].[545]

Conservatives of the time (known as Republicans) held that the Federalists were "squinting towards monarchy," and they were correct. Today we could also say that they were "squinting towards socialism." While it is true that monarchy and socialism are different systems, and are in some ways, in fact, opposing ideas, they do have one major attribute in common: both divest the people of their political power and put it in the hands of either a royal family (absolute monarchy)[546] or the central government (absolute socialism).[547] Both, in other words, are a

form of tyranny: an oppressive political system in which absolute position and power are vested in a single person (monarchy) or a consolidated government (socialism).[548] It is for this reason that many of the Federalists' liberal principles, ideas, and doctrines would later combine to help develop the political theories known as American socialism, collectivism, and communism.[549]

One of President Lincoln's many radical military men: German socialist-communist and Union General Joseph Wedemeyer, a personal friend of communists Karl Marx and Friedrich Engels. Like thousands of other Forty-Eighters, after the failed European socialist revolution Wedemeyer immigrated to the U.S. (in 1851), and joined the Republican Party (Liberal), formed by American liberals, radicals, and European revolutionaries in 1854.

In Europe in 1848 such leftist ideologies were officially ushered in by a number of populist revolts against monarchies in Sicily, Germany, the Austrian Empire, Italy, and France, as well as by the publication of *The Communist Manifesto* by radical German socialists Karl Marx and Friedrich Engels. But the European Revolutions of 1848 were unsuccessful, and the disillusioned liberal revolutionaries who had sought the violent overthrow of established government began to seek a new home from where they might try again.[550] For many that new home was the United States of America, and thousands of angry discontented socialists began arriving on our shores within months of their failed "revolution."[551]

We will recollect that a number of these radical European Liberals, known as the "Forty-Eighters," helped create the Republican Party in 1854 and aided in the writing of its platform. We will also recall that in 1860 this same group helped Lincoln win the presidency, and even joined his administration and his armies to further the cause of liberalism in America. The Emancipation Proclamation, as well as the "Civil War" and its "slavery was the cause" myth, were inspired by South-hating, anti-Christian socialists who worked with Lincoln and his constituents.

An 1895 pro-Republican Party illustration employing three bicyclists. The one in the back right represents the Populist Party (radicals), who cannot get his bike over the rough terrain. The one on the left, the Democratic Party (then Conservative), has run over a broken bottle and burst her front tire. Neither can keep up with the Republican Party (then Liberal), the cyclist leading the way.

By the 1880s, liberalism mixed with a strong current of populism, reaching fever pitch in the U.S., with Liberals demanding "a more equitable distribution of the mounting wealth of the country" (a socialist doctrine known today as "economic equality"). Chief among the progressive complainants were Eastern wage-earners and Western farmers, who, in their anger and dissatisfaction, began forming scores of political parties (such as the Corn Growers Association, the United Laborites, and the National Farmers Alliance) around their hostility toward Wall Street and big corporations. By fusing their various ideas into one massive and powerful socialist voting block, they became known as "fusionists."[552]

In 1889 the principle of "fusion" took on new life at the Liberals' St. Louis Convention (a gathering of labor, agrarian, and liberal elements), where "the new radical party," the Populist Party got its official start. Comprised of everything from feminists and farmers to reformers and socialists,[553] the intentions of America's "most colorful party"[554] were to whip up discontent among the masses, particularly the laboring masses, and eliminate the established political parties and replace them with a "people's government."[555]

The elections of 1890 only further intensified the coming political revolution. Buck describes the period this way:

> The events of 1890 constituted not only a political revolt but a social upheaval in the West. Nowhere was the overturn more complete than in Kansas. If the West in general was uneasy, Kansas was in the throes of a mighty convulsion; it was swept as by the combination of a tornado and a prairie fire. As a sympathetic commentator of later days puts it, "It was a religious revival, a crusade, a pentecost of politics in which a tongue of flame sat upon every man, and each spake as the spirit gave him utterance." All over the State, [day-long] meetings were held in schoolhouses, churches, and public halls.[556]

An 1896 political cartoon of politically Liberal presidential candidate William Jennings Bryan during his countrywide train campaign. Bryan uses a bellows to "blow" excerpts from his speeches at farmers from the back of a caboose as it passes by. A group of newspaper reporters accompany the candidate. On the bellows are the words "16 to 1," Bryan's solution to the economic problems caused by the Panic of 1893: unlimited coinage of silver at a ratio to gold of 16 to 1.

The swell of support among laborers and farmers for populism and fusionism grew rapidly, and in 1891 another leftist party was formed: The Peoples' Party of the United States of America. The fact that it had a number of similarities to the Republican Party (Liberals) of 1854 put it in instant conflict with Conservatives (then the Democrats), for they attributed their personal economic condition to "the deliberate, malevolent persecution of the capitalists."[557]

As these varied groups came together, they met, marched, protested, and discussed, finally forging a unified agenda. They would strive for *the complete takeover and transformation of the Democratic Party, at the time the Conservative Party!*

It is hard for us today, from a 21st-Century perspective, to understand why a large, disparate organization of 19th-Century Liberals, radicals, and labor groups would want to subdue, annex, seize, and ultimately control the party of their sworn enemy. Perhaps it was an attempt to absorb and ultimately destroy the American conservative movement; or maybe the Populists believed that by assuming the party name "Democratic" they would have more political clout at the polls.

The 1892 People's Party candidates for president, James B. Weaver of Ohio (top), and for vice president, James G. Field (bottom), a former Confederate officer from Virginia. The title of this campaign poster is: "Equal Rights to All; Special Privileges to None."

Not surprisingly, these left-wing malcontents felt an affinity with Conservative Founder Thomas Jefferson[558] and his notions of personal independence, unencumbered opportunity, and just recompense for an honest day's work. Yet their belief that the government should help alleviate their financial problems, an early form of "social politics," went against the conservative Jeffersonian (that is *classical* Liberal) philosophy of *laissez faire*[559]—a doctrine which states that true societal happiness and liberty are only possible if each person follows his or her own "enlightened self-interest," *without government aid or interference.*[560] Such was the complex nature of this

Victorian left-wing faction, the Populist Party.

The desire and need to form a "fusion" between the radical Liberals and the Democrats (Conservatives) continued to increase. Helping to spearhead the effort was the Peoples Party (Liberal), which nominated Bryan at their St. Louis Convention on July 22, 1896.[561] Revealingly, as noted, the Peoples Party had numerous similarities with the 1854 Republican Party that had been launched by Liberals, socialists, and various progressives after the collapse of the Whig Party (Liberals) around 1852. Among these resemblances there was an appeal to a "discontented class" preoccupied with its own personal complaints about the "system" rather than with the good of the country as a whole; a class made up of "victims" who felt that their economic misfortune was due to the wealthy and powerful; and lastly, groups of partyless "wild-eyed radicals" who merely wanted to stir up trouble and antagonize Conservatives.[562]

As the months passed, Populists (far left Liberals) and Democrats (Conservatives) began to merge in a number of states, with both sides supporting and voting for one another. One result of the "strange bedfellows" created by this bizarre partnership at the time was, as discussed, the election of our 24th president and the last Conservative of the *Democratic* Party, Grover Cleveland, to a second presidential term in 1892.[563]

U.S. President Grover Cleveland. In 1892 he became the last Conservative put forth by the Democratic Party, which, in 1896, became the Liberal party.

It is clear what advantage this fusion gave to the Populists and their agrarian and labor members. But how did teaming up with radicals and progressives benefit the Conservatives, the Democratic Party? By joining forces the two parties hoped to have enough voting power to overcome the Republicans (the establishment Liberals) in the 1896 election.

But would mere hope be enough to motivate the Democrats (the Conservatives) to agree to co-nominate the liberal candidate of the Populists, progressive Democrat William Jennings Bryan? No one knows for sure, but my own theory is as follows.

William Jennings Bryan: politically liberal, socially conservative, what I call a "reverse libertarian."

Generally speaking, the definition of a libertarian is someone who is politically conservative and socially liberal. Bryan was what I would call a "reverse libertarian,"[564] for he was politically liberal and socially conservative. To put it another way, in the political arena he leaned to the far left, while in the social arena he leaned to the far right. Indeed, though a political progressive, Bryan was a fundamentalist Christian who would later become a household name acting as the prosecuting attorney for Tennessee in the famous Scopes Trial of 1925—where he argued for the teaching of creationism over evolution in public schools.[565] I believe that the Democrats, the Conservatives, in joining with the Populist Party (far left Liberals) in an attempt to beat the Republicans (mainstream Liberals), justified their support of Bryan by focusing on the Populist nominee's Christian conservatism. The Populist Party did the opposite. They made this bargain with the Devil for the same reason, but justified their decision by focusing on Bryan's political liberalism.[566]

All of this was backed by Democrat Bryan himself, who stringently urged his party to combine with the Populist faction.[567] Hopkins describes the inner workings of the dual party ploy this way:

> In order to get the full combined vote for Bryan, who was the nominee of both parties, an arrangement was perfected between the Democrats and Populists in twenty-eight States by which each had a proportionate representation on the electoral ticket.[568]

Unfortunately for the Democrats (Conservatives), they did not realize that they were being swindled; that a massive leftist plot was underfoot to absorb them and drive them out of power!

A year later the financial Panic of 1893 struck,[569] an economic depression that left a trail of collapsing banks, factory shutdowns, languishing trade, house foreclosures, homeless "tramps," soup kitchens,[570] vast unemployment, labor unrest, riots, strikes, and a general state of "industrial paralysis" across the country. Liberal discontent and anger toward the "system" reached an all time high, further coalescing the working classes in their "struggle" against capitalism and its corporate leaders. Simultaneously, the Democratic Party (still Conservative) itself was now splitting into two groups over President Cleveland's support of the gold standard: the conservative leaning Gold Democrats and the liberal leaning Silver Democrats. This further weakened the party, with many Western and Southern Democrats now going fully over to the ever popular silverite Bryan, the "despotic" leader of the Populists (far left Liberals), and heartily supported by socialist leaders such as Eugene V. Debs[571]—the man who would later found the American Socialist Party in 1901.[572]

Radical socialist leader Eugene V. Debs: founder of the American Socialist Party in 1901 and a supporter of Democratic presidential candidate William Jennings Bryan in 1896.

Over the next year the political power of the Populists continued to strengthen, and by 1894 they had increased their vote by over 40 percent. Due to the Populists' and the Democrats' (Conservatives') mutual support of agrarian interests (farming, granges, and associated agricultural alliances), millions of farmers with socialist inclinations continued pouring into the Democratic Party (Conservative). In this way the influence of the Liberals eventually began to outpace that of the Conservatives within the party—who were still unaware of the dangerous and deceptive takeover that was gradually undermining them.[573] By the Fall of 1894 thousands more disgruntled Democrats had joined hands with their Populist compatriots.[574]

The Populists' gambit, to win the upcoming 1896 election by repudiating Cleveland's gold standard, by seizing upon "the agrarian discontent" in the Western and Southern states, and by slowly assimilating themselves into the Democratic Party, seemed to be working.[575]   Stanwood describes the "unique," "sensational," and "unexampled shifting of the line between parties" that occurred during the 1896 campaign season:

> . . . events so shaped themselves as to render the contest one of the sharpest, most memorable, and for a brief season the most doubtful, of all that have taken place since the election of Mr. Lincoln in 1860. That which brought about the change was the intrusion of the silver question into the canvass as the dominant issue, in opposition to the wishes and efforts of those who, in each of the old historic parties, had previously exercised a controlling influence in its councils. It is easy to understand why they took this attitude of opposition. As apostles of the gospel of success, they dreaded the division which a plain and unmistakable pronouncement on the subject of silver would cause. The Populist party [far left Liberals] alone was united on that issue. The growing strength of that organization had filled all the old politicians with alarm. In some of the Western States it had even become formidable to the extent of outnumbering both the old parties combined. It was evident that, if the silver question were to become the foremost issue in the canvass, the old policy of a "straddling" platform would not do; since in that case all those who were resolved to have free coinage at all hazards would flock to the Populist standard. Out of this situation developed a sensational contest for the control of the Democratic [still Conservative] organization.
>
> . . . Affairs were in this interesting situation when the time arrived [in the Spring of 1896] for holding the national conventions. The results of these great assemblies were surprising to those even who had gauged accurately the intensity of the public feeling on the silver question. Never before were conventions so inharmonious, and never were there so many "splits" and "bolts" in parties.
>
> . . . It long had been evident that this canvass was to witness an unexampled shifting of the line between parties. In those parts of the country where the silver idea was almost universally dominant, there had been an instant bolt of Republicans [still Liberals] from the platform of the St. Louis convention. And now a revolt of Democrats [still Conservatives] set in, not only greater in extent than any other in the history of American politics, but distinctly unlike all others.   Many of the oldest and most consistent Democratic [Conservative] journals proclaimed in emphatic terms their determination not to continue their support of the party, and not a few of them boldly advocated the election of [Conservative] Mr. [William] McKinley. The dissension extended to all parts of the country; and, although it was most pronounced in the Eastern section, it was so widespread that even in Kentucky, where the victory of the Silver wing had virtually enabled that faction to carry its point in the national convention, there was at the beginning of the canvass not one daily newspaper that advocated the election of [Liberal] Mr. Bryan.

The canvass so remarkably begun continued to be unique and sensational to the end. The Republicans [Liberals] who seceded from the convention at St. Louis, and most of those who agreed with them on the silver question, made common cause with the Democrats [Conservatives]. The dissident Democrats were divided in their course of action, but were animated by one and the same purpose, namely, to defeat the regular candidates of their own party in the only possible way, by helping the election of Mr. McKinley. Where a separate organization seemed to promise to draw away more votes from Mr. Bryan, they rallied around the "National Democratic" [Party] standard [a new and short-lived Conservative party devoted to the ideals of Conservative Thomas Jefferson]. Where direct support of the Republican [Liberal] candidates seemed necessary, they were ready to give that support. Many of them participated in the nomination of National Democratic candidates [Conservatives] for office, and even addressed audiences on the stump in favor of them, in order to draw away votes from Mr. Bryan; but they themselves voted for [Conservative] McKinley. The Prohibition party, never large, was divided; the faction which had insisted at the national convention, that the question of the sale of intoxicating liquor was the great issue before the people, could not hold its own members to that position; the other faction was strongly attracted, in a body, toward the coalesced forces of Free Silver. Even the Populists [far left Liberals] were in a state of hopeless dissension. It was apparent to the merest tyro [beginner] in politics that a separate electoral ticket in any State for Bryan and [Liberal Populist Thomas E.] Watson was as little in favor of Bryan as the ticket for [Conservative National Democrat John M.] Palmer and [Conservative National Democrat and former Confederate officer Simon B.] Buckner. In short, the "Middle-of-the-road" programme was one of practical though undeclared hostility to the head of the ticket it professed to support. This fact was recognized by many of the leaders of the party, especially by those who had been intrusted with authority to speak in the name of the party. Mr. Watson, the candidate for Vice President, reproached them for taking a course which he regarded as resulting in a sacrifice of himself, of the principles of the Populist party, and of its separate organization. It does not seem unjust to them to surmise that they were, in fact, chiefly desirous of the election of Mr. Bryan, and that at any cost to Mr. Watson they would do that which they thought would contribute most to the success of the head of the ticket.

Former Confederate officer Simon B. Buckner, 1896 vice presidential candidate for the moderately Conservative National Democratic Party, which opposed Bryan.

At first sight the action of the Democratic [Conservative] convention, in taking a position where a great number of the members of the party could not support [a Liberal] platform and candidates without a tremendous sacrifice of principle, might seem the height of political folly. Examined more carefully and critically, the reason of their action and the justification of it are obvious. The [Liberal] leaders in the Silver movement had no hope of success in a canvass based on the tariff issue. There was therefore nothing to lose by shifting the field of contest. In taking a firm stand in favor of free coinage, these men doubtless had two things in view, as to both of which the event showed their judgment to have been sound: first, that, whether it were self consistent or not, the great body of the party would continue to support the ticket; and, secondly, that an addition of the Populist [far left] vote to the Democratic [Conservative] vote would in many of the States convert a minority into a majority.[576]

Finally, toward the end of the campaign of 1896, the Populists and their radical Liberal members achieved their goal of fully "capturing" the disintegrating Democratic Party (Conservative), after which they denounced its conservative leaders, rewrote its platform, and formally dedicated themselves to the doctrine of populism.[577] Extraordinarily, the new "Democratic" platform literally rejected every domestic policy it had been promoting and following for the previous four years.[578]

The new Populist-Democratic coalition, known collectively as the "Popocrats," had gotten its way. On July 10, 1896, the newly reversed, now *Liberal*, Democratic

In 1896 William McKinley became the first Conservative presidential candidate chosen by the Republican Party of 1854, formerly the Liberal party.

Party officially settled on politically liberal (but religiously conservative) Democrat William Jennings Bryan of Illinois, whose powerful "cross of gold" speech before the Democratic Convention helped make him known to every schoolboy and girl.[579] Conversely, if it hoped to have any chance of getting in the White House, the Republican Party, formerly Liberal, now had no choice but to switch its platform as well. For by going left, the Democrats literally forced Republicans into taking a more conservative stance.[580] Hence, on June 17, 1896, the newly reversed, now *Conservative*, Republican Party nominated politically moderate Conservative William McKinley of Ohio.

But the ultimate victory for the Liberal Popocrats, a Democratic president, was not to be. The now Liberal Democrats, who idolized Liberal Founding Father Alexander Hamilton, ended up replicating the demise of his party, the Federalist (Liberal) Party: their 19th-Century left-wing politics had alienated much of Middle America, which handed a win to the now conservative Republicans. With the support of nearly every newspaper in the country (even many Democratic ones),[581] and the ingenious campaign management of Marcus A. Hanna, Conservative McKinley became our 25th president, eventually serving two terms, laying the groundwork for three more Republican presidential victories—until the election of Liberal Democrat Woodrow Wilson in 1912. Of the 1896 election Stanwood writes:

> At the close of the canvass the people were wrought up to the highest pitch of excitement. Never before was the display of political emblems so profuse. The city streets were decorated from end to end with huge flags and banners bearing the names of the candidates. Lithograph portraits of McKinley or of Bryan were exhibited in the front windows of dwellings and shops. Buttons showing the familiar features were worn in the lapels of their coats by hundreds of thousands, if not by millions, of men and boys.
>
> Almost fourteen million citizens went to the polls. The number of votes given was 13,936,957,—by far the largest number ever cast at a popular election in any country. Throughout the country the polling was orderly. Although the indications of a great Republican [now Conservative] victory had been apparent for weeks, even months, to the most casual observer, many of the [Liberal] supporters of Mr. Bryan entertained hopes, some of them were even confident, of success to the last. The earliest returns gave assurance of an overwhelming majority for Mr. McKinley, and the prognostication was confirmed as one State after another was heard from. The Eastern, Middle, and Central Northwestern States were carried by the Republicans [now Conservatives], without an exception, by unprecedented majorities. The South even was not "solid" for Bryan. Only during the Reconstruction period had the Republicans [then Liberals] ever obtained any electoral votes in the States from Delaware to Texas. Now Delaware, Maryland, and West Virginia gave McKinley substantial majorities; and even Kentucky, the "dark

Our 25th president, Republican William McKinley, a Conservative.

and bloody ground" of the Democratic [then Conservative] conflict between the Gold and the Silver forces, yielded him a narrow margin. No northern State east of the Missouri River gave Bryan a single electoral vote, and even on the Pacific slope the Republicans [now Conservatives] won California and Oregon.

On the other hand the Democrats [now Liberals] wrested from the Republicans [now Conservatives] Kansas and Nebraska, together with the whole group of mining States, except California; and their majority in such States as Arkansas, Alabama, Missouri, and Texas, was immense.

. . . The electoral count took place on the 10th of February, 1897. It was conducted in accordance with the law, and was strictly without incident. The inauguration of Mr. McKinley on the 4th of March was made the occasion of a great popular demonstration by the Republicans [now Conservatives], who flocked to Washington in large numbers to witness the ceremony.

The site of the Republican Convention at St. Louis, Missouri, 1896.

The immediate subsidence of excitement after the result of the election was ascertained, and the good-humored acceptance of that result by all save a few grievously disappointed leaders of the defeated party, [the Democrats, now Liberals,] is not a new experience in American political life. We have seen it after other historic struggles. The Federalists [Liberals] thought that all was lost when [Conservative Thomas] Jefferson was elected [in 1800]. [In 1828 Conservative Andrew] Jackson's triumph seemed to his [Liberal] opponents a victory of evil over good. The Democrats [then Conservatives] lost faith in popular government when [Liberal William Henry] Harrison was chosen [in 1840]. To the supporters of [Conservative] Mr. [Samuel J.] Tilden the declaration that [Liberal] Mr. [Rutherford B.] Hayes was elected [in 1876] was nothing short of a great political crime. Yet after a momentary loss of temper all these good people recovered themselves and devoted their energies to the public service with zeal and with undiminished hope and confidence. So it was in 1896.

In some respects the result was the greatest trial of the temper of the defeated party [the now Liberal Democrats] the country has ever known. The [scheming] aims of the Democratic party were,—not to use the phrase offensively,—in a certain sense revolutionary. They were intended to array the weak, the poor, the debtors, the employed, against the [Conservative] men who were designated as plutocrats. The failure of such an attack is sometimes almost as dangerous to society as its success. The fact that, when the American people had spoken at the polls upon questions that involved the highest interests of society, the decision was quietly accepted as conclusive until a new occasion should arise for passing upon them in the orderly American way, is most creditable to them, and a happy augury for the future.[582]

McKinley's 1896 win was largely attributed to Marcus A. Hanna, the brilliant chairman of the National Republican Committee.

Up until the 1890s, the Democratic Party (then Conservative) and the Republican Party (then Liberal) had maintained their respective platforms based on heritage and culture. But while McKinley was something of minor figure in all of this (and was largely swept along by currents and tides over which he had little control), Bryan proved to be a much more direct force, actively helping to coalesce the disenfranchised agrarian and labor elements in the West and South—which threw off factional equilibrium and weakened traditional party ties. This opened the door for the greatest political upheaval and reversal in American history, with the once Conservative Democratic Party becoming Liberal and the once Liberal Republican Party becoming Conservative.

Thus the Gilded Age (1878-1900), as Mark Twain referred to it, came to a close with a loud bang: the major realignment of America's two primary parties.[583]

On Halloween, a few days before the November 1896 election, a psychic scries her mirror and sees the image of the winner: William McKinley. American politics would never be the same.

5

FROM MCKINLEY TO TRUMP 1896 TO 2016

FROM THE YEAR 1896 ONWARD, America's two main political parties have retained their respective ideologies, the Republicans embracing a conservative outlook, the Democrats maintaining a liberal viewpoint.

To place our modern parties in their proper perspective within the framework of our study—and for those who are not familiar with American political history, or those who would simply like to refresh their memory—we will now briefly go through the list of the remaining U.S. presidential candidates, from our 25th chief executive in 1896 to our 45th chief executive in 2017. Note that, as I have done throughout this entire book, I list the birth states of the candidates rather than the states they were politically associated with later in their lives. And again, the terms "conservative" and "liberal" as applied to our politicians must

McKinley's First Inauguration, March 4, 1897.

be considered as general rather than literal in meaning. Hence, my emphasis on party affiliations.

Let us begin where we left off.

The 1896 election (our 28th): Conservative Republican William McKinley of Ohio wins with 7,035,638 popular votes and 271 electoral votes, over Liberal Democrat William Jennings Bryan of Illinois, who receives 6,467,946 popular votes and 176 electoral votes. McKinley becomes our 25th president.

Our 26th president, Republican Theodore Roosevelt, a Conservative.

The 1900 election (our 29th): Conservative Republican William McKinley of Ohio wins with 7,219,530 popular votes and 292 electoral votes, over Liberal Democrat William Jennings Bryan of Illinois, who receives 6,358,071 popular votes and 155 electoral votes. McKinley enters his second term as our 25th president. He is assassinated in 1901, however, and his vice president, Theodore Roosevelt of New York, becomes our 26th president.

The 1904 election (our 30th): Conservative Republican Theodore Roosevelt of New York wins with 7,628,834 popular votes and 336 electoral votes, over Liberal Democrat Alton B. Parker of New York, who receives 5,084,401 popular votes and 140 electoral votes. Roosevelt enters his second term as our 26th president.

The 1908 election (our 31st): Conservative Republican William H. Taft of Ohio wins with 7,679,006 popular votes and 321 electoral votes, over Liberal Democrat William Jennings Bryan of Illinois, who receives 6,409,106 popular votes and 162 electoral votes. Taft becomes our 27th president.

Our 27th president, Republican William H. Taft, a Conservative.

The 1912 election (our 32nd): Liberal Democrat Woodrow Wilson of Virginia wins with 6,286,820 popular votes and 435 electoral votes, over Conservative Republican William H. Taft of Ohio, who receives 3,483,922 popular votes and 8 electoral votes. Wilson becomes our 28th president.

The 1916 election (our 33rd): Liberal Democrat Woodrow Wilson of Virginia wins with 9,129,606 popular votes and 277 electoral votes, over Conservative Republican Charles E. Hughes of New York, who receives 8,538,221 popular votes and 254 electoral votes. Wilson enters his second term as our 28th president.

Our 28th president, Democrat Woodrow Wilson, a Liberal.

The 1920 election (our 34th): Conservative Republican Warren G. Harding of Ohio wins with 16,152,200 popular votes and 404 electoral votes, over Liberal Democrat James M. Cox of Ohio, who receives 9,147,353 popular votes and 127 electoral votes. Harding becomes our 29th president, but dies in office in 1923. His vice president, Conservative Republican Calvin Coolidge of Vermont, becomes our 30th president.

The 1924 election (our 35th): Conservative Republican Calvin Coolidge of Vermont wins with 15,725,016 popular votes and 382 electoral votes, over Liberal Democrat John W. Davis of West Virginia, who receives 8,385,586 popular votes and 136 electoral

Our 29th president, Republican Warren G. Harding, a Conservative.

votes. Coolidge enters his second term as our 30th president.

The 1928 election (our 36th): Conservative Republican Herbert Hoover of Iowa wins with 21,392,190 popular votes and 444 electoral votes, over Liberal Democrat Alfred E. Smith of New York, who receives 15,016,443 popular votes and 87 electoral votes. Hoover becomes our 31st president.

The 1932 election (our 37th): Liberal Democrat Franklin D. Roosevelt of New York

Our 30th president, Republican Calvin Coolidge, a Conservative.

Our 31ˢᵗ president, Republican Herbert Hoover, a Conservative.

wins with 22,821,857 popular votes and 472 electoral votes, over Conservative Republican Herbert Hoover of Iowa, who receives 15,761,841 popular votes and 59 electoral votes. Roosevelt becomes our 32ⁿᵈ president.

The 1936 election (our 38ᵗʰ): Liberal Democrat Franklin D. Roosevelt of New York wins with 27,751,597 popular votes and 523 electoral votes, over Conservative Republican Alf M. Landon of Pennsylvania, who receives 16,679,583 popular votes and 8 electoral votes. Roosevelt enters his second term as our 32ⁿᵈ president.

The 1940 election (our 39ᵗʰ): Liberal Democrat Franklin D. Roosevelt of New York wins with 27,243,466 popular votes and 449 electoral votes, over Conservative Republican Wendell Willkie of Indiana, who receives 22,304,755 popular votes and 82 electoral votes. Roosevelt enters his third term as our 32ⁿᵈ president.

The 1944 election (our 40ᵗʰ): Liberal Democrat Franklin D. Roosevelt of New York wins with 25,602,505 popular votes

Our 32ⁿᵈ president, Democrat Franklin D. Roosevelt, a Liberal.

and 432 electoral votes, over Conservative Republican Thomas E. Dewey of Michigan, who receives 22,006,278 popular votes and 99 electoral votes. Roosevelt enters his fourth term as our 32ⁿᵈ president, but dies in office in 1945. His vice president, Liberal Democrat Harry S. Truman of Missouri, becomes our 33ʳᵈ president. (Note: in 1951 the 22ⁿᵈ Amendment was added to the U.S. Constitution, limiting the president to two four-year terms.)

Our 33ʳᵈ president, Democrat Harry S. Truman, a Liberal.

The 1948 election (our 41ˢᵗ): Liberal Democrat Harry S. Truman of Missouri wins with 24,105,812 popular votes and 303 electoral votes, over Conservative Republican Thomas E. Dewey, who receives 21,970,065 popular votes and 189 electoral votes. Truman enters his second term as our 33rd president.

The 1952 election (our 42nd): Conservative Republican Dwight D. Eisenhower of Texas wins with 33,936,234 popular votes and 442 electoral votes, over Liberal Democrat Adlai E. Stevenson of California, who receives 27,314,992 popular votes and 89 electoral votes. Eisenhower becomes our 34th president.

Our 34th president, Republican Dwight D. Eisenhower, a Conservative.

The 1956 election (our 43rd): Conservative Republican Dwight D. Eisenhower of Texas wins with 35,590,472

popular votes and 457 electoral votes, over Liberal Democrat Adlai E. Stevenson of California, who receives 26,031,322 popular votes and 73 electoral votes. Eisenhower enters his second term as our 34th president.

The 1960 election (our 44th): Liberal Democrat John F. Kennedy of Massachusetts wins with 34,227,096 popular votes and 303 electoral votes, over Conservative Republican Richard M. Nixon of California, who receives 34,108,546 popular votes and 219 electoral votes.

Our 35th president, Democrat John F. Kennedy, a Liberal.

Kennedy becomes our 35th president. He is assassinated in 1963, however, and his vice president, Lyndon B. Johnson of Texas, becomes our 36th president.

The 1964 election (our 45th): Liberal Democrat Lyndon B. Johnson of Texas wins with 43,126,506 popular votes and 486 electoral votes, over Conservative Republican Barry M. Goldwater of Arizona, who receives 27,176,799 popular votes and 52 electoral

Our 36th president, Democrat Lyndon B. Johnson, a Liberal.

Our 37th president, Republican Richard M. Nixon, a Conservative.

votes. Johnson enters his second term as our 36th president.

The 1968 election (our 46th): Conservative Republican Richard M. Nixon of California wins with 31,785,480 popular votes and 301 electoral votes, over Liberal Democrat Hubert H. Humphrey of South Dakota, who receives 31,275,166 popular votes and 191 electoral votes. Nixon becomes our 37th president.

The 1972 election (our 47th): Conservative Republican Richard M. Nixon of California wins with 47,165,234 popular votes and 520 electoral votes, over Liberal Democrat George S. McGovern of South Dakota, who receives 29,168,110 popular votes and 17 electoral votes. Nixon enters his second term as our 37th president. In 1974 he resigns over Watergate and various other scandals, however, and his vice president, Gerald R. Ford of Nebraska, becomes our 38th president.

Our 38th president, Republican Gerald R. Ford, a Conservative.

The 1976 election (our 48th): Liberal Democrat Jimmy Carter of Georgia wins with 40,825,839 popular votes and 297 electoral votes, over Conservative Republican Gerald R. Ford of Nebraska, who receives 39,147,770 popular votes and 240 electoral votes. Carter becomes our 39th president.

Our 39th president, Democrat Jimmy Carter, a Liberal.

The 1980 election (our 49th): Conservative Republican Ronald Reagan of Illinois wins with 43,899,248 popular votes and 489 electoral votes, over Liberal Democrat Jimmy Carter of Georgia, who receives 35,481,435 popular votes and 49 electoral votes. Reagan becomes our 40th president.

The 1984 election (our 50th): Conservative Republican Ronald Reagan of

California wins with 54,281,858 popular votes and 525 electoral votes, over Liberal Democrat Walter F. Mondale of Minnesota, who receives 37,457,215 popular votes and 13 electoral votes. Reagan enters his second term as our 40th president.

The 1988 election (our 51st): Conservative Republican George H. W. Bush of Massachusetts wins with 47,946,422 popular votes and 426 electoral votes, over Liberal Democrat Michael S. Dukakis of Massachusetts, who receives 41,016,429 popular votes and 111 electoral votes. Bush becomes our 41st president.

Our 40th president, Republican Ronald Reagan, a Conservative.

The 1992 election (our 52nd): Liberal Democrat Bill Clinton of Arkansas wins with 44,908,233 popular votes and 370 electoral votes, over Conservative Republican George H. W. Bush of Massachusetts, who receives 39,102,282 popular votes and 168 electoral votes. Clinton becomes our 42nd president.

The 1996 election (our 53rd): Liberal Democrat Bill Clinton of Arkansas wins with 45,628,667 popular votes and

Our 41st president, Republican George H. W. Bush, a Conservative.

379 electoral votes, over Conservative Republican Bob Dole of Kansas, who receives 37,869,435 popular votes and 159 electoral votes. Clinton enters his second term as our 42nd president.

The 2000 election (our 54th): Conservative Republican George W. Bush (son of President George H. W. Bush) of Connecticut wins with 50,456,002 popular votes and 271 electoral votes, over Liberal Democrat Al Gore of Washington, D.C., who receives 50,999,897

Our 42nd president, Democrat Bill Clinton, a Liberal.

Our 43rd president, Republican George W. Bush, a Conservative.

popular votes and 266 electoral votes. Bush becomes our 43rd president.

The 2004 election (our 55th): Conservative Republican George W. Bush of Connecticut wins with 62,028,285 popular votes and 286 electoral votes, over Liberal Democrat John Kerry of Colorado, who receives 59,028,109 popular votes and 251 electoral votes. Bush enters his second term as our 43rd president.

The 2008 election (our 56th): Liberal Democrat Barack H. Obama of Hawaii wins with 69,499,428 popular votes and 365 electoral votes, over Conservative Republican John McCain of Panama, who receives 59,950,323 popular votes and 173 electoral votes. Obama becomes our 44th president.

Our 44th president, Democrat Barack H. Obama, a Liberal.

The 2012 election (our 57th): Liberal Democrat Barack H. Obama of Hawaii wins with 65,918,507 popular votes and 332 electoral votes, over Conservative Republican Mitt Romney of Michigan, who receives 60,934,407 popular votes and 206 electoral votes. Obama enters his second term as our 44th president.

The 2016 election (our 58th): Conservative Republican Donald J. Trump of New York wins with 62,979,636 popular votes and 304 electoral votes, over Liberal Democrat Hillary Clinton of Illinois, who receives 65,844,610 popular votes and 227 electoral votes. Trump becomes our 45th president.

Our 45th president, Republican Donald J. Trump, a Conservative.

6

A REVIEW OF THE FACTS

ABRAHAM LINCOLN WAS A LIBERAL, and Jefferson Davis was a Conservative, and our examination of the presidential history of both the United States of America and the Confederate States of America has proven these facts with an overabundance of irrefutable evidence. Let us now summarize.

The 1860 Republican Party of Lincoln—which has no connection to today's Republican Party—was a political descendant of the left-wing 18th-Century Federalist Party. It was founded in 1854 by Liberals (then sometimes known as "fusionists"), who revered Liberal Founding Father Alexander Hamilton and who were associated with communist Karl Marx.[584] They, along with various types of socialists, radicals, collectivists, and revolutionaries, wrote its platform, served as delegates at the 1860 Republican convention, zealously campaigned for Lincoln, a big government Liberal with socialistic leanings,[585] and were instrumental in getting him into the White House.[586]

The author's cousin, Confederate Vice President and Democrat Alexander H. Stephens: a Southern Conservative.

More proof of the original

Republican Party's liberal foundations comes from the facts that Lincoln idolized the radical leaders of the European socialist revolution of 1848,[587] while the radical progressive members of the party agreed with socialists and communists that the American "Civil War" was a "revolutionary movement" (Marx), a "radical revolution" (Thaddeus Stevens), and a "social revolution" (James A. Garfield).[588]

The 1860 Democratic Party of Jefferson Davis—which has no connection to today's Democratic Party—is a political descendant of the right-wing 18th-Century Democratic-Republican Party. It was founded in 1828 by Conservatives who followed in the footsteps of Conservative Founding Father Thomas Jefferson. Democratic President Davis was the foremost Victorian Conservative during the Civil War period. A small government Conservative with libertarian leanings, he will always be honorably known to us here in the traditional South as "the Patriot of Patriots."[589]

Evidence for the conservatism of the original Democratic Party (of 1828) is abundant and clear. In the mid 1800s, for example, the conservative wing of the party was known as "the States' Rights Party,"[590] while Democrats themselves referred to each other as "conservatives" (particularly in the South),[591] "confederates," "anti-centralists," or "constitutionalists" (the latter because they favored rigorous adherence to

U.S. President William McKinley, in 1896 the first Conservative Republican since the party's inception in 1854.

the original Constitution—which tacitly guaranteed states' rights—as created by the Founding Fathers). In sharp contrast, the Republicans of the Civil War era called themselves "liberals," "nationalists," "centralists," or "consolidationists" (the latter three because they wanted to nationalize

William Jennings Bryan, in 1896 the Democratic Party's first Liberal presidential nominee, and the first political progressive to add a populist plank to the party's platform since its inception in 1828.

the central government and consolidate political power in Washington, D.C.).[592] Due to the 19th-Century Republicans' (Liberals') hatred of the Constitution (which they derogatorily referred to as a "worthless"[593] "scrap of paper"),[594] Democrats (Conservatives) of that era called them "radicals"[595] (that is, revolutionaries), or more accurately, the "Anti-Constitutional Party."[596]

Thus in the year 1900, even after the two main parties had switched platforms (in 1896), Conservative President Grover Cleveland was still being correctly described as a "Jackson Democrat" and Liberal Benjamin Harrison as a "Lincoln Republican."[597] Extending this line of reasoning, it is because of the reversal of the parties in 1896 that it would be wholly incorrect to refer to Cleveland as "Clinton Democrat" and Harrison as a "Reagan Republican."

Since in our post-truth political world these facts are new to most of my readers,[598] let us further demystify them by viewing them from the perspective of the American Revolutionary War. If Confederate President Jefferson Davis and his *conservative* Southern constituents (the Democrats of 1861) had been alive in 1775, they would have sided with George Washington and the American colonists, who sought to secede from the tyrannical government of Great Britain; if Union President Abraham Lincoln and his *liberal* Northern constituents (the Republicans of 1861) had been alive at that time, they would have sided with King George III and the English monarchy, who sought to maintain the American colonies as possessions of the British Empire.

It is due to this very comparison that Southerners often refer to the "Civil War" as the Second American Revolutionary War, for

the struggle between the [Liberal] advocates of a [strong] central government and the [Conservative] champions of states' rights was a repetition of the struggle between the [Conservative] colonists and the [Liberal] British government which led to the Revolution.[599]

Thousands of Victorian eyewitnesses attest to this fact. On May 30, 1861, one of them, Mrs. R. L. Hunt of New Orleans, Louisiana, sent a letter to her brother, Salmon P. Chase (at the time a Liberal), Lincoln's Secretary of the Treasury, which contains the following pertinent comments. "Dear brother," she began in defense of the South:

Lincoln's Secretary of the Treasury Salmon P. Chase.

Do not delude yourself or others with the notion that war can maintain the Union. . . . With these [the rifle, sword, and cannon] you propose to subjugate the entire free people of the South, while you mock them with the declaration that your object is to maintain a Union which no longer exists. Is this wise, just, quite in keeping with the spirit of Christianity and of liberty, and with the lofty character of the United States? Would you desire a union of compulsion, a union to be maintained by the bayonet, a union with hatred and revenge filling the hearts of the North and of the South? I hope you would not. But if you would, the thing is impossible. You can never subjugate the South—never.

Her people are high-spirited, martial, and intelligent. Educated in the school of American liberty, they value the right of self-government above all price. . . . They view the attempt to conquer them and to compel them to submit to the government of their victors as an effort of high-handed tyranny and oppression. You may for the moment have an advantage in wealth and numbers. But . . . the North is fighting for subjugation and domination, the South for liberty and independence. It is precisely like the great revolutionary struggle of 1776 against the tyranny of Great Britain—a struggle for liberty on one side and for despotism on the other. How can you expect victory in such a cause?[600]

Thus,

absolutely convinced of the righteousness of their cause, the South entered the [civil] war as a holy crusade, repeating the language of the men of 1776 and resolved to defend their liberty and independence to the last man and the last dollar.[601]

It is obvious then why, in the early 20th Century, former Confederates spoke of 18th-Century Federalist Alexander Hamilton as a big government or centralizing Liberal, while acknowledging that Thomas Jefferson and the Republicans were "now Democrats," the Conservatives of the Civil War period,[602] men committed to states' rights and a literal and strict interpretation of the Constitution.[603] This is made more clear by the fact that, as we have seen, in his day Conservative Jefferson was a member of the Democratic-Republican Party, which,

Conservative icon, Republican Thomas Jefferson.

after his death, "dropped the name 'Republican' which it had borne during his life, and assumed the name 'Democrat.'"[604] To recap, let us recall the words of Meriwether:

> Not until 1854 did the [Liberal] men of the Federal and Whig persuasion unite and organize a party and take the name "Republican." The Republican [Liberal] party of the 1860s was the legitimate offspring of the old New England Federalists [early American big government Liberals], and inherited all its progenitor's faiths, hopes, hates and purposes, viz: Passion for power, fear and hate of Democracy [here meaning conservatism], hate of the Union . . . and the strong persistent determination to break the Union asunder and form of the Northeast section a Northeastern Confederacy. All these ideas belonged to the old Federalists [Liberals] of New England, and were handed down to the Republican [Liberal] party in 1854.[605]

These party designations were particularly evident in the so-called "New South" shortly after Lincoln's War, as historian Holland Thompson comments:

> The political organization [the Democrats] to which allegiance was demanded was generally called the Conservative party, and the Republican [Liberal] party was universally called the Radical party. The term Conservative was adopted partly as a contrast, partly because the peace party had been so called during the War, and especially because the name Democrat was obnoxious to so many old Whigs [antebellum Liberals]. It was not until 1906 that the term Conservative was officially dropped from the title of the dominant party in Alabama [the Democratic Party].[606]

Conservative William McKinley.

Lastly, it is important to drive home the point that the conservative Republican Party and the liberal Democratic Party that we are so familiar with today, did not arise until 1896, when the then *liberal* Republican Party switched to a *conservative* platform and nominated Conservative capitalist William McKinley of Ohio (who was supported by conservative former Confederate soldiers)[607] as its presidential nominee. That same year the then *conservative* Democratic Party switched to a *progressive* platform, nominating the Liberal "fusion candidate" William Jennings Bryan of Illinois as its presidential nominee,[608] whose populist platform Conservatives charged rested on a cornerstone of "chartered communism,"[609] written by a party made up of "socialists, anarchists and demagogues of a dangerous type."[610]

This major realignment in American politics is why the Border States (Delaware, Maryland, West Virginia, Kentucky, and Missouri) did not begin to be carried by Republican candidates until 1896,[611] and it is why the election of 1896, for both positive and negative reasons, has been called "the most important in U.S. history since Lincoln's War";[612] "the most unique and remarkable in the experience of this country, or of any other";[613] and the year when party ties, "which had usually been strong as steel, became ropes of sand."[614] "There was," writes Platt, a "general shifting of the old party lines and a 'bolting' from all of the party candidates."[615] In 1900, McClure, who participated in this spectacular election, described it this way:

Political Liberal William Jennings Bryan, "out for a morning ride" at his Nebraska farm.

No mere party contest in the history of the country, and indeed no other contest, with the single exception of the issue of secession and civil war, ever exhibited so large a measure of political independence as is shown in the vote for President in 1896.[616]

Of our ever changing political name game, American President Martin Van Buren wrote:

> The names of . . . [our] parties, like those of their predecessors in older countries, have from time to time been changed, from suggestions of policy or from accidental causes. Men of similar and substantially unchanged views and principles have, at different periods of English history, been distinguished as Cavaliers or Roundheads, as Jacobites or Puritans and Presbyterians, as Whigs or Tories. Here [in the U.S.], with corresponding consistency in principle, the same men have at different periods been known as Federalists, Federal Republicans, and Whigs, or as Anti- Federalists, Republicans, and Democrats. But no changes of name have indicated . . . a change or material modification of the true character and principles of the [two primary] parties themselves.[617]

The truth has now been established about the American "Civil War." The Confederacy was a traditional republic under the leadership of small government Conservative, Democratic President Jefferson Davis, whose citizens were mainly Conservatives fighting to retain the original government and Constitution of the Founding Fathers. The Union was

a progressive nation under the leadership of big government Liberal, Republican President Abraham Lincoln, whose citizens were mainly Liberals fighting to overturn the original government and Constitution of the Founding Fathers.

Thus, the Republican Party today is the Democratic Party of the Civil War Era. The Democratic Party today is the Republican Party of the Civil War Era. This means, in turn, that our modern Republican Party is in no way connected or even loosely related to the Republican Party of 1861; and our modern Democratic Party is in no way connected or even loosely related to the Democratic Party of 1861.

U.S. President, Republican Abraham Lincoln, the most powerful Liberal during the Civil War Era.

Modern Conservatives who attribute the freeing of the slaves to the "Conservative Republican Party," invoke the name "Lincoln" and glorify him in interviews and speeches, and conservative groups and organizations who name themselves after Lincoln, are all committing heinous crimes against authentic history. Likewise, those who denigrate the "Liberal Democratic Party" of the 1860s as the founder of the KKK and the "pro-slavery party," or refer to Democrat Davis as a Liberal, do a great injustice to the Truth.

C.S. President, Democrat Jefferson Davis, to traditional Southerners the greatest of all the American Conservatives.

Without a basic understanding of these facts, the American "Civil War" will forever remain incomprehensible, and thus its lessons will be lost. This work, and my companion volume, *Lincoln's War: The Real Cause, the Real Winner, the Real Loser*, supplies the missing key to unfolding this understanding. With God's blessings, may it spread far and wide.

The End

APPENDICES

*Four Different Ways of Looking at the
History of America's Two-Party System*

The Democratic (Conservative) C.S. cabinet in 1861. From left to right: Stephen Russell Mallory (secretary of the navy), Judah Philip Benjamin (attorney general), LeRoy Pope Walker (secretary of war), Jefferson Davis (president), Robert Edward Lee (general-in-chief of Confederate forces), John Henninger Reagan (postmaster general), Christopher Gustavus Memminger (secretary of the treasury), Alexander Hamilton Stephens (vice president), Robert Augustus Toombs (secretary of state).

The Republican (Liberal) U.S. cabinet in 1861. From left to right: Montgomery Blair (postmaster general), Caleb Blood Smith (secretary of the interior), Salmon Portland Chase (secretary of the treasury), Abraham Lincoln (president), William Henry Seward (secretary of state), Simon Cameron (secretary of war), Edward Bates (attorney general), Gideon Welles (secretary of the navy). Hannibal Hamlin (vice president) and Ulysses S. Grant (commanding general of Union forces) are missing.

APPENDIX A

U.S. PRESIDENTS, PARTY AFFILIATIONS, & TERMS

At a Glance

1. George Washington: Federalist (Liberal), served 1789-1797.
2. John Adams: Federalist (Liberal), served 1797-1801.
3. Thomas Jefferson: Republican (Conservative), served 1801-1809.
4. James Madison: Republican (Conservative), served 1809-1817.
5. James Monroe: Republican (Conservative), served 1817-1825.
6. John Quincy Adams: Republican (Conservative), served 1825-1829.
7. Andrew Jackson: Democrat (Conservative), served 1829-1837.
8. Martin Van Buren: Democrat (Conservative), served 1837-1841.
9. William Henry Harrison: Whig (Liberal), served 1841-1841 (died in office).
10. John Tyler: Whig (Liberal), served 1841-1845.
11. James Knox Polk: Democrat (Conservative), served 1845-1849.
12. Zachary Taylor: Whig (Liberal), served 1849-1850 (died in office).
13. Millard Fillmore: Whig (Liberal), served 1850-1853.
14. Franklin Pierce: Democrat (Conservative), served 1853-1857.
15. James Buchanan: Democrat (Conservative), served 1857-1861.
16. Abraham Lincoln: Republican (Liberal), served 1861-1865 (died in office).
17. Andrew Johnson: National Union (Republican/Liberal), served 1865-1869.
18. Ulysses Simpson Grant: Republican (Liberal), served 1869-1877.
19. Rutherford Birchard Hayes: Republican (Liberal), served 1877-1881.
20. James Abram Garfield: Republican (Liberal), served 1881-1881 (died in office).
21. Chester Alan Arthur: Republican (Liberal), served 1881-1885.
22. Stephen Grover Cleveland: Democrat (Conservative), served 1885-1889.
23. Benjamin Harrison: Republican (Liberal), served 1889-1893.
24. Stephen Grover Cleveland: Democrat (Conservative), served 1893-1897.
25. William McKinley: Republican (Conservative), served 1897-1901 (died in office).
26. Theodore Roosevelt: Republican (Conservative), served 1901-1909.
27. William Howard Taft: Republican (Conservative), served 1909-1913.
28. Thomas Woodrow Wilson: Democrat (Liberal), served 1913-1921.
29. Warren Gamaliel Harding: Republican (Conservative), served 1921-1923 (died in office).
30. John Calvin Coolidge: Republican (Conservative), served 1923-1929.
31. Herbert Clark Hoover: Republican (Conservative), served 1929-1933.
32. Franklin Delano Roosevelt: Democrat (Liberal), served 1933-1945 (died in office).
33. Harry S. Truman: Democrat (Liberal), served 1945-1953.
34. Dwight David Eisenhower: Republican (Conservative), served 1953-1961.
35. John Fitzgerald Kennedy: Democrat (Liberal), served 1961-1963 (died in office).
36. Lyndon Baines Johnson: Democrat (Liberal), served 1963-1969.
37. Richard Milhous Nixon: Republican (Conservative), served 1969-1974.
38. Gerald Rudolph Ford: Republican (Conservative), served 1974-1977.
39. James Earl Carter, Jr.: Democrat (Liberal), served 1977-1981.
40. Ronald Wilson Reagan: Republican (Conservative), served 1981-1989.
41. George Herbert Walker Bush: Republican (Conservative), served 1989-1993.
42. William Jefferson Clinton: Democrat (Liberal), served 1993-2001.
43. George Walker Bush: Republican (Conservative), served 2001-2009.
44. Barack Hussein Obama II: Democrat (Liberal), served 2009-2017.
45. Donald John Trump: Republican (Conservative), served 2017-   .

APPENDIX B

A TIMELINE OF AMERICA'S
TWO MAIN PARTIES IN BRIEF

With the Terms, Names, & Political Persuasion of the Parties of Our Presidents

Hundreds of political parties have come and gone throughout our history. Unfortunately for the modern student of politics, the names by which they designated themselves were often not well thought out, and therefore were inappropriate and misleading—as this very book has demonstrated. For example, some party names were invented by their critics and were meant to be deceptive, and thus purposefully offensive or bewildering to the public. Worst of all, in some cases the same name was used by different factions, parties who had little in common, or even held opposing views.

To help alleviate this confusion, in the following timeline I use political platforms to identify a presidential party rather than its official name, the same technique I have used throughout this work. As I have emphasized, our presidential nominees, as well as our elected presidents and their parties, have rarely been either completely conservative or completely liberal, and would therefore be more correctly considered conservative-leaning or liberal-leaning. Nevertheless, the designations I have given to the political persuasions of the two main parties in this appendix hold true.

Timeline

The Federalist Party, our first liberal party, is founded in 1789—an outgrowth of the Federalists of 1787 who lived in the U.S.A. during the Confederation period (1781-1789).

★ 1st President: 1789-1797: Federalist Party - Liberal

The Democratic-Republican Party, our first conservative party, is founded in 1792. Members tend to use only the name "Republicans," while their opponents refer to them as "Democrats." In any event, the word "Democrat" is dropped from the party title during the French Revolution (1789-1799) when it begins to fall into disrepute.

★ 2ⁿᵈ President: 1797-1801: Federalist Party - Liberal

After ruling the White House from 1789 to 1801, the Federalist Party begins to weaken and dissolve around 1800. For a brief peaceful period there is only one major party and all Americans consider themselves "Republicans," that is, Conservatives.

★ 3ʳᵈ President: 1801-1809: Republican Party - Conservative
★ 4ᵗʰ President: 1809-1817: Republican Party - Conservative

In the 1816 election the Federalist Party puts up its last presidential nominee.

★ 5ᵗʰ President: 1817-1825: Republican Party - Conservative

Due to several election losses in a row as well as charges of being "unpatriotic," by 1820 the Federalist Party has disappeared.

★ 6ᵗʰ President: 1825-1829: Republican Party - Conservative

During the 1828 election year the Republican Party, the main conservative party, splits in two, the liberal-leaning faction becoming the "National Republicans," the conservative-leaning faction resuscitating the old discarded name "Democrat," which had fallen into disrepute during the French Revolution.

★ 7ᵗʰ President: 1829-1837: Democratic Party - Conservative

In 1834 the newly formed Whig Party (Liberal) replaces the National Republican Party (Liberal), both descendants of the defunct Federalist Party (Liberal).

★ 8ᵗʰ President: 1837-1841: Democratic Party - Conservative

By the late 1830s, national, state, county, and town parties are connected via congressional districts, which send select delegates to state and national conventions. America is now in possession of a true and complete party system.

★ 9th President: 1841-1841: Whig Party - Liberal
★ 10th President: 1841-1845: Whig Party - Liberal
★ 11th President: 1845-1849: Democratic Party - Conservative
★ 12th President: 1849-1850: Whig Party - Liberal
★ 13th President: 1850-1853: Whig Party - Liberal

Lacking focus and public support, the Whig Party disbands around 1852.

★ 14th President: 1853-1857: Democratic Party - Conservative

In 1854 former Whigs and other partyless Liberals and socialists form a new party. Using "Republican," the name that was dropped by the Democratic-Republicans in 1828, they, intentionally misleadingly, become the Republican Party (Liberal).

★ 15th President: 1857-1861: Democratic Party - Conservative

Abraham Lincoln, a Republican (Liberal), becomes president of the U.S.A. Jefferson Davis, a Democrat (Conservative), becomes president of the C.S.A.

★ 16th President: 1861-1865: Republican Party - Liberal
★ 17th President: 1865-1869: National Union Party - Liberal
★ 18th President: 1869-1877: Republican Party - Liberal
★ 19th President: 1877-1881: Republican Party - Liberal
★ 20th President: 1881-1881: Republican Party - Liberal
★ 21st President: 1881-1885: Republican Party - Liberal
★ 22nd President: 1885-1889: Democratic Party - Conservative
★ 23rd President: 1889-1893: Republican Party - Liberal
★ 24th President: 1893-1897: Democratic Party - Conservative

Finally, the two main parties switch platforms during the 1896 election: the Democrats (formerly Conservative) become Liberals, the Republicans (formerly Liberals) become Conservatives—transforming into the parties we are familiar with today.

★ 25th President: 1897-1901: Republican Party - Conservative
★ 26th President: 1901-1909: Republican Party - Conservative
★ 27th President: 1909-1913: Republican Party - Conservative
★ 28th President: 1913-1921: Democratic Party - Liberal
★ 29th President: 1921-1923: Republican Party - Conservative
★ 30th President: 1923-1929: Republican Party - Conservative
★ 31st President: 1929-1933: Republican Party - Conservative
★ 32nd President: 1933-1945: Democratic Party - Liberal
★ 33rd President: 1945-1953: Democratic Party - Liberal
★ 34th President: 1953-1961: Republican Party - Conservative
★ 35th President: 1961-1963: Democratic Party - Liberal
★ 36th President: 1963-1969: Democratic Party - Liberal
★ 37th President: 1969-1974: Republican Party - Conservative
★ 38th President: 1974-1977: Republican Party - Conservative
★ 39th President: 1977-1981: Democratic Party - Liberal
★ 40th President: 1981-1989: Republican Party - Conservative
★ 41st President: 1989-1993: Republican Party - Conservative
★ 42nd President: 1993-2001: Democratic Party - Liberal
★ 43rd President: 2001-2009: Republican Party - Conservative
★ 44th President: 2009-2017: Democratic Party - Liberal
★ 45th President: 2017-   : Republican Party - Conservative

Thomas Jefferson, age 47.

APPENDIX C
KEY EVENTS IN THE EVOLUTION
OF THE TWO PARTIES

❦ 1789: The Federalist Party, or Hamiltonians (after Alexander Hamilton), our first Liberal party, is founded—an outgrowth of the Federalists of 1787, who lived in the U.S.A. during the Confederation period (1781-1789). Their conservative opponents, the Jeffersonians (after Thomas Jefferson), also begin to coalesce and emerge at this time. The Federalists disrespectfully (and inaccurately) call them the Antifederalist Party. Being only loosely organized and based on local rather than national politics, neither faction is yet an official party.

❦ 1792: The Democratic-Republican Party, our first Conservative party, is founded around the Antifederalist Party. Its members tend to use only the name "Republicans," while their Liberal opponents, the Federalists, refer to them as "Democrats." During the French Revolution (1789-1799) the word "Democrat" is dropped from the party title because it had begun to fall into disrepute.

❦ 1800: After ruling the White House from 1789 to 1801, the Federalist Party (Liberal) begins to dissolve due to lack of organization and focus. For a brief peaceful period there is only one major party, the Republican Party (Conservative), and all Americans now consider themselves "Republicans."

❦ 1816: During this election the Federalist Party (Liberal) puts up its last presidential nominee: Rufus King of New York.

❦ 1820: By this year the Federalist Party has disappeared.

❦ 1828: During the election this year the Republican Party, the main Conservative party, splits in two, the liberal-leaning faction going by the name of the "National Republicans," the conservative-leaning faction resuscitating the old discarded name "Democrat," which had become discredited during the French Revolution.

❦ 1834: The newly formed Whig Party (Liberal) replaces the National Republican Party (Liberal), both descendants of the defunct Federalist Party (Liberal).

❦ Late 1830s: National, state, county, and town parties are connected via congressional districts, which send select delegates to state and national conventions. America is now in possession of a true and complete party system.

❦ 1852: The Whig Party (Liberal) dissolves around this time due to the absence of a central cohesive platform.

❦ 1854: Former Whigs and other partyless Liberals and socialists form a new party. Using the name that was dropped by the Democratic-Republicans in 1828, they become the Republican Party (Liberal). It must be strongly emphasized here that the 1854 Republican Party (Liberal) has no connection to the 1792 Republican Party (Conservative) of Thomas Jefferson, the 1896 Republican Party (Conservative) of William McKinley, the 1980 Republican Party (Conservative) of Ronald Reagan, or the 2016 Republican Party (Conservative) of Donald Trump. The Republican Party of 1854 was an entirely new creation, one formed by Liberals, socialists, and various radical left-wingers, using a discarded and inappropriate name, "Republican," intended to mislead. This, the 1854 Republican Party (Liberal), died out in 1896 and was replaced that year by the modern Democratic Party (Liberal).

❦ 1856: Big government Liberal Abraham Lincoln, a former member of the now extinct Whig Party (Liberal), joins the newly formed Republican Party (Liberal).

❦ 1860: Lincoln, a new member of the Republican Party (Liberal), is elected president of the U.S.A. (by the Electoral College) with a minority of popular votes in the North and with none in the South.

❦ 1861: Small government constitutionalist Jefferson Davis, a Democrat (Conservative), is unanimously chosen to become president of the C.S.A.

❦ 1896: During the campaign and election this year, the two main parties switch platforms: the Democrats (formerly Conservative) become Liberals, the Republicans (formerly Liberals) become Conservatives—changing into the parties we are familiar with today.

In other words, the 1854 Republican Party (Liberal) of Lincoln, Ulysses S. Grant, and James A. Garfield, died out in 1896, and was replaced by a modern version of the 1789 Federalist Party (Liberal) of John Adams and the 1854 Whig Party (Liberal) of William H. Harrison and Millard Fillmore. This is what we now know as the current Democratic Party (Liberal).

Simultaneously, the 1828 Democratic Party (Conservative) of Andrew Jackson, Franklin Pierce, and Grover Cleveland, died out in 1896, replaced by a modern version of the 1792 Republican Party (Conservative) of Thomas Jefferson and the 1828 Democratic Party (Conservative) of Andrew Jackson, James K. Polk, James Buchanan, and Jefferson Davis. This is what we now know as the current Republican Party (Conservative).

U.S. Supreme Court (top), Senate Chamber (bottom).

APPENDIX D

ELECTION YEARS, PARTY NAMES, & WINNERS

58 Elections - 45 Presidents

Showing the Changing Names of the Two Main Parties

- NOTE IN PARTICULAR THE 11TH AND 28TH ELECTIONS -

ELECTION NUMBER	ELECTION YEAR	CONSERVATIVE PARTY	LIBERAL PARTY	WINNER Key: Lib/Liberal, Con/Conservative
1	1788	Anti-Federalist	Federalist	Federalist (Lib)
2	1792	Democratic-Republican	Federalist	Federalist (Lib)
3	1796	Democratic-Republican	Federalist	Federalist (Lib)
4	1800	Republican	Federalist	Republican (Con)
5	1804	Republican	Federalist	Republican (Con)
6	1808	Republican	Federalist	Republican (Con)
7	1812	Republican	Federalist	Republican (Con)
8	1816	Republican	Federalist	Republican (Con)
9	1820	Republican	None	Republican (Con)
10	1824	Republican	None	Republican (Con)
11	1828	Democratic	National Republican	Democratic (Con)
12	1832	Democratic	National Republican	Democratic (Con)
13	1836	Democratic	Whig	Democratic (Con)
14	1840	Democratic	Whig	Whig (Lib)
15	1844	Democratic	Whig	Democratic (Con)
16	1848	Democratic	Whig	Whig (Lib)
17	1852	Democratic	Whig	Democratic (Con)
18	1856	Democratic	Republican	Democratic (Con)
19	1860	Democratic	Republican	Republican (Lib)
20	1864	Democratic	National Union	National Union (Lib)

21	1868	Democratic	Republican	Republican (Lib)
22	1872	Democratic	Republican	Republican (Lib)
23	1876	Democratic	Republican	Republican (Lib)
24	1880	Democratic	Republican	Republican (Lib)
25	1884	Democratic	Republican	Democratic (Con)
26	1888	Democratic	Republican	Republican (Lib)
27	1892	Democratic	Republican	Democratic (Con)
28	1896	Republican	Democratic	Republican (Con)
29	1900	Republican	Democratic	Republican (Con)
30	1904	Republican	Democratic	Republican (Con)
31	1908	Republican	Democratic	Republican (Con)
32	1912	Republican	Democratic	Democratic (Lib)
33	1916	Republican	Democratic	Democratic (Lib)
34	1920	Republican	Democratic	Republican (Con)
35	1924	Republican	Democratic	Republican (Con)
36	1928	Republican	Democratic	Republican (Con)
37	1932	Republican	Democratic	Democratic (Lib)
38	1936	Republican	Democratic	Democratic (Lib)
39	1940	Republican	Democratic	Democratic (Lib)
40	1944	Republican	Democratic	Democratic (Lib)
41	1948	Republican	Democratic	Democratic (Lib)
42	1952	Republican	Democratic	Republican (Con)
43	1956	Republican	Democratic	Republican (Con)
44	1960	Republican	Democratic	Democratic (Lib)
45	1964	Republican	Democratic	Democratic (Lib)
46	1968	Republican	Democratic	Republican (Con)
47	1972	Republican	Democratic	Republican (Con)
48	1976	Republican	Democratic	Democratic (Lib)

49	1980	Republican	Democratic	Republican (Con)
50	1984	Republican	Democratic	Republican (Con)
51	1988	Republican	Democratic	Republican (Con)
52	1992	Republican	Democratic	Democratic (Lib)
53	1996	Republican	Democratic	Democratic (Lib)
54	2000	Republican	Democratic	Republican (Con)
55	2004	Republican	Democratic	Republican (Con)
56	2008	Republican	Democratic	Democratic (Lib)
57	2012	Republican	Democratic	Democratic (Lib)
58	2016	Republican	Democratic	Republican (Con)

The White House of the C.S.A., Richmond, Virginia, official residence of President Jefferson Davis, 1861-1865.

The White House of the U.S.A., Washington, D.C., official residence of President Abraham Lincoln, 1861-1865.

NOTES

1. See e.g., Seabrook, TQJD, pp. 30, 38, 76.
2. See e.g., J. Davis, RFCG, Vol. 1, pp. 55, 422; Vol. 2, pp. 4, 161, 454, 610. Besides using the term "Civil War" himself, President Davis cites numerous other individuals who use it as well.
3. See e.g., Confederate Veteran, March 1912, Vol. 20, No. 3, p. 122.
4. Minutes of the Eighth Annual Meeting, July 1898, p. 87.
5. Bernhard, pp. 61, 80-81.
6. Bernhard, p. 110.
7. Seward, p. 85.
8. Garraty, p. 210.
9. See e.g., Bernhard, p. 139.
10. See e.g., Faulkner, pp. 141, 155.
11. Bernhard, p. 270.
12. Bernhard, p. 298. Note: Once thought of as a "classical liberal" economic system, today *laissez-faire* is more generally considered a conservative philosophy promoting government nonintervention in economic matters.
13. Muzzey, Vol. 1, p. 135.
14. Faulkner, p. 150.
15. See W. Wilson, DAR, passim. Wilson's desire to clamp down on the American press came during and because of World War I. Muzzey, Vol. 2, pp. 537, 662.
16. *La Follette's Weekly Magazine*, Vol. 3, No. 1, January 7, 1911, p. 13.
17. Muzzey, Vol. 2, p. 529. My paraphrasal.
18. Garraty, p. 330.
19. For more on Lincoln's many war crimes, which included unlawfully shutting down the governments of states like Maryland (and arresting and imprisoning their entire legislatures), censoring the press, torturing and killing American citizens, and illegally suspending *habeas corpus*, see Seabrook, AL, passim; Seabrook, LW, passim.
20. In reality, Lincoln, a lifelong black colonizationist, had nothing to do with ending slavery; the institution was abolished by the Thirteenth Amendment, which was ratified eight months *after* his death. See Seabrook, AL, passim.
21. Davis was not connected to the founding of what I call the "Reconstruction KKK" (which is not in any way associated with the modern KKK). While those who did found it were indeed Democrats, the Democrats at the time were conservatives. Lastly, the Reconstruction KKK, which lasted only from late 1865 to early 1869, was not a racist organization, but rather a conservative, anti-Liberal, pro-Constitution group, one that was not only comprised of thousands of black supporters, but which ran an all-black KKK chapter in Nashville, as just one example. See Seabrook, NBFATKKK, passim.
22. Nelson, p. 778.
23. Morison and Commager, Vol. 1, p. 469.
24. It is a fact that some of President Andrew Jackson's beliefs, practices, and policies were *not* conservative in nature. But this phenomenon is true of nearly all of our presidents: none have been purely conservative or purely liberal. Overall, Jackson would certainly be considered more conservative than not by today's standards. In any event, as this very book demonstrates, the Democrat Party of that era *was* conservative in nature, and Jackson was its highest elected leader.
25. Wayne, MacKenzie, and Cole, p. 249.
26. Leavitt, p. 18.
27. S. S. McPherson, p. 13.
28. Halloran, pp. 29-31, 50-51.
29. F. Curtis, Vol. 1, p. 65.
30. Bernhard, p. 316.
31. Burns, pp. 134-136, 376.
32. M. Van Buren, p. 6.
33. Macy, p. 32.
34. W. MacDonald, pp. 42-43.
35. Beard, epigraph.

36. J. S. Brown, p. 9.
37. Garraty, p. 196.
38. Bernhard, p. 12.
39. Marshall, Vol. 2, p. 402.
40. Macy, p. 24.
41. Bedford and Colbourn, p. 109.
42. Bernhard, p. 8.
43. Morison and Commager, Vol. 1, p. 334.
44. Faulkner, p. 141.
45. W. MacDonald, p. 140.
46. Bedford and Colbourn, p. 109.
47. Burns, pp. 135, 379.
48. S. M. Hamilton, Vol. 5, p. 346.
49. Carey, title page.
50. C. C. Lee, p. 252.
51. Garraty, p. 209.
52. McLaughlin, Vol. 10, p. 291.
53. A. Johnson, p. 39.
54. M. Van Buren, pp. 85-87.
55. Beard, pp. 27, 32.
56. F. Curtis, Vol. p. 17.
57. J. S. Brown, p. 9.
58. H. A. Washington, Vol. 4, p. 451.
59. Bailey, p. 71.
60. J. S. Brown, pp. 9-10.
61. W. L. Wilson, pp. 17-18, 30.
62. Seabrook, LW, p. 68.
63. J. S. Young, p. 92.
64. Muzzey, Vol. 1, p. 551.
65. J. S. Brown, p. 14.
66. Davidson, Vol. 2, p. 321.
67. Muzzey, Vol. 1, p. 590.
68. McRee, Vol. 2, p. 285.
69. Wagstaff, Vol. 1, pp. 64-65.
70. Harvey, pp. 77-78.
71. Bernhard, p. 157.
72. Garraty, p. 195.
73. Seabrook, C101, pp. 85-86.
74. Morison and Commager, Vol. 1, p. 331.
75. Seabrook, C101, pp. 106-107.
76. Rawle, pp. 9, 93, 296-297.
77. Jefferson Davis, Vol. 1, p. 145.
78. H. A. Washington, Vol. 8, p. 3.
79. W. L. Wilson, p. 59.
80. Beard, pp. 34-74.
81. Beard, pp. 34-74.
82. W. L. Wilson, pp. 20-23, 36, 40.
83. Bernhard, pp. 173-176.
84. Foley, p. 756.
85. Faulkner, p. 140.
86. Bernhard, pp. 62-63.
87. Hopkins, pp. 5, 6.
88. Morison and Commager, Vol. 1, pp. 331, 336.
89. Bernhard, p. 98.
90. W. L. Wilson, p. 44.

91. Bernhard, pp. 63, 297.
92. McMillan, p. 24.
93. W. L. Wilson, pp. 44-45.
94. Garraty, p. 210.
95. Morison and Commager, Vol. 1, pp. 331, 336.
96. Muzzey, Vol. 1, p. 163.
97. For more on this period of U.S. history, see Seabrook, TAOCE, passim.
98. Kimball, p. 366.
99. W. L. Wilson, pp. 54-55.
100. Hopkins, pp. 9-10.
101. Muzzey, Vol. 1, p. 163.
102. Muzzey, Vol. 1, p. 336.
103. Garraty, p. 310; Faulkner, p. 141.
104. Hall, p. 13.
105. A. Johnson, pp. 107-108.
106. Bernhard, pp. 109, 122.
107. W. L. Wilson, p. 55.
108. W. L. Wilson, pp. 55-56.
109. H. S. Randall, Vol. 2, pp. 78-79.
110. W. L. Wilson, pp. 60, 64.
111. W. L. Wilson, p. 59. This is a paraphrasal of Jefferson's actual words.
112. J. H. Moore, pp. 163-164.
113. W. L. Wilson, p. 65.
114. Beard, p. 13.
115. Garraty, p. 211.
116. Faulkner, p. 142.
117. Bernhard, p. 191.
118. McLaughlin and Hart, Vol. 1, pp. 576-577.
119. Hopkins, p. 14.
120. W. L. Wilson, p. 77.
121. See e.g., Bernhard, pp. 271, 273, 276, 302, 311.
122. M. Van Buren, p. 436.
123. Hunt, p. 21.
124. Morison and Commager, Vol. 1, pp. 363-364, 370.
125. Garraty, p. 209; Muzzey, Vol. 1, p. 163.
126. Martin, p. 152.
127. Martin, p. 165.
128. Garraty, p. 210.
129. J. S. Young, pp. 58-59.
130. Faulkner, p. 156.
131. W. L. Wilson, p. 80.
132. John Davis, p. 177.
133. Tucker, Vol. 2, pp. 89-92.
134. Garraty, p. 218.
135. F. Curtis, Vol. 1, p. 53.
136. F. Curtis, Vol. 1, pp. 53-54.
137. F. Curtis, Vol. 1, p. 54.
138. For other references to the Republican Party and the Federalist Party in the year 1800, see e.g., Bernhard, pp. 271, 273, 276.
139. W. L. Wilson, pp. 92, 95.
140. W. L. Wilson, p. 96.
141. F. Curtis, Vol. 1, p. 40.
142. Hill, p. 118.
143. Garraty, pp. 249-250.
144. Bonura, p. 66.

145. Buell and Lennox, s.v. "Congressional Caucus."
146. Faulkner, p. 186.
147. W. L. Wilson, pp. 101-103.
148. M. Van Buren, p. 416.
149. See Schurz, passim.
150. Morison and Commager, Vol. 1, pp. 439-441.
151. W. L. Wilson, p. 103.
152. Seabrook, AL, p. 507.
153. A. Johnson, p. 309.
154. Faulkner, p. 193.
155. Ormsby, p. 189; Hopkins, pp. 41-42; Faulkner, p. 204.
156. W. L. Wilson, pp. 109-110.
157. Claflin, p. 46; Muzzey, Vol. 1, p. 163.
158. W. L. Wilson, pp. 110-112.
159. Muzzey, Vol. 1, p. 344.
160. Benton, Vol. 1, p. 111.
161. Ormsby, p. 185.
162. W. L. Wilson, pp. 112-113, 117.
163. Burns, p. 323.
164. Burns, Peltason, Cronin, Magleby, and O'Brien, p. 31.
165. Faulkner, p. 198.
166. Hopkins, p. 51.
167. F. Curtis, Vol. 1, p. 65.
168. F. Curtis, Vol. 1, pp. 64, 65.
169. Hall, p. 166.
170. Cole, pp. 17-18; Benton, Vol. 1, p. 47.
171. W. L. Wilson, p. 126.
172. Muzzey, Vol. 1, p. 387.
173. Macy, pp. 32-34.
174. Faulkner, pp. 194-198.
175. Jameson, DOUSH, s.v. "Whigs." For those interested in a deeper discussion of the origins and meaning of the term "Whig," the name given to the Federalist or Liberal Party in 1828, the following is from England's *The Penny Cyclopedia* of 1843, which dates the word's origins back to ancient Scotland: "In the article 'Tory' is quoted the account of the origin of that term, given by Roger North, in his *Examen*. In his Life of his brother, the Lord Keeper Guildford, subsequently written, North says:—'I have heard his lordship discourse much of ignominious distinctions, and particularly that of Whig and Tory. I have given the History of this party distinction in the *Examen*, where I have showed that the faction began the game, and not the loyal party, as some now would persuade us; so shall say only, that when the Exclusion Bill, to disinherit the Duke of York, was brought forth, all the factious people and their libels chimed in to defame the duke; and among other topics, that of entertaining the Irishmen was one. Whereupon his friends were termed bogtrotters, wild Irish, or, which means the same thing, Tories. And there was such a pregnancy of contempt in that word as made it current; and the loyalists had it at every turn, with the epithets of damned, confounded, and the like. His lordship observed that the loyalists were not at all ashamed of the name, but took and owned it as their honour; which he said was the best way to frustrate the wicked intent of the other side, which was to cast an ignominy upon them. And so the primitive Christians did; for that which the heathen cast in their faces as the greatest reproach, they accounted their glory, which was the cross. But it was not long before the Tories made full payment by the term Whig.' To this we may add that *Tory* is said to be the Irish word *Torec*, that is, 'Give me,' which was the summons of surrender used by the banditti to whom the name was originally applied. . . . in a debate on the state of Ireland, Major Morgan is reported as saying, 'We have three beasts to destroy that lay burthens upon us. First is a public Tory, on whose head we lay, and upon a private Tory. Your army cannot catch them; the Irish bring them in; brothers and cousins cut one another's throats. Second beast is a priest, on whose head we lay; if he be eminent, more. Third beast, the wolf, on whom we lay a head, if a dog; if a bitch.' By a public Tory here is probably meant a leader captain; by a private, one of the common banditti. It seems not unlikely that Tory island, on the coast of Donegal, and another at the confluence of the rivers Shannon and Fergus, may have derived their names from having been haunts or strongholds of these lawless bands. Of the two terms, it was Tory, according to North, that was first applied as a political nickname; and

this is probably a correct statement in so far as regards their employment in that sense in England after the Restoration. It is commonly stated to have been in 1679, after the prorogation which defeated the first exclusion bill, that the two parties called at first Petitioners and Abhorrers (that is, petitioners for parliament being reassembled and signers of counter-petitions expressing abhorrence of the proceedings of the exclusionists), were soon alter designated derisively or contumeliously by one another Whigs and Tories. After various other epithets had been adopted and abandoned, as not sufficiently bitter or contemptuous, the Tories retorted upon their opponents, who had given them that name, by the term Whig, 'which,' says North, 'was very significative, as well as ready, being vernacular in Scotland (from whence it was borrowed) for corrupt and sour whey.' In point of fact, whig, according to the Scottish lexicographers, is not whey, but the slightly acidulated serum of butter-milk. Quite a different account from this however is given by Burnet. In his *History of His Own Time*, under the year 1648, that writer says, 'The south-west counties of Scotland have seldom corn enough to serve them round the year; and the northern parts producing more than they need, those in the west came in the summer to buy at Leith the stores that come from the north; and from a word *whiggam*, used in driving their horses, all that drove were called *whiggamors* and shorter, the *whiggs*. Now, in that year, after the news came down of Duke Hamilton's defeat, the ministers animated their people to rise and march to Edinburgh; and they came up marching on the head of their parishes, with an unheard-of fury, praying and preaching all the way as they came. The Marquis of Argyle and his party came and bearded them, they being about 6000. This was called the "whiggamors' inroad"; and ever after that all that opposed the court came in contempt to be called whiggs; and from Scotland the word was brought into England, where it is now one of our unhappy terms of distinction.' There can be little doubt that this is the true origin of the name Whig, and that it was really its previous application to the Scotch Covenanters that led to its revival as a designation for the opponents of the court in England in 1679. Kirkton, in his *History of the Church of Scotland from the Restoration to 1678*, says, under the year 1667, 'The poor people, who were in contempt called Whiggs, became name-fathers to all that owned one honest interest in Britain, who were called Whiggs, after them, even at the court of England: so strangely doth providence improve man's mistakes for the furthering of the Lord's purposes.' It may be indeed, as has been sometimes stated that the original Scotch Whigs were so called, not, as Burnet says, from the word they used in driving their horses, but from their common drink being *whig*, or sour milk; and the term may also have seemed to the English Tories of 1679 to carry a peculiar significancy and appropriateness in reference to the sour and rigid temper which they attributed to their opponents, and the want of cordiality and substance with which they changed their principles, independently of its previous application to the Covenanters. There may have appeared to the common feeling, too, to be something of fitness in giving an Irish name to the reckless and warm-blooded assertors of the royal prerogative, and a Scotch one to the more cool aid argumentative wranglers for popular rights. It may be said with considerable truth that, nationally or generally, the Irish are Tories and the Scotch are Whigs by temperament or mental constitution. With regard to the party opinions of the Whigs, it is scarcely necessary to add anything to what has been stated under the word Tory. The Whigs of the last century and a half are generally viewed as the representatives of the friends of reform or change in the ancient constitution of the country, ever since the popular element became active in the legislature, whether they were called puritans, nonconformists, round-heads, covenanters, or by any other name. Down to the Revolution of 1688 the object of this reform party was to make such change; since that event, it least till recently, it has principally been to maintain the change then made. Of course however this party, like all other parties, has both shifted or modified its professions, principles, and modes of action within certain limits from time to time, in conformity with the continual variation of circumstances, and has seldom been without several shades of opinion among the persons belonging to it in the tame age. These differences have been sometimes less, sometimes more distinctive; at one time referring to matters of apparently mere temporary policy, as was thought to be the case when the Whigs of the last age, soon after the breaking out of the French revolution, split info two sections, which came to be known as the Old and the New Whigs; at another, seeming to involve so fundamental a discordance of ultimate views and objects, if not of first principles, as perhaps to make it expedient for one extreme of the party to drop the name of Whig altogether, and to call itself something else, as we have seen the Radicals do in our own day. All parties in politics indeed are liable to be thus drawn or forced to shift their ground from time to time; even that party whose general object is to resist change and to preserve what exists, although it has no doubt a more definite course marked out for it than the opposite party, must still often, as Burke expresses it, vary its means to secure the unity of its end; besides, upon no principles will precisely the same objects seem the most desirable or important at all times. But the innovating party, or party of the movement, is more especially subject to this change of views, aims, and character: it can, properly speaking, have no fixed principles; as soon as it begins to assume or profess such, it loses its true character and really passes into its opposite. Accordingly, in point of fact, much of what was once Whiggism has now become Toryism or

Conservatism, the changes in the constitution which were formerly sought for being now attained; and, on the other hand, as new objects have presented themselves to it. Whiggism has, in so far as it retains its proper character, put on new aspects, and even taken to itself new names. The expression, an Old Whig, is almost self-contradictory; it means, if anything, one who was once a Whig, but is so no longer." G. Long, Vol. 27, s.v. "Whig."

176. Benton, Vol. 1, pp. 111-112.
177. McLaughlin and Hart, Vol. 1, p. 581.
178. W. L. Wilson, pp. 126-127.
179. Morison and Commager, Vol. 1, p. 468.
180. W. L. Wilson, p. 130.
181. W. L. Wilson, p. 130.
182. Seabrook, AL, pp. 203-205.
183. Seabrook, EYWTAAAATCWIW, p. 371.
184. Seabrook, CFF, p. 162.
185. Seabrook, EYWTAASIW, p. 549.
186. Seabrook, EYWTATCWIW, pp. 99-101.
187. Seabrook, EYWTAASIW, p. 576.
188. See Muzzey, Vol. 1, pp. 388-391.
189. Seabrook, LW, p. 44.
190. W. L. Wilson, p. 130.
191. Morison and Commager, Vol. 1, p. 567.
192. Burns, p. 380.
193. W. L. Wilson, pp. 132-134.
194. W. L. Wilson, pp. 134-136.
195. W. L. Wilson, pp. 138-140.
196. Stanwood, p. 215.
197. See Muzzey, Vol. 1, p. 441.
198. Faulkner, pp. 328-329.
199. W. L. Wilson, pp. 151-152.
200. W. L. Wilson, pp. 152-153.
201. W. L. Wilson, pp. 154-155.
202. Seabrook, EYWTAASIW, pp. 595-621.
203. See Muzzey, Vol. 1, pp. 466-467.
204. W. L. Wilson, p. 157.
205. Holt, p. 910.
206. F. Curtis, Vol. 1, p. 135.
207. W. L. Wilson, p. 157.
208. W. L. Wilson, p. 158.
209. Harvey, pp. 2-3.
210. Morison and Commager, Vol. 1, p. 645. For more on the pro-Choice slavery politics of the antebellum Conservatives, see W. L. Wilson, pp. 170-171.
211. Douglas, p. 13; W. L. Wilson, pp. 161-162.
212. W. L. Wilson, pp. 162-163. When asked about their organization they responded: "I know nothing."
213. Morison and Commager, Vol. 1, pp. 647-648.
214. Benson and Kennedy, p. 143.
215. See Gross, passim. See also Muzzey, Vol. 1, p. 470.
216. F. Curtis, Vol. 1, p. 145.
217. Seabrook, EYWTATCWIW, p. 195.
218. For a detailed discussion of the Reconstruction KKK, see Seabrook, NBFATKKK, passim.
219. F. Curtis, Vol. 1, pp. 145-146.
220. Benson and Kennedy, p. 139.
221. Palmer and Colton, pp. 469-507. For more on the Forty-Eighters, and Victorian German-American culture in general, see Wittke, passim; Efford, passim; Lorenzkowski, passim; Zucker, passim; Frizzell, passim.
222. Garraty, pp. 226-227.
223. Schapiro, p. 346.

224. Ming, p. 202.
225. Seabrook, LW, p. 78.
226. Benson and Kennedy, pp. 142, 201.
227. F. Curtis, Vol. 1, pp. 227-228.
228. Harvey, p. 7.
229. Morison and Commager, Vol. 1, p. 647.
230. Muzzey, Vol. 1, pp. 491-492. We will note here that along with Wisconsin, six other states claim to be the "birthplace of the Republican Party."
231. Boller and Story, p. 180.
232. Lause, ASSHOTCW, p. 43.
233. Lause, YA, p. 1.
234. Commons, p. 484.
235. Ghent, p. 34.
236. Muzzey, Vol. 1, p. 491.
237. W. L. Wilson, p. 163.
238. F. Curtis, Vol. 1, pp. 1-2.
239. Faulkner, p. 344.
240. Blasi, Freeman, and Kruse, p. 38.
241. DuBois and Mathews, pp. 146-148.
242. Hearn, p. 33.
243. Ilisevich, p. 117.
244. Commons, p. 484.
245. F. Curtis, Vol. 1, p. 176.
246. Benson and Kennedy, pp. 41, 51-73.
247. Hopkins, p. 94.
248. Benson and Kennedy, p. 143.
249. W. L. Wilson, pp. 165-166.
250. W. L. Wilson, p. 166.
251. W. L. Wilson, p. 166.
252. Benson and Kennedy, pp. 146-147, 163-164, 199-201.
253. W. L. Wilson, pp. 169-170.
254. Faulkner, p. 375.
255. Muzzey, Vol. 1, p. 520.
256. Harvey, p. 11.
257. Macy, p. 247; Faulkner, p. 346; F. Curtis, Vol. 1, p. 271.
258. Horrocks, p. 20.
259. Seabrook, AL, p. 271.
260. Hacker, p. 580.
261. Garraty and McCaughey, p. 241; H. U. Faulkner, p. 374.
262. W. B. Garrison, CWTFB, p. 145.
263. Jameson, TAHR, p. 788.
264. Seabrook, AL, pp. 571-572.
265. Hacker, p. 580.
266. W. B. Garrison, CWTFB, p. 145.
267. Burns, Peltason, Cronin, Magleby, and O'Brien, p. 151.
268. Seabrook, EYWTAASIW, pp. 182-183, 212-213.
269. Nicolay and Hay, ALCW, Vol. 2, p. 1.
270. Muzzey, Vol. 1, pp. 491-492.
271. E. McPherson, PHUSAGR, p. 105.
272. See Spooner, NT, No. 6, p. 54.
273. Seabrook, LW, passim.
274. Seabrook, AL, pp. 41, 57-58, 76, 80, 183.
275. W. B. Garrison, ACW, pp. 194-195.
276. DeGregorio, s.v. "Abraham Lincoln" (p. 237).
277. Donald, L, p. 249; DeGregorio, s.v. "Abraham Lincoln" (p. 238).

278. Wood, pp. 47, 237.
279. Current, TLNK, p. 200.
280. W. B. Garrison, TLNOK, p. 75.
281. Simmons, s.v. "Lincoln, Abraham."
282. Christian, p. 25.
283. Muzzey, Vol. 1, p. 523.
284. See Seabrook, C101, passim.
285. Seabrook, EYWTATCWIW, pp. 35-39.
286. Seabrook, LW, pp. 58, 76, 109.
287. Muzzey, Vol. 1, p. 517.
288. Ormsby, pp. 13, 46.
289. W. L. Wilson, pp. 176-179.
290. Muzzey, Vol. 1, p. 519.
291. Muzzey, Vol. 1, pp. 421, 522.
292. Seabrook, EYWTAASIW, pp. 549-645.
293. See Seabrook, NBFATKKK, passim.
294. Muzzey, Vol. 1, p. 538.
295. Seabrook, EYWTATCWIW, p. 110. See also pp. 30-32, 44-45. See also Muzzey, Vol. 1, p. 603.
296. W. L. Wilson, pp. 179-180.
297. Modern socialists also dislike the Declaration of Independence, in this case because it promotes the "bourgeois" idea of "private property and its logical corollaries, competitive industry and individual liberty." Hillquit, SITAP, p. 79.
298. Rutherford, TOH, p. ix.
299. J. G. Randall, p. 79.
300. J. H. Moore, p. 163.
301. Bryan, LAS, p. 279.
302. Faulkner, p. 136.
303. Rutherford, TOH, p. 28.
304. Seabrook, AL, pp. 27, 68.
305. Macy, p. 247; Faulkner, p. 346; F. Curtis, Vol. 1, p. 271.
306. Seabrook, AL, pp. 67-68.
307. For Lincoln's war crimes specifically, see Seabrook, AL, pp. 293-318.
308. See Muzzey, Vol. 2, pp. 40, 59.
309. Seabrook, LW, pp. 72-73.
310. For the facts about the South, the North, the KKK, and Reconstruction, see Seabrook, NBFATKKK, passim.
311. See Benson and Kennedy, passim.
312. Frayssé, p. 141.
313. Another example was German born Dr. Theodore Canisius of Illinois, who had affiliations with the Forty-Eighters and with various radicals, such as Giuseppe Garibaldi. As I show, Lincoln and Canisius became business partners prior to the 1860 election. See F. Curtis, Vol. 1, pp. 337-338; Herriott, p. 62; Harry Nelson Gay, "Lincoln's Offer of a Command to Garibaldi: Light on a Disputed Point of History," *The Century Illustrated Monthly Magazine*, November 1907, Vol. 75, No. 1, pp. 71-73.
314. Seabrook, HJADA, p. 68.
315. See DiLorenzo, LU, pp. 149-155.
316. Seabrook, EYWTATCWIW, pp. 120-121.
317. Seabrook, AL, p. 182.
318. Biagini, p. 76.
319. Borchard, passim.
320. Maltsev, p. 285.
321. Seabrook, AL, pp. 506-507.
322. Benson and Kennedy, pp. 158-159.
323. Seabrook, L, pp. 113-114.
324. Sarna and Shapell, p. 46.
325. For more on the Victorian German-American press, see Wittke, passim; Geitz, passim.
326. M. E. Page, Vol. 1, s.v. "Garibaldi, Giuseppe."

327. Caroti, passim; Gregor, p. 29.

328. H. Nelson Gay, "Lincoln's Offer of a Command to Garibaldi," *The Century Magazine*, November 1907, Vol. 75, No. 1, p. 72.

329. Donald, L, p. 242.

330. Silverman, p. 69.

331. Holzer, p. 149.

332. Seabrook, TGYC, p. 60.

333. Basler, TCWOAL, Vol. 1, pp. 112, 278-279, 438-439, 441; Vol. 2, pp. 115, 251, 371.

334. Harry Nelson Gay, "Lincoln's Offer of a Command to Garibaldi: Light on a Disputed Point of History," *The Century Illustrated Monthly Magazine*, November 1907, Vol. 75, No. 1, pp. 63-74.

335. Avrich, p. 18.

336. Sotheran, p. 293.

337. J. M. McPherson, BCOF, p. 138. For more on Greeley and socialism see Sotheran, passim.

338. Benson and Kennedy, p. 71.

339. J. H. Wilson, pp. xi, 182-193.

340. Fraysse, p. 141.

341. Benson and Kennedy, pp. 172-174, 186-188.

342. Muzzey, Vol. 2, p. 11.

343. J. M. McPherson, ALATSAR, pp. 5-6.

344. Mendel, p. 586.

345. Fraysse, pp. 141-142.

346. Kamman, pp. 41, 61. See also p. 43.

347. Warner, GIB, s.v. "Max Weber."

348. Warner, GIB, s.v. "Francis Channing Barlow"; Welch, passim.

349. Blackburn, p. 25.

350. Basler, TCWOAL, Vol. 5, p. 272.

351. Basler, TCWOAL, Vol. 5, p. 272.

352. Warner, GIB, s.v. "Alexander Sandor Asboth."

353. Friedman, p. 132.

354. Warner, GIB, s.v. "Alexander Schimmelfennig."

355. Marcus, Vol. 3, p. 21. The German spelling of his surname is Busch.

356. Warner, GIB, s.v. "Franz Sigel."

357. Reichstein, pp. 92-95, passim.

358. McNitt, p. 225.

359. Warner, GIB, s.v. "Albin Francisco Schoepf."

360. Roba, pp. 1, 9; Benson and Kennedy, p. 146.

361. Warner, GIB, s.v. "Peter Joseph Osterhaus." See also Townsend, passim.

362. Bonansinga, passim.

363. After the War socialist Salomon continued to work for the U.S. government under the administrations of Presidents Hayes, Garfield, and Arthur. Warner, GIB, s.v. "Friedrich Salomon."

364. Warner, GIB, s.v. "Julius Stahel"; s.v. "Louis (Ludwig) Blenker." Like many other anti-American European leftists, Stahel was buried in Arlington Cemetery.

365. Kaplan, p. 215.

366. Diedrich, p. 305.

367. Warner, GIB, s.v. "Carl Schurz."

368. See e.g., F. Curtis, Vol. 1, p. 444. See also pp. 353, 359, 364.

369. Neilson, s.v. "Schurz, Carl."

370. Muzzey, Vol. 2, p. 107.

371. Schurz, Vol. 2, pp. 393-396.

372. Hillquit, HOSITUS, p. 170.

373. Seabrook, LW, passim.

374. See Benson and Kennedy, pp. 51-73, 285.

375. Fraysse, p. 141. In English the name of the newspaper is *Illinois State Advertiser*.

376. Blackburn, p. 1.

377. It was Marx who said that "all history is a struggle between social classes." Berkin and Wood, p. 89.

378. Benson and Kennedy, pp. 58-59.
379. J. M. McPherson, ALATSR, p. 24.
380. C. Miller, p. 157.
381. Sotheran, p. 95.
382. Sotheran, p. 95.
383. Thornton and Ekelund, p. 99.
384. DeGregorio, s.v. "Franklin D. Roosevelt" (p. 498).
385. Napolitano, pp. 131-138.
386. Mussey, Vol. 2, p. 108.
387. Benson and Kennedy, pp. 145-146.
388. Mendel, pp. 583-584.
389. Hillquit, HOSITUS, p. 56.
390. Fourierism, named after French socialist Charles Fourier, is a type of "utopian socialism" that led to the founding of numerous failed communes, such as Brook Farm in West Roxbury, Massachusetts, which thrived from 1841 to 1847. His "ideal communities" were known as "phalansteries." Mendel, p. 580.
391. Sotheran, p. 192.
392. Hartzell, p. 1.
393. Basler, TCWOAL, Vol. 4, p. 283.
394. Simon, Vol. 9, p. 645.
395. Mendel, p. 586.
396. Stevenson, pp. 104, 117-118, 121, 193.
397. Stevenson, p. 193.
398. McAfee, p. 33; DePalma, p. 135. Also see Remsburg, passim.
399. Rowan, pp. 5, 354-361.
400. Spingola, p. 428.
401. Roba, p. 10.
402. Silverman, pp. 38-40.
403. Spingola, p. 428.
404. Browder, p. 5.
405. McCarty is incorrect. The word socialist was coined in 1833; the word socialism in 1839. See Mish, s.v. "socialist"; s.v. "socialism."
406. McCarty, title page. Emphasis added.
407. McCarty, p. 4. Emphasis added.
408. McCarty, p. 14. Emphasis added.
409. McCarty, p. 15.
410. E. McPherson, TPHOTUSDTGR, p. 135.
411. Schlüter, pp. 174-175.
412. Boller and Story, p. 167.
413. Schlüter, p. 175.
414. Schlüter, p. 184.
415. Schlüter, p. 181.
416. Schlüter, pp. 181-182.
417. Schlüter, p. 11.
418. Schlüter, p. 184.
419. J. M. McPherson, BCOF, p. 138. For more on Greeley and socialism see Sotheran, passim.
420. J. H. Wilson, pp. xi, 182-193.
421. Swift, p. 150.
422. Snay, p. 56.
423. Benson and Kennedy, p. 71.
424. Snay, p. 56.
425. Codman, pp. 17, 43, 104-105, 155, 183, 189, 237, 242, 312.
426. Constitution of the Brook Farm Association, p. 10.
427. Boller and Story, p. 142.
428. Swift, pp. 17-19, 22, 23, 25, 145-152.
429. Russell, pp. 187-191.

430. Swift, pp. 263-270.

431. Russell, p. 272.

432. Sotheran, p. 192.

433. For more on the many similarities between Lincoln and Hitler, see Seabrook, CFF, pp. 287-291.

434. Marx and Engels, p. 45.

435. Seabrook, AL, pp. 282, 300, 507.

436. Marx and Engels, p. 45.

437. Seabrook, CFF, p. 288.

438. Marx and Engels, p. 45.

439. Thornton and Ekelund, p. 99.

440. Muzzey, Vol. 1, p. 607.

441. Marx and Engels, p. 45.

442. Thornton and Ekelund, p. 99.

443. Muzzey, Vol. 2, p. 28.

444. Marx and Engels, pp. 45-46.

445. Thornton and Ekelund, p. 99.

446. Marx and Engels, p. 46.

447. Seabrook, AL, p. 530. My paraphrasal.

448. Marx and Engels, p. 46.

449. Morse, s.v. "Education in the United States."

450. Seabrook, AL, pp. 495-504. Also see Remsburg, passim.

451. See e.g., Marx and Engels, pp. 33, 44, 49; Hillquit and Ryan, pp. vi-vii. Says socialist Morris Hillquit: "The majority of socialists find it difficult, if not impossible, to reconcile their general philosophic views with the doctrines and practices of dogmatic religious creeds." Hillquit and Ryan, p. 261.

452. Morse, s.v. "Education in the United States." Note: The Department of Education was briefly combined with an even larger communistic body, the disastrous, bloated, governmental boondoggle known as The Department of Health, Education, and Welfare. But it has since grown so oversized that it has been made an agency in its own right, and is now an autonomous entity once again: The Department of Education.

453. For more on the Articles of Confederation, see Seabrook, TAOCE, passim.

454. Etheredge, p. 167.

455. Boortz, p. 51.

456. This quote is attributed to Lord Tytler, and has not been verified.

457. J. C. Hamilton, Vol. 2, p. 440.

458. Muzzey, Vol. 1, pp. 348-349.

459. Hamilton, Madison, and Jay, p. 61.

460. For more on this topic and its connection to both the U.S.A. and C.S.A., see Seabrook, C101, passim.

461. Etheredge, p. 167.

462. See supra, pp. 9-14.

463. See Carey, passim.

464. Carey, p. 270.

465. Carey, p. 270.

466. Carey, pp. 270-271.

467. Meriwether, pp. 91-95, 135-137. Emphasis added.

468. Rutherford, TOH, pp. 27-28. Emphasis added.

469. Rutherford, TOH, p. 28. Emphasis added.

470. Rutherford, TOH, pp. 27-28. Emphasis added.

471. Rutherford, TOH, p. 28.

472. Rutherford, TOH, p. 28.

473. Rutherford, TOH, p. 29.

474. Rutherford, TOH, p. 29.

475. Rutherford, TOH, p. 29. Emphasis added.

476. Rutherford, TOH, pp. 29-30. Emphasis added.

477. Confederate Veteran, June 1918, Vol. 26, No. 6, p. 240. Emphasis added.

478. Faulkner, p. 397.

479. See Woodworth, p. 290; Lytle, pp. 271-272; N. Bradford, p. 490; Sword, CLH, pp. 33-35; Groom, pp. 49-54; J. M. McPherson, NCW, pp. 305-306; Warner, GG, s.v. "John Bell Hood." In Margaret Mitchell's powerful and factual Confederate epic, *Gone With the Wind*, Southern belle Scarlett O'Hara says of Hood: "He left the damn Yankees to go through us with nothing but schoolboys and convicts and Home Guards to protect us." Mitchell, p. 475. Hood's incompetence at Atlanta that July boosted Lincoln's sagging ratings, helping to assure the unscrupulous president of a second victory at the polls in November.

480. Had Hood won Atlanta, Lincoln would have lost in 1864 to his rivals the Democrats (then the Conservatives), whose platform denounced the War as a "failure" and advocated an immediate end to hostilities. Some 120 million Southerners would be living in peace, prosperity, safety, and happiness under the Confederate Flag. See Hendelson, s.v. "Lincoln, Abraham."

481. See Seabrook, C101, passim.

482. Seabrook, TGYC, p. 48.

483. Hacker, p. 589.

484. C. Adams, p. 58; W. B. Garrison, TLNOK, pp. 193-197.

485. L. Johnson, p. 127.

486. Donald, LR, p. 65.

487. W. B. Garrison, TLNOK, p. 215.

488. Hansen, pp. 58-59; K. L. Hall, s.v. "Lincoln, Abraham." Lincoln's unlawful acts stirred up a number of court cases. See K. L. Hall, s.v. "Prize Cases."

489. Denney, p. 25.

490. W. C. Davis, HD, pp. 79-80.

491. It is illegal for a section of a state to secede from the parent state without the parent state's approval. Virginia never authorized the secession of West Virginia. Seabrook, L, pp. 763, 877.

492. W. B. Garrison, TLNOK, pp. 193-197.

493. Lincoln knew this particular action was unconstitutional, which is why he brought the issue up with his cabinet members on December 23, 1862. Nicolay and Hay, ALCW, Vol. 2, p. 283. See also Nicolay and Hay, ALCW, Vol. 2, pp. 285-287, where Lincoln resorts to his usual tortured logic to justify his action regarding the secession of West Virginia.

494. Donald, LR, p. 79.

495. Napolitano, pp. 69-70.

496. Seabrook, AL, p. 291.

497. Christian, p. 26.

498. Mitgang, p. 402. My paraphrasal.

499. My paraphrasals.

500. Mitgang, pp. 403, 404. My paraphrasal.

501. For more on Lincoln's behavior during his presidency, see Seabrook, AL, passim.

502. Blaine, Vol. 2, p. 49.

503. Muzzey, Vol. 1, pp. 592-593.

504. See Faulkner, p. 375.

505. Muzzey, Vol. 1, pp. 598-599.

506. Muzzey, Vol. 1, p. 603.

507. W. L. Wilson, p. 184.

508. Faulkner, p. 375.

509. Seabrook, LW, pp. 19-20.

510. Boller and Story, p. 180.

511. Seabrook, AL, pp. 419-420.

512. Seabrook, NBFATKKK, passim.

513. W. L. Wilson, p. 185.

514. W. L. Wilson, p. 188.

515. Hofstadter, GIIAH, p. 15.

516. W. L. Wilson, p. 193.

517. W. L. Wilson, p. 194.

518. W. L. Wilson, p. 198.

519. W. L. Wilson, p. 198.

520. Benson and Kennedy, p. 71.

521. Diedrich, p. 305.

522. S. G. O'Brien, s.v. "Schurz, Carl."
523. W. L. Wilson, p. 200.
524. W. L. Wilson, p. 199.
525. For more on the topic of Northern and Liberal crimes against the South, see Seabrook, TUC, passim; Seabrook, AL, passim.
526. Seabrook, AL, pp. 551-553.
527. W. L. Wilson, p. 213.
528. W. L. Wilson, p. 221.
529. W. L. Wilson, pp. 222-225.
530. McClure, OPAHWMT, p. 332.
531. DeGregorio, pp. 336-337.
532. McClure, OPAHWMT, p. 333.
533. McClure, OPAHWMT, p. 334.
534. DeGregorio, p. 345.
535. McClure, OPAHWMT, p. 343.
536. McClure, OPAHWMT, pp. 337-338.
537. DeGregorio, p. 331.
538. Kane, pp. 253-254.
539. Faulkner, p. 538.
540. For more clarification on this striking 1896 realignment of the two major parties, see the Appendices, and in particular, Appendix D.
541. For more on this topic, see Seabrook, C101, passim.
542. West, pp. 521-522.
543. Muzzey, Vol. 1, pp. 164-165.
544. Vandenberg, p. 211.
545. Muzzey, Vol. 1, pp. 163-164.
546. Mish, s.v. "monarch"; s.v. "monarchy."
547. Mish, s.v. "socialism."
548. See Mish, s.v. "tyranny."
549. See I. Howe, p. 107.
550. Kaplan, p. 215.
551. Seabrook, LW, p. 112.
552. Muzzey, Vol. 2, pp. 228-229.
553. Buck, p. 94.
554. Nevins and Commager, p. 328.
555. Muzzey, Vol. 2, p. 230.
556. Buck, p. 134.
557. Muzzey, Vol. 2, p. 232.
558. Nevins and Commager, p. 329.
559. Muzzey, Vol. 2, pp. 233, 237.
560. Palmer and Colton, p. 429.
561. Platt, p. 258.
562. Muzzey, Vol. 2, pp. 232-233, 235.
563. Muzzey, Vol. 2, pp. 231, 239, 246-247.
564. I coined this term because there was nothing else as suitable.
565. Bryan's equally famous opponent, the attorney for the defendant (John Scopes), was Clarence Darrow.
566. My personal theory.
567. Nevins and Commager, p. 329.
568. Hopkins, p. 207.
569. Norton, Katzman, Escott, Chudacoff, Paterson, and Tuttle, pp. 575-579.
570. Nevins and Commager, p. 330.
571. Muzzey, Vol. 2, pp. 257-258, 263-264, 274-275, 479.
572. Berkin and Wood, p. 89.
573. Muzzey, Vol. 2, p. 247.
574. Nevins and Commager, p. 331.

575. Faulkner, p. 539.
576. Stanwood, pp. 526, 528, 550, 561-562.
577. Muzzey, Vol. 2, p. 247. See also pp. 268, 275, 276.
578. Faulkner, p. 539.
579. For the full speech, see Bryan, LAS, pp. 247-252.
580. Faulkner, p. 541.
581. Berkin and Wood, p. 116.
582. Stanwood, pp. 565-566, 569.
583. Unger, p. 581
584. Burns, pp. 549, 553. As their name indicates, though mainly progressive, fusionists embraced bits and pieces from various other political parties.
585. Seabrook, LW, pp. 73-83, passim.
586. Benson and Kennedy, pp. 145-146.
587. J. M. McPherson, ALATSAR, pp. 23-24.
588. J. M. McPherson, ALATSAR, pp. 5-6.
589. Seabrook, LW, pp. 121, 297.
590. See J. W. Jones, TDMV, pp. 144, 200-201, 273.
591. Bedford and Colbourn, p. 323.
592. See Seabrook, TAHSR, passim. See also Stephens, ACVOTLW, Vol. 1, pp. 10, 12, 148, 150-151, 157-158, 161, 170, 192, 206, 210, 215, 219, 221-222, 238-240, 258-260, 288, 355, 360, 370, 382-384, 516, 575-576, 583, 587; Vol. 2, pp. 28-30, 32-33, 88, 206, 258, 631, 648; Pollard, LC, p. 178; J. H. Franklin, pp. 101, 111, 130, 149; Nicolay and Hay, ALCW, Vol. 1, p. 627.
593. Bryan, LAS, p. 279.
594. Rutherford, TOH, p. ix.
595. Muzzey, Vol. 2, p. 140.
596. Stephens, ACVOTLW, Vol. 2, p. 33.
597. McClure, OPAHWMT, p. 361.
598. "Post-truth politics" is a political environment in which public opinion is shaped by emotion and personal belief rather than objective facts. We can thank the Liberal-controlled media, with its aggressive and largely uneducated bastion of socialists, communists, and anarchists, for this form of intellectual dishonesty.
599. Muzzey, Vol. 1, p. 112.
600. Seabrook, LW, pp. 63-64.
601. Muzzey, Vol. 1, p. 551.
602. Minutes of the Twelfth Annual Meeting, April 1902, p. 75.
603. Muzzey, Vol. 2, pp. 38, 78.
604. Meriwether, p. 93.
605. Meriwether, p. 93.
606. A. R. Thompson, pp. 11-12.
607. Rove, pp. 336, 372.
608. See Muzzey, Vol. 2, pp. 274-293; Boyd, passim; Bryan, TFB, passim.
609. Magliocca, p. 106.
610. Unger, p. 579; R. H. Williams, TDPACP, p. 234.
611. Muzzey, Vol. 2, p. 140.
612. Muzzey, Vol. 2, p. 290. My paraphrasal. For more on the election of 1896, see Boyd, pp. 501-554.
613. Hopkins, p. 213.
614. Hopkins, p. 209.
615. Platt, p. 259.
616. McClure, OPAHWMT, pp. 392-393.
617. M. Van Buren, pp. 7-8.

BIBLIOGRAPHY

Note: My pro-South readers are to be advised that the majority of the books listed here are anti-South in nature (some extremely so), and were written primarily by liberal elitist, socialist, communist, and Marxist authors who loathe the South, and typically the United States and the U.S. Constitution as well. Despite this, as a scholar I find these titles indispensable, for *an honest evaluation of Lincoln's War is not possible without studying both the Southern and the Northern versions*—an attitude, unfortunately, completely lacking among pro-North historians (who read and study only their own ahistorical version). Still, it must be said that the material contained in these often mean-spirited works is largely the result of a century and a half of Yankee myth, falsehoods, cherry-picking, slander, anti-South propaganda, outright lies, and junk research, as modern pro-North writers merely copy one another's errors without ever looking at the original 19th-Century sources. This type of literature, filled as it is with both misinformation and disinformation, is called "scholarly" and "objective" by pro-North advocates. In the process, the mistakes and lies in these fact-free, fault-ridden, South-shaming, historically inaccurate works have been magnified over the years, and the North's version of the "Civil War" has come to be accepted as the only legitimate one. Indeed, it is now the only one known by most people. That over 95 percent of the titles in my bibliography fall into the anti-South category is simply a reflection of the enormous power and influence that the pro-North movement—our nation's cultural ruling class—has long held over America's education system, libraries, publishing houses, and media (paper and electronic). My books serve as a small rampart against the overwhelming tide of anti-South Fascists, Liberals, and political elites, all who are working hard to obliterate Southern culture and guarantee that you will never learn the Truth about Lincoln and his War on the Constitution and the American people.

Abbott, John Stevens Cabot. *The Life of General Ulysses S. Grant*. Boston, MA: B. B. Russell, 1868.

Abernathy, Thomas P. *The South in the New Nation, 1789-1819*. Baton Rouge, LA: Louisiana State University Press, 1961.

Adams, Charles. *When in the Course of Human Events: Arguing the Case for Southern Secession*. Lanham, MD: Rowman and Littlefield, 2000.

Adams, Henry (ed.). *Documents Relating to New-England Federalism, 1800-1815*. Boston, MA: Little, Brown, and Co., 1877.

Adams, Nehemiah. *A South-side View of Slavery: Three Months at the South, in 1854*. Boston, MA: T. R. Marvin, 1855.

Anderson, Dale. *The Republican Party: The Story of the Grand Old Party*. Minneapolis, MN: Compass Point Books, 2007.

Andrews, Elisha Benjamin. *The United States in Our Own Time: A History From Reconstruction to Expansion*. 1895. New York, NY: Charles Scribner's Sons, 1903 ed.

Andrews, Sidney. *The South Since the War: As Shown by Fourteen Weeks of Travel and Observation*. Boston, MA: Ticknor and Fields, 1866.

Angle, Paul M. (ed.). *The Complete Lincoln-Douglas Debates of 1858*. Chicago, IL: University of Chicago Press, 1991.

Annunzio, Frank (chairman). *The Capitol: A Pictorial History of the Capitol and of the Congress*. Washington, D.C.: U.S. Joint Committee on Printing, 1983.

Anonymous. *Life of John C. Calhoun: Presenting a Condensed History of Political Events, From 1811 to 1843*. New York, NY: Harper and Brothers, 1843.

Ashe, Samuel A'Court. *A Southern View of the Invasion of the Southern States and War of 1861-1865*. 1935. Crawfordville, GA: Ruffin Flag Co., 1938 ed.

Ashworth, John. *Slavery, Capitalism, and Politics in the Antebellum Republic.* 2 vols. New York, NY: Cambridge University Press, 2007.

Bailey, Thomas A. *A Diplomatic History of the American People.* 1940. New York, NY: Appleton-Century-Crofts, 1970 ed.

Bailyn, Bernard. *The Origins of American Politics.* New York, NY: Random House, 1968.

Bailyn, Bernard, Robert Dallek, David Brion Davis, David Herbert Donald, John L. Thomas, and Gordon S. Wood. *The Great Republic: A History of the American People.* 1977. Lexington, MA: D. C. Heath and Co., 1992 ed.

Baker, George E. (ed.). *The Works of William H. Seward.* 5 vols. 1861. Boston, MA: Houghton, Mifflin and Co., 1888 ed.

Bancroft, Frederic, and William A. Dunning (eds.). *The Reminiscences of Carl Schurz.* 3 vols. New York, NY: McClure Co., 1909.

Banks, Noreen. *Early American Almanac.* New York, NY: Bantam, 1975.

Banner, James M. *To the Hartford Convention: The Federalists and the Origins of Party Politics in Massachusetts, 1789-1815.* New York, NY: Alfred A. Knopf, 1969.

Bartlett, Irving H. *John C. Calhoun: A Biography.* New York, NY: W. W. Norton, 1994.

——. *Wendell Phillips: Brahmin Radical.* Boston, MA: Beacon Press, 1961.

Barton, William E. *The Soul of Abraham Lincoln.* New York, NY: George H. Doran, 1920.

Basler, Roy Prentice (ed.). *Abraham Lincoln: His Speeches and Writings.* 1946. New York, NY: Da Capo Press, 2001 ed.

—— (ed.). *The Collected Works of Abraham Lincoln.* 9 vols. New Brunswick, NJ: Rutgers University Press, 1953.

Bateman, William O. *Political and Constitutional Law of the United States of America.* St. Louis, MO: G. I. Jones and Co., 1876.

Baxter, Maurice G. *Henry Clay and the American System.* Lexington, KY: University Press of Kentucky, 2004.

Beard, Charles A. *Economic Origins of Jeffersonian Democracy.* New York, NY: Macmillan, 1915.

Bedford, Henry F., and Trevor Colbourn. *The Americans: A Brief History.* 1972. New York, NY: Harcourt Brace Jovanovich, 1980 ed.

Beer, Thomas. *The Mauve Decade: American Life at the End of the Nineteenth Century.* New York, NY: Garden City Publishing, 1926.

Benedict, Michael Les. *The Impeachment and Trial of Andrew Johnson.* New York, NY: W. W. Norton and Co., 1973.

Bennett, Lerone, Jr. *Forced Into Glory: Abraham Lincoln's White Dream.* Chicago, IL: Johnson Publishing Co., 2000.

Benson, Al, Jr., and Walter Donald Kennedy. *Lincoln's Marxists.* Gretna, LA: Pelican, 2011.

Benson, Lee. *The Concept of Jacksonian Democracy: New York as a Test Case.* Princeton, NJ: Princeton University Press, 1970.

Benton, Thomas Hart. *Thirty Years' View; or A History of the Working of the American Government for Thirty Years, From 1820 to 1850.* 2 vols. New York, NY: D. Appleton and Co., 1854.

Bergh, Albert Ellery (ed.). *The Writings of Thomas Jefferson.* 20 vols. Washington, D.C.: Thomas Jefferson Memorial Association of the U.S., 1905.

Berkin, Carol, and Leonard Wood. *Land of Promise: A History of the United States: From 1865.* Glenview, IL: Scott, Foresman and Co., 1983.

Bernhard, Winfred E. A. (ed.). *Political Parties in American History, Vol. 2, 1789-1828.* New York, NY: G. P. Putnam's Sons, 1973.

Beschloss, Michael R. *Presidential Courage: Brave Leaders and How They Changed America, 1789-1989.* New York, NY: Simon and Schuster, 2007.

Beveridge, Albert Jeremiah. *Abraham Lincoln: 1809-1858.* 2 vols. Boston, MA: Houghton Mifflin, 1928.

Biagini, Eugenio F. *Liberty, Entrenchment and Reform: Popular Liberalism in the Age of Gladstone, 1860-1880.* 1992. Cambridge, UK: Cambridge University Press, 2002 ed.

Binkley, Wilfred E. *American Political Parties: Their Natural History.* New York, NY: Alfred A. Knopf, 1963.

Black, Chauncey F. *Essays and Speeches of Jeremiah S. Black.* New York, NY: D. Appleton and Co., 1886.

Blackburn, Robin. *An Unfinished Revolution: Karl Marx and Abraham Lincoln.* London, UK: Verso, 2011.

Blaine, James G. *Twenty Years in Congress: From Lincoln to Garfield.* 2 vols. Norwich, CT: Henry Bill Publishing Co., 1884-1886.

Blasi, Joseph, Richard Freeman, and Douglas Kruse. *The Citizen's Share: Putting Ownership Back Into Democracy.* New Haven, CT: Yale University Press, 2013.

Bliss, William Dwight Porter (ed.). *The Encyclopedia of Social Reform.* New York, NY: Funk and Wagnalls, 1897.

Boller, Paul F., Jr., and Ronald Story. *A More Perfect Union: Documents in U.S. History.* 2 vols. Boston, MA: Houghton Mifflin, 1984.

Bonansinga, Jay. *Pinkerton's War: The Civil War's Greatest Spy and the Birth of the U.S. Secret Service.* Guilford, CT: Lyons Press, 2012.

Bone, Hugh A. *American Politics and the Party System.* New York, NY: McGraw-Hill, 1970.

Bonura, Michael A. *Under the Shadow of Napoleon: French Influence on the American Way of Warfare From the War of 1812 to the Outbreak of World War II.* New York, NY: New York University Press, 2012.

Boortz, Neal. *The Terrible Truth About Liberals: America's Rude Awakening.* 1988. Atlanta, GA: Longstreet Press, 2001 ed.

Borchard, Gregory A. *Abraham Lincoln and Horace Greeley.* Carbondale, IL: Southern Illinois University Press, 2011.

Borden, Morton. *Parties and Politics in the Early Republic, 1789-1815.* New York, NY: Thomas Y. Crowell, 1967.

Bowen, Catherine Drinker. *John Adams and the American Revolution.* 1949. New York, NY: Grosset and Dunlap, 1977 ed.

Bowman, John S. (ed.). *The Civil War Day by Day: An Illustrated Almanac of America's Bloodiest War.* 1989. New York, NY: Dorset Press, 1990 ed.

——. *Encyclopedia of the Civil War* (ed.). 1992. North Dighton, MA: JG Press, 2001 ed.

Boyd, James P. *Parties, Problems, and Leaders of 1896: An Impartial Presentation of Living National Questions.* Chicago, IL: Publishers' Union, 1896.

Bradford, James C. (ed.). *Atlas of American Military History.* New York, NY: Oxford University Press, 2003.

Bradford, Ned (ed.). *Battles and Leaders of the Civil War.* 1-vol. ed. New York, NY: Appleton-Century-Crofts, 1956.

Brant, Irving. *James Madison: Father of the Constitution, 1787-1800.* Indianapolis, IN: Bobbs-Merrill Co., 1950.

Brinkley, Alan. *The Unfinished Nation: A Concise History of the American People.* 1993. Boston, MA: McGraw-Hill, 2000 ed.

Brockett, Linus Pierpont. *The Life and Times of Abraham Lincoln, Sixteenth President of the United States.* Philadelphia, PA: Bradley and Co., 1865.

Brodie, Fawn McKay. *Thaddeus Stevens: Scourge of the South.* New York, NY: W. W. Norton, 1966.

——. *Thomas Jefferson: An Intimate History.* 1974. New York, NY: Bantam, 1981 ed.

Brooks, Gertrude Zeth. *First Ladies of the White House.* Chicago, IL: Charles Hallberg and Co., 1969.

Browder, Earl. *Lincoln and the Communists*. New York, NY: Workers Library Publishers, Inc., 1936.

Brown, James Sayles. *Partisan Politics: The Evil and the Remedy*. Philadelphia, PA: J. P. Lippincott, 1897.

Brown, Lydia Lawrence. *The Decay of the Federalist Party*. Madison, WI: University of Wisconsin, 1923.

Brown, Stuart G. *The First Republicans: Political Philosophy and Public Policy in the Party of Jefferson and Madison*. Syracuse, NY: Syracuse University Press, 1954.

Bryan, William Jennings. *The First Battle: A Story of the Campaign of 1896*. Chicago, IL: W. B. Conkey Co., 1896.

———. *Life and Speeches of Hon. Wm. Jennings Bryan*. Baltimore, MD: R. H. Woodward Co., 1900.

Bryce, James. *The American Commonwealth*. 3 vols. London, UK: Macmillan and Co., 1888.

Buchanan, James. *The Works of James Buchanan*. 12 vols. Philadelphia, PA: J. B. Lippincott Co., 1911.

Buchanan, Patrick J. *A Republic, Not an Empire: Reclaiming America's Destiny*. Washington, D.C.: Regenry, 1999.

Buck, Solon J. *The Agrarian Crusade: A Chronicle of the Farmer in Politics*. New Haven, CT: Yale University Press, 1921.

Buell, Richard, Jr., and Jeffers Lennox. *Historical Dictionary of the Early American Republic*. Lanham, MD: Rowman and Littlefield, 2017.

Burgess, John William. *Reconstruction and the Constitution: 1866-1876*. New York, NY: Charles Scribner's Sons, 1903.

Burlingame, Michael. *The Inner World of Abraham Lincoln*. Champaign, IL: University of Illinois Press, 1997.

Burns, James MacGregor. *The Vineyard of Liberty*. New York, NY: Alfred A. Knopf, 1982.

Burns, James MacGregor, J. W. Peltason, Thomas E. Cronin, David B. Magleby, and David M. O'Brien. *Government By the People*. 1952. Upper Saddle River, NJ: 2002 ed.

Calvert, Thomas H. *The Federal Statutes Annotated*. 10 vols. Northport, NY: Edward Thompson, 1905.

Carey, Mathew. *The Olive Branch: or, Faults on Both Sides, Federal and Democratic - A Serious Appeal on the Necessity of Mutual Forgiveness and Harmony*. 1814. Middlebury, VT: William Slade, 1816 ed.

Carlton, Frank Tracy. *Organized Labor in America*. New York, NY: D. Appleton and Co., 1920.

Carman, Harry J., and Harold C. Syrett. *A History of the American People - Vol. 1: To 1865*. 1952. New York, NY: Alfred A. Knopf, 1958 ed.

Caroti, Marcello. *Garibaldi the First Fascist: The Roots of Fascism in the Italian Risorgimento*. Milan, Italy: self-published, 2015.

Chambers, Mortimer, Raymond Grew, David Herlihy, Theodore K. Rabb, and Isser Woloch. *The Western Experience, to 1715*. New York, NY: Alfred A. Knopf, 1974.

Chambers, William N. *Political Parties in a New Nation: The American Experience, 1776-1809*. New York, NY: Oxford University Press, 1963.

Charles, Joseph E. *The Origins of the American Party System: Three Essays*. Williamsburg, VA: Institute of Early American History and Culture, 1956.

Cherny, Robert W. *A Righteous Cause: The Life of William Jennings Bryan*. Norman, OK: University of Oklahoma Press, 1994.

Chesnut, Mary. *A Diary From Dixie: As Written by Mary Boykin Chesnut, Wife of James Chesnut, Jr., United States Senator from South Carolina, 1859-1861, and Afterward an Aide to Jefferson Davis and a Brigadier-General in the Confederate Army*. (Isabella D. Martin and Myrta Lockett Avary, eds.). New York, NY: D. Appleton and Co., 1905 ed.

Chinard, Gilbert. *Honest John Adams*. Boston, MA: Little, Brown and Co., 1961.

Christian, George L. *Abraham Lincoln: An Address Delivered Before R. E. Lee Camp, No. 1 Confederate Veterans at Richmond, VA, October 29, 1909.* Richmond, VA: L. H. Jenkins, 1909.

Claflin, Alta Blanche (ed.). *Political Parties in the United States 1800-1914: A List of References.* New York, NY: New York Public Library, 1915.

Clark, L. Pierce. *Lincoln: A Psycho-Biography.* New York, NY: Charles Scribner's Sons, 1933.

Cluskey, Michael W. (ed.). *The Political Text-Book, or Encyclopedia.* Philadelphia, PA: Jas. B. Smith, 1859 ed.

Cmiel, Kenneth. *Democratic Eloquence: The Fight Over Popular Speech in Nineteenth-Century America.* Berkeley, CA: University of California Press, 1990.

Codman, John Thomas. *Brook Farm: Historic and Personal Memoirs.* Boston, MA: Arena, 1894.

Coe, Joseph. *The True American.* Concord, NH: I. S. Boyd, 1840.

Coffin, Charles Carleton. *Abraham Lincoln.* New York, NY: Harper and Brothers, 1893.

Coit, Margaret L. *John C. Calhoun: American Portrait.* Boston, MA: Sentry, 1950.

Cole, Arthur Charles. *The Whig Party in the South.* Washington, D.C.: The American Historical Society, 1914.

Collier, Christopher, and James Lincoln Collier. *Decision in Philadelphia: The Constitutional Convention of 1787.* 1986. New York, NY: Ballantine, 1987 ed.

Collins, Elizabeth. *Memories of the Southern States.* Taunton, UK: J. Barnicott, 1865.

Commons, John Rogers. *Horace Greeley and the Working Class Origins of the Republican Party.* Boston, MA: Ginn and Co., 1909.

Conner, Frank. *The South Under Siege, 1830-2000: A History of the Relations Between the North and the South.* Newnan, GA: Collards Publishing Co., 2002.

Constitution of the Brook Farm Association for Industry and Education, West Roxbury, Mass. Boston, MA: self-published, 1844.

Cooke, Alistair. *Alistair Cooke's America.* 1973. New York, NY: Alfred A. Knopf, 1984 ed.

Cooper, William J., Jr. *Jefferson Davis, American.* New York, NY: Vintage, 2000.

Coulter, Ann. *Guilty: Liberal "Victims" and Their Assault on America.* New York, NY: Three Rivers Press, 2009.

Countryman, Edward. *The American Revolution.* 1985. New York, NY: Hill and Wang, 1993 ed.

Cousins, Norman (ed.). *In God We Trust: The Religious Beliefs and Ideas of the American Founding Fathers.* New York, NY: Harper and Brothers, 1958.

Crallé, Richard Kenner. (ed.). *The Works of John C. Calhoun.* 6 vols. New York: NY: D. Appleton and Co., 1853-1888.

Craven, John J. *Prison Life of Jefferson Davis.* New York: NY: Carelton, 1866.

Crotty, William J. (ed.). *Approaches to the Study of Party Organization.* Boston, MA: Allyne and Bacon, 1968.

Cummins, Joseph. *Anything For a Vote: Dirty Tricks, Cheap Shots, and October Surprises in U.S. Presidential Campaigns.* Philadelphia, PA: Quirk, 2007.

Cunningham, Noble E., Jr. *The Jeffersonian Republicans: The Formation of Party Organization, 1789-1801.* Chapel Hill, NC: University of North Carolina Press, 1957.

Current, Richard N. *The Lincoln Nobody Knows.* 1958. New York, NY: Hill and Wang, 1963 ed.

——. (ed.) *The Confederacy* (Information Now Encyclopedia). 1993. New York, NY: Macmillan, 1998 ed.

Curti, Merle, Willard Thorpe, and Carlos Baker (eds.). *American Issues: The Social Record.* 1941. Chicago, IL: J. B. Lippincott, 1960 ed.

Curtis, Francis. *The Republican Party: A History of Its Fifty Years' Existence and a Record of Its Measures and Leaders, 1854-1904.* 2 vols. New York, NY: G. P. Putnam's Sons, 1904.

Curtis, George Ticknor. *Life of James Buchanan: Fifteenth President of the United States.* 2 vols. New York, NY: Harper and Brothers, 1883.

Curtis, William Eleroy. *Abraham Lincoln*. Philadelphia, PA: J. B. Lippincott Co., 1902.

Dabney, Robert Lewis. *A Defense of Virginia and the South*. Dahlonega, GA: Confederate Reprint Co., 1999.

Dahl, Robert A. *A Preface to Democratic Theory*. Chicago, IL: University of Chicago Press, 1956.

Dangerfield, George. *The Era of Good Feelings.*. New York, NY: Harcourt, Brace and World, 1952.

——. *The Awakening of American Nationalism: 1815-1828*. New York, NY: Harper and Row, 1965.

Daniel, John M. *The Richmond Examiner During the War*. New York, NY: John M. Daniel, 1868.

Daniel, John W. *Life and Reminiscences of Jefferson Davis by Distinguished Men of His Time*. Baltimore, MD: R. H. Woodward, and Co., 1890.

Darling, Arthur B. *Political Changes in Massachusetts, 1824-1848: A Study of Liberal Movements in Politics*. New Haven, CT: Yale University Press, 1925.

Dauer, Manning J. *The Adams Federalists*. Baltimore, MD: Johns Hopkins Press, 1968.

Daugherty, James. *Abraham Lincoln*. 1943. New York, NY: Scholastic Book Services, 1966 ed.

Davidson, Marshall B. *Life in America*. 2 vols. 1951. Boston, MA: Houghton Mifflin, 1974 ed.

Davis, Jefferson. *The Rise and Fall of the Confederate Government*. 2 vols. New York, NY: D. Appleton and Co., 1881.

Davis, John. *Travels of Four Years and a Half in the United States of America, During 1798, 1799, 1800, 1801, and 1802*. London, UK: self-published, 1803.

Davis, Michael. *The Image of Lincoln in the South*. Knoxville, TN: University of Tennessee Press, 1971.

Davis, Varina. *Jefferson Davis: Ex-President of the Confederate States of America - A Memoir by His Wife*. 2 vols. New York, NY: Belford Co., 1890.

Davis, William C. *Jefferson Davis: The Man and His Hour*. New York, NY: Harper Collins, 1991.

——. *An Honorable Defeat: The Last Days of the Confederate Government*. New York, NY: Harcourt, 2001.

——. *Look Away: A History of the Confederate States of America*. 2002. New York, NY: Free Press, 2003 ed.

Dawson, Sarah Morgan. *A Confederate Girl's Diary*. London, UK: William Heinemann, 1913.

Dean, Henry Clay. *Crimes of the Civil War, and Curse of the Funding System*. Baltimore, MD: William T. Smithson, 1869.

De Angelis, Gina. *It Happened in Washington, D.C.* Guilford, CT: Globe Pequot Press, 2004.

Dearing, Mary R. *Veterans in Politics: The Story of the G. A. R.* Baton Rouge, LA: Louisiana State University Press, 1952.

DeCaro, Louis A., Jr. *Fire From the Midst of You: A Religious Life of John Brown*. New York, NY: New York University Press, 2002.

DeConde, Alexander. *Entangling Alliance: Politics and Diplomacy Under George Washington*. Durham, NC: Duke University Press, 1958.

DeGregorio, William A. *The Complete Book of U.S. Presidents*. 1984. New York, NY: Barricade, 1993 ed.

Denney, Robert E. *The Civil War Years: A Day-by-Day Chronicle of the Life of a Nation*. 1992. New York, NY: Sterling Publishing, 1994 ed.

Denson, John V. (ed.). *Reassessing the Presidency: The Rise of the Executive State and the Decline of Freedom*. Auburn, AL: Mises Institute, 2001.

DePalma, Margaret C. *Dialogue on the Frontier: Catholic and Protestant Relations, 1793-1883*. Kent, OH: The Kent State University Press, 2004.

Derosa, Marshall L. *The Confederate Constitution of 1861: An Inquiry into American Constitutionalism*. Columbia, MO: University of Missouri Press, 1991.

Desty, Robert. *The Constitution of the United States*. San Francisco, CA: Sumner Whitney and Co., 1881.

Dicey, Edward. *Six Months in the Federal States.* 2 vols. London, UK: Macmillan and Co., 1863.

Diedrich, Maria. *Love Across Color Lines: Ottilie Assing and Frederick Douglass.* New York, NY: Hill and Wang, 1999.

DiLorenzo, Thomas J. *Lincoln Unmasked: What You're Not Supposed to Know About Dishonest Abe.* New York, NY: Crown Forum, 2006.

——. *Hamilton's Curse: How Jefferson's Archenemy Betrayed the American Revolution—and What It Means for America Today.* New York, NY: Crown Forum, 2008.

Dinkins, James. *1861 to 1865: Personal Recollections and Experiences in the Confederate Army, by an "Old Johnnie".* Cincinnati, OH: Robert Clarke, 1897.

Dinnerstein, Leonard, and Kenneth T. Jackson. *American Vistas: 1877 to the Present.* New York, NY: Oxford University Press, 1979.

Donald, David Herbert. *Lincoln Reconsidered: Essays on the Civil War Era.* 1947. New York, NY: Vintage Press, 1989 ed.

——. *Lincoln.* New York, NY: Simon and Schuster, 1995.

Douglas, Stephen Arnold. *Speeches of Senator S. A. Douglas on the Occasion of His Public Receptions by the Citizens of New Orleans, Philadelphia, and Baltimore.* Washington, D.C.: Lemuel Towers, 1859.

DuBois James T., and Gertrude S. Mathews. *Galusha A. Grow: Father of the Homestead Law.* Boston, MA: Houghton Mifflin Co., 1917.

Dunbar, Rowland (ed.). *Jefferson Davis, Constitutionalist: His Letters, Papers, and Speeches.* 10 vols. Jackson, MS: Mississippi Department of Archives and History, 1923.

Durant, Will, and Ariel Durant. *The Age of Reason Begins: A History of European Civilization in the Period of Shakespeare, Bacon, Montaigne, Rembrandt, Galileo, and Descartes: 1558-1648.* New York, NY: Simon and Schuster, 1961.

Duverger, Maurice. *Political Parties: Their Organization and Activity in the Modern State.* New York, NY: Barnes and Noble, 1954.

Early, Jubal A. *A Memoir of the Last Year of the War for Independence in the Confederate States of America.* Lynchburg, VA: Charles W. Button, 1867.

Eaton, Clement. *Henry Clay and the Art of American Politics.* Boston, MA: Little, Brown and Co., 1957.

Eaton, John, and Ethel Osgood Mason. *Grant, Lincoln and the Freedmen: Reminiscences of the Civil War, With Special Reference to the Work of the Contrabands and Freedmen of the Mississippi Valley.* New York, NY: Longmans, Green, and Co., 1907.

Edmonds, Franklin Spencer. *Ulysses S. Grant.* Philadelphia, PA: George W. Jacobs and Co., 1915.

Efford, Alison Clark, *German Immigrants, Race, and Citizenship in the Civil War Era.* Cambridge, UK: Cambridge University Press, 2013.

Eldersveld, Samuel J. *Political Parties: A Behavioral Analysis.* Chicago, IL: Rand McNally and Co., 1964.

Elliot, Jonathan. *The Debates in the Several State Conventions on the Adoption of the Federal Constitution, As Recommended by the General Convention at Philadelphia in 1787.* 5 vols. Philadelphia, PA: J. B. Lippincott, 1891.

Elliott, E. N. *Cotton is King, and Pro-Slavery Arguments: Comprising the Writings of Hammond, Harper, Christy, Stringfellow, Hodge, Bledsoe, and Cartwright, on this Important Subject.* Augusta, GA: Pritchard, Abbott and Loomis, 1860.

Ellis, Joseph J. *American Sphinx: The Character of Thomas Jefferson.* 1996. New York, NY: Vintage, 1998 ed.

——. *Founding Brothers: The Revolutionary Generation.* 2000. New York, NY: Vintage, 2002 ed.

Emerson, Bettie Alder Calhoun. *Historic Southern Monuments: Representative Memorials of the Heroic Dead of the Southern Confederacy.* New York, NY: Neale Publishing Co., 1911.

Encyclopedia Britannica: A New Survey of Universal Knowledge. 1768. Chicago, IL/London, UK: Encyclopedia Britannica, 1955 ed.

Engels, Friedrich. *The Development of Socialism From Utopia to Science.* 1877. New York, NY: Labor News Co., 1892 ed.

Engs, Robert F., and Randall M. Miller (eds.). *The Birth of the Grand Old Party: The Republicans' First Generation.* Philadelphia, PA: University of Pennsylvania Press, 2002.

Escott, Paul D. (ed.). *North Carolinians in the Era of the Civil War and Reconstruction.* Chapel Hill, NC: University of North Carolina Press, 2008.

Etheredge, Robert C. *The American Challenge: Preserving the Greatness of America in the 21st Century.* Orinda, CA: Mira Vista Press, 2011.

Evans, Clement Anselm (ed.). *Confederate Military History: A Library of Confederate States History, in Twelve Volumes, Written By Distinguished Men of the South.* 12 vols. Atlanta, GA: Confederate Publishing Co., 1899.

Evans, Lawrence B. (ed.). *Writings of George Washington.* New York, NY: G. P. Putnam's Sons, 1908.

Farrand, Max. *The Records of the Federal Convention of 1787.* 3 vols. New Haven, CT: Yale University Press, 1911.

Faulkner, Harold Underwood. *American Political and Social History.* 1937. New York, NY: Appleton-Century-Crofts, 1948 ed.

Fehrenbacher, Don E. (ed.). *Abraham Lincoln: A Documentary Portrait Through His Speeches and Writings.* New York, NY: Signet, 1964.

——. *Lincoln in Text and Context: Collected Essays.* Stanford, CA: Stanford University Press, 1987.

——. (ed.) *Abraham Lincoln: Speeches and Writings, 1859-1865.* New York, NY: Library of America, 1989.

Findlay, Bruce, and Esther Findlay. *Your Rugged Constitution: How America's House of Freedom is Planned and Built.* 1950. Stanford, CA: Stanford University Press, 1951 ed.

Fischer, David H. *The Revolution of American Conservatism: The Federalist Party in the Era of Jeffersonian Democracy.* New York, NY: Harper and Row, 1969.

Fiske, John. *The Critical Period of American History, 1783-1789.* Boston, MA: Houghton, Mifflin and Co., 1889.

Fite, Emerson David. *Social and Industrial Conditions in the North During the Civil War.* New York, NY: Macmillan, 1910.

——. *The Presidential Election of 1860.* New York, NY: MacMillan, 1911.

Foley, John P. (ed.). *The Jeffersonian Cyclopedia: A Comprehensive Collection of the Views of Thomas Jefferson.* New York, NY: Funk and Wagnalls, 1900.

Foner, Eric. *Free Soil, Free Labor, Free Men: The Ideology of the Republican Party Before the Civil War.* New York, NY: Oxford University Press, 1970.

——. *Reconstruction: America's Unfinished Revolution, 1863-1877.* 1988. New York, NY: Harper and Row, 1989 ed.

Ford, Paul Leicester (ed.). *The Works of Thomas Jefferson.* 12 vols. New York, NY: G. P. Putnam's Sons, 1904.

Ford, Worthington Chauncey (ed.). *A Cycle of Adams Letters.* 2 vols. Boston, MA: Houghton Mifflin, 1920.

Forman, S. E. *The Life and Writings of Thomas Jefferson.* Indianapolis, IN: Bowen-Merrill, 1900.

Fowler, John D. *The Confederate Experience Reader: Selected Documents and Essays.* New York, NY: Routledge, 2007.

Fowler, William Chauncey. *The Sectional Controversy; or Passages in the Political History of the United States, Including the Causes of the War Between the Sections.* New York, NY: Charles Scribner, 1864.

Fox, Dixon R. *The Decline of Aristocracy in the Politics of New York, 1801-1840.* New York, NY:

Harper and Row, 1965.

Franklin, Benjamin. *The Life and Writings of Benjamin Franklin.* 2 vols. Philadelphia, PA: McCarty and Davis, 1834.

——. *The Complete Works of Benjamin Franklin.* 10 vols. New York, NY: G. P. Putnam's Sons, 1887.

Franklin, John Hope. *Reconstruction After the Civil War.* Chicago, IL: University of Chicago Press, 1961.

Frayssé, Olivier. *Lincoln, Land, and Labor, 1809-1860.* Urbana, IL: University of Illinois Press, 1988.

Friedman, Jean E. *Abraham Lincoln and the Virtues of War: How Civil War Families Challenged and Transformed Our National Values.* Santa Barbara, CA: Praeger, 2015.

Frizzell, Robert W. *Independent Immigrants: A Settlement of Hanoverian Germans in Western Missouri.* Columbia, MO: University of Missouri Press, 2007.

Furnas, J. C. *The Americans: A Social History of the United States, 1587-1914.* New York, NY: G. P. Putnam's Sons, 1969.

Garibaldi, Giuseppe. *Garibaldi: An Autobiography.* (Edited by Alexandre Dumas.) London, UK: Routledge, Warne, and Routledge, 1861.

Garraty, John A. *The American Nation: A History of the United States to 1877.* 1966. New York, NY: Harper and Row, 1971 ed.

Garraty, John A., and Robert A. McCaughey. *A Short History of the American Nation.* 1966. New York, NY: HarperCollins, 1989 ed.

Garrison, Webb B. *The Lincoln No One Knows: The Mysterious Man Who Ran the Civil War.* Nashville, TN: Rutledge Hill Press, 1993.

——. *Civil War Curiosities: Strange Stories, Oddities, Events, and Coincidences.* Nashville, TN: Rutledge Hill Press, 1994.

——. *The Amazing Civil War.* Nashville, TN: Rutledge Hill Press, 1998.

Garrison, Wendell Phillips, and Francis Jackson Garrison. *William Lloyd Garrison, 1805-1879.* 4 vols. New York, NY: Century Co., 1889.

Garrison, William Lloyd. *Thoughts on African Colonization.* Boston, MA: Garrison and Knapp, 1832.

Gazley, John G. *American Opinion of German Unification, 1848-1871.* New York, NY: Columbia University Press, 1926.

Geer, John G., Wendy J. Schiller, Jeffrey A. Segal, and Richard Herrera. *Gateways to Democracy: An Introduction to American Government.* 2012. Boston, MA: Cengage Learning, 2016 ed.

Geitz, Henry (ed.). *The German-American Press.* Madison, WI: Max Kade Institute for German-American Studies, 1992.

Ghent, William James (ed.). *Appeal Socialist Classics* (issues 1-12). Girard, KS: Appeal to Reason, 1916.

Giddens-White, Bryon. *National Elections and the Political Process.* Chicago, IL: Heinemann Library, 2006.

Gilmore, James Roberts. *Personal Recollections of Abraham Lincoln and the Civil War.* Boston, MA: L. C. Page and Co., 1898.

Golay, Michael. *A Ruined Land: The End of the Civil War.* New York, NY: John Wiley and Sons, 1999.

Goodman, Paul. *The Democratic-Republicans of Massachusetts: Politics in a Young Republic.* Cambridge, MA: Harvard University Press, 1964.

Goodwyn, Lawrence. *Democratic Promise: The Populist Movement in America.* New York, NY: Oxford University Press, 1976.

Gordon, Armistead Churchill. *Figures From American History: Jefferson Davis.* New York, NY: Charles Scribner's Sons, 1918.

Gould, Lewis L. *The Presidency of William McKinley*. Lawrence, KS: University Press of Kansas, 1980.

Graham, John Remington. *A Constitutional History of Secession*. Gretna, LA: Pelican Publishing Co., 2003.

———. *Blood Money: The Civil War and the Federal Reserve*. Gretna, LA: Pelican Publishing Co., 2006.

Grant, Ulysses Simpson. *Personal Memoirs of U. S. Grant*. 2 vols. 1885-1886. New York, NY: Charles L. Webster and Co., 1886.

Greeley, Horace (ed.). *The Writings of Cassius Marcellus Clay*. New York, NY: Harper and Brothers, 1848.

———. *A History of the Struggle for Slavery Extension or Restriction in the United States From the Declaration of Independence to the Present Day*. New York, NY: Dix, Edwards and Co., 1856.

———. *The American Conflict: A History of the Great Rebellion in the United States, 1861-1865*. 2 vols. Hartford, CT: O. D. Case and Co., 1867.

Greenhow, Rose O'Neal. *My Imprisonment and the First Year of Abolition Rule at Washington*. London, UK: Richard Bentley, 1863.

Gregor, A. James. *Young Mussolini and the Intellectual Origins of Fascism*. Berkeley, CA: University of California Press, 1979.

Grimsley, Mark. *The Hard Hand of War: Union Military Policy Toward Southern Civilians, 1861-1865*. 1995. Cambridge, UK: Cambridge University Press, 1997 ed.

Grissom, Michael Andrew. *Southern By the Grace of God*. 1988. Gretna, LA: Pelican Publishing Co., 1995 ed.

Groom, Winston. *Shrouds of Glory - From Atlanta to Nashville: The Last Great Campaign of the Civil War*. New York, NY: Grove Press, 1995.

Gross, Michael B. *The War Against Catholicism: Liberalism and the Anti-Catholic Imagination in Nineteenth-Century Germany*. Ann Arbor, MI: University of Michigan Press, 2004.

Grun, Bernard. *The Timetables of History: A Horizontal Linkage of People and Events*. 1946. New York, NY: Touchstone, 1982 ed.

Guelzo, Allen C. *Abraham Lincoln As a Man of Ideas*. Carbondale, IL: Southern Illinois University Press, 2009.

Hacker, Louis Morton. *The Shaping of the American Tradition*. New York, NY: Columbia University Press, 1947.

Hall, Benjamin Franklin. *The Republican Party and its Presidential Candidates*. New York, NY: Miller, Orton and Mulligan, 1856.

Hall, Kermit L. (ed). *The Oxford Companion to the Supreme Court of the United States*. New York, NY: Oxford University Press, 1992.

Halloran, Fiona Deans. *Thomas Nast: The Father of Modern Political Cartoons*. Chapel Hill, NC: University of North Carolina Press, 2012.

Hamilton, Alexander, James Madison, and John Jay. *The Federalist*. Washington, D.C.: Masters, Smith and Co., 1852.

Hamilton, John C. (ed.). *The Works of Alexander Hamilton; Comprising His Correspondence, and His Political and Official Writings, Exclusive of the Federalist, Civil, and Military*. 7 vols. New York, NY: John F. Trow, 1850.

Hamilton, Stanislaus Murray (ed.). *The Writings of James Monroe: Including a Collection of His Public and Private Papers and Correspondence Now for the First Time Printed*. 7 vols. New York, NY: G. P. Putnam's Sons, 1901.

Hamilton, Neil A. *Rebels and Renegades: A Chronology of Social and Political Dissent in the United States*. New York, NY: Routledge, 2002.

Hammond, Bray. *Banks and Politics in America from the Revolution to the Civil War*. Princeton, NJ: Princeton University Press, 1957.

Handlin, Oscar (ed.). *Readings in American History: Vol. 1 - From Settlement to Reconstruction*. 1957. New York, Alfred A. Knopf, 1970 ed.

Hannity, Sean. *Let Freedom Ring: Winning the War of Liberty Over Liberalism*. New York, NY: Harper Collins, 2002.

Hansen, Harry. *The Civil War: A History*. 1961. Harmondsworth, UK: Mentor, 1991 ed.

Harding, Samuel Bannister. *The Contest Over the Ratification of the Federal Constitution in the State of Massachusetts*. New York, NY: Longmans, Green, and Co., 1896.

Harrell, David Edwin, Jr., Edwin S. Gaustad, John B. Boles, Sally Foreman Griffith, Randall M. Miller, and Randall B. Woods. *Unto a Good Land: A History of the American People*. Grand Rapids, MI: William B. Eerdmans, 2005.

Hart, Albert Bushnell (ed.). *American History Told by Contemporaries*. 5 vols. New York, NY: Macmillan, 1908.

Hartzell, Josiah. *The Genesis of the Republican Party*. Canton, OH: n.p., 1890.

Harvey, Charles Mitchell. *Republican National Convention, St Louis, June 16th to 18th, 1896*. St. Louis, MO: Haas Publishing, 1896.

Hawthorne, Julian (ed.). *Orations of American Orators*. 2 vols. New York, NY: Colonial Press, 1900.

Hawthorne, Julian, James Schouler, and Elisha Benjamin Andrews. *United States, From the Discovery of the North American Continent Up to the Present Time*. 9 vols. New York, NY: Co-operative Publication Society, 1894.

Hayes, Carlton J. H., Marshall Whited Baldwin, and Charles Woolsey Cole. *History of Europe*. 1949. New York, NY: Macmillan Co., 1950 ed.

Hearn, Chester G. *The Impeachment of Andrew Johnson*. Jefferson, NC: McFarland and Co., 1993.

Helper, Hinton Rowan. *The Impending Crisis of the South: How to Meet It*. New York, NY: A. B. Burdick, 1860.

Hendelson, William H. (ed). *Funk and Wagnalls New Encyclopedia*. New York, NY: Funk and Wagnalls, 1973 ed.

Herndon, William H., and Jesse W. Weik. *Abraham Lincoln: The True Story of a Great Life*. 2 vols. New York, NY: D. Appleton and Co., 1892.

Herriott, Frank Irving. *The Premises and Significance of Abraham Lincoln's Letter to Theodore Canisius*. Chicago, IL: Jahrbuch der Deutsch-Amerikanischen Historischen, Gesellschaft von Illinois, Vol. 15, 1915.

Hertz, Emanuel. *Abraham Lincoln: A New Portrait*. 2 Vols. New York, NY: H. Liveright, 1931.

——. *The Hidden Lincoln*. New York, NY: Blue Ribbon Works, 1940.

Hervey, Anthony. *Why I Wave the Confederate Flag, Written By a Black Man: The End of Niggerism and the Welfare State*. Oxford, UK: Trafford Publishing, 2006.

Hesseltine, William B. *Lincoln and the War Governors*. New York, NY: Alfred A. Knopf, 1948.

Hickey, William. *The Constitution of the United States*. Philadelphia, PA: T. K. and P. G. Collins, 1853.

Hicks, John D. *The Populist Revolt: A History of the Farmers' Alliance and the People's Party*. Minneapolis, MN: University of Minnesota Press, 1931.

Hildreth, Richard. *The White Slave: Another Picture of Slave Life in America*. Boston, MA: Adamant Media Corp., 2001.

Hill, Kenneth L. *An Essential Guide to American Politics and the American Political System*. Bloomington, IN: Author House, 2012.

Hillquit, Morris. *History of Socialism in the United States*. 1903. New York, NY: Funk and Wagnalls, 1910 ed.

——. *Socialism in Theory and Practice*. New York, NY: Macmillan, 1909.

Hillquit, Morris, and John A. Ryan. *Socialism: Promise or Menace?* New York, NY: Macmillan, 1914.

Hitler, Adolf. *Mein Kampf.* 2 vols. 1925, 1926. New York: NY: Reynal and Hitchcock, 1941 English translation ed.

Hoffman, Michael A., II. *They Were White and They Were Slaves: The Untold History of the Enslavement of Whites in Early America.* Dresden, NY: Wiswell Ruffin House, 1993.

Hoffman, William S. *Andrew Jackson and North Carolina Politics.* Chapel Hill, NC: University of North Carolina Press, 1958.

Hofstadter, Richard. *The American Political Tradition, and the Men Who Made It.* New York, NY: Alfred A. Knopf, 1948.

———. *The Age of Reform: From Bryan to FDR.* New York, NY: Alfred A. Knopf, 1955.

———. (ed.) *Great Issues in American History: From Reconstruction to the Present Day, 1864-1969.* 1958. New York, NY: Vintage, 1969 ed.

Holland, Josiah Gilbert. *The Life of Abraham Lincoln.* Springfield, MA: Gurdon Bill, 1866.

Holt, Michael F. *The Rise and Fall of the American Whig Party: Jacksonian Politics and the Onset of the Civil War.* Oxford, UK: Oxford University Press, 1999.

Holzer, Harold. *Lincoln President-Elect: Abraham Lincoln and the Great Secession, Winter 1860-1861.* New York, NY: Simon and Schuster, 2008.

Hopkins, James Herron. *History of Political Parties in the United States.* New York, NY: G. P. Putnam's Sons, 1900.

Horrocks, Thomas A. *Lincoln's Campaign Biographies.* Carbondale, IL: Southern Illinois University Press, 2014.

Howe, Irving (eds.). *Essential Works of Socialism.* 1970. New York, NY: Bantam, 1971 ed.

Howe, John R., Jr. *Changing Political Thought of John Adams.* Princeton, NJ: Princeton University Press, 1966.

Hunt, Gaillard (ed.). *The First Forty Years of Washington Society.* New York, NY: Charles Scribner's Sons, 1906.

Ilisevich, Robert D. *Galusha A. Grow: The People's Candidate.* Pittsburgh, PA: University of Pittsburgh Press, 1988.

Ingersoll, Thomas G., and Robert E. O'Connor. *Politics and Structure: Essentials of American National Government.* North Scituate, MA: Duxbury Press, 1979.

Jameson, John Franklin (ed.). *Dictionary of United States History.* Philadelphia, PA: Historical Publishing Co., 1908.

———. (ed.). *The American Historical Review.* Vol. 16, October 1910 to July 1911. London, UK: Macmillan, 1911.

Jefferson, Thomas. *Notes on the State of Virginia.* Boston, MA: H. Sprague, 1802.

———. *Thomas Jefferson's Farm Book.* (Edwin Morris Betts, ed.). Charlottesville, VA: Thomas Jefferson Memorial Foundation, 1999.

Jenkins, John S. *The Life of James Knox Polk, Late President of the United States.* Auburn, NY: James M. Alden, 1850.

Jensen, Merrill. *The New Nation: A History of the United States During the Confederation, 1781-1789.* New York, NY: Vintage, 1950.

———. *The Articles of Confederation: An Interpretation of the Social-Constitutional History of the American Revolution, 1774-1781.* Madison, WI: University of Wisconsin Press, 1959.

Jensen, Richard. *The Winning of the Midwest: Social and Political Conflict, 1888-1896.* Chicago, IL: University of Chicago Press, 1971.

Johannsen, Robert Walter. *Lincoln, the South, and Slavery: The Political Dimension.* Baton Rouge, LA: Louisiana State University Press, 1991.

Johnson, Allen (ed.). *Readings in Constitutional History, 1776-1876.* Boston, MA: Houghton Mifflin Co., 1912.

———. *Union and Democracy.* Boston, MA: Houghton Mifflin Co., 1915.

Johnson, Benjamin Heber. *Making of the American West: People and Perspectives.* Santa Barbara, CA:

ABC-Clio, 2007.

Johnson, Clint. *The Politically Incorrect Guide to the South (and Why It Will Rise Again)*. Washington, D.C.: Regnery, 2006.

Johnson, Ludwell H. *North Against South: The American Iliad, 1848-1877*. 1978. Columbia, SC: Foundation for American Education, 1993 ed.

Johnson, Oliver. *William Lloyd Garrison and His Times*. 1879. Boston, MA: Houghton Mifflin and Co., 1881 ed.

Johnson, Paul. *A History of the American People*. 1997. New York, NY: Harper Collins, 1999 ed.

Johnson, Robert Underwood (ed.). *Battles and Leaders of the Civil War*. 4 vols. New York, NY: The Century Co., 1884-1888.

Johnstone, Huger William. *Truth of War Conspiracy, 1861*. Idylwild, GA: H. W. Johnstone, 1921.

Jones, John William. *Personal Reminiscences, Anecdotes, and Letters of Gen. Robert E. Lee*. New York, NY: D. Appleton and Co., 1874.

——. *The Davis Memorial Volume; Or Our Dead President, Jefferson Davis and the World's Tribute to His Memory*. Richmond, VA: B. F. Johnson, 1889.

Jones, Stanley Llewellyn. *The Presidential Election of 1896*. Madison, WI: University of Wisconsin Press, 1964.

Josephson, Matthew. *The Politicos, 1865-1896*. New York, NY: Harcourt, Brace and World, 1938.

Julian, George Washington. *Speeches on Political Questions*. New York, NY: Hurd and Houghton, 1872.

Kamman, William Frederic. *Socialism in German American Literature*. Philadelphia, PA: Americana Germanica Press, 1917.

Kane, Joseph Nathan. *Facts About the Presidents: A Compilation of Biographical and Historical Data*. 1959. New York, NY: Ace, 1976 ed.

Kaplan, Justin. *Mr. Clemens and Mark Twain: A Biography*. New York, NY: Simon and Schuster, 1966.

Kass, Alvin. *Politics in New York State, 1800-1830*. Syracuse, NY: Syracuse University Press, 1965.

Katcher, Philip. *The Civil War Source Book*. 1992. New York, NY: Facts on File, 1995 ed.

Kazin, Michael. *A Godly Hero: The Life of William Jennings Bryan*. New York, NY: Anchor, 2006.

Kelly, Alfred H., Winfred A. Harbison, and Herman Belz. *The American Constitution: Its Origins and Development* (Vol. 2). 1965. New York, NY: W.W. Norton, 1991 ed.

Key, Valdimer O., Jr. *Politics, Parties, and Pressure Groups*. New York, NY: Thomas Y. Crowell, 1964.

Kimball, Everett. *The National Government of the United States*. Boston, MA: Ginn and Co., 1920.

King, Charles R. (ed.). *The Life and Correspondence of Rufus King*. 6 vols. New York, NY: G. P. Putnam's Sons, 1897.

King, Edward. *The Great South: A Record of Journeys*. Hartford, CT: American Publishing Co., 1875.

Kleppner, Paul. *The Cross of Culture: A Social Analysis of Midwestern Politics, 1850-1900*. New York, NY: Free Press, 1970.

Koenig, Louis W. *Bryan: A Political Biography of William Jennings Bryan*. New York, NY: Putnam's Sons, 1971.

Kurtz, Stephen G. *The Presidency of John Adams: The Collapse of Federalism, 1795-1800*. Cranbury, NJ: A. S. Barnes, 1961.

Lamon, Ward Hill. *The Life of Abraham Lincoln: From His Birth to His Inauguration as President*. Boston, MA: James R. Osgood and Co., 1872.

——. *Recollections of Abraham Lincoln: 1847-1865*. Chicago, IL: A. C. McClurg and Co., 1895.

Lancaster, Bruce, and J. H. Plumb. *The American Heritage Book of the Revolution*. 1958. New York, NY: Dell, 1975 ed.

La Palombara, Joseph, and Myron Weiner (eds.). *Political Parties and Political Development*. Princeton, NJ: Princeton University Press, 1966.

Lause, Mark A. *Young America: Land, Labor, and the Republican Community*. Urbana, IL: University of Illinois Press, 2005.

——. *A Secret Society History of the Civil War*. Urbana, IL: University of Illinois Press, 2011.

Lawton, G. W. *The American Caucus System: Its Origin, Purpose and Utility - Questions of the Day*. New York, NY: Putnam, 1885.

Leavitt, Amie Jane. *A History of the Republican Party*. Hockessin, DE: Mitchell Lane, 2013.

Lee, Charles Carter. *Observations on the Writings of Thomas Jefferson*. Philadelphia, PA: Judah Dobson, 1839.

Lee, Robert E., Jr. *Recollections and Letters of General Robert E. Lee*. New York, NY: Doubleday, Page and Co., 1904.

Leech, Margaret. *Reveille in Washington, 1860-1865*. 1941. Alexandria, VA: Time-Life Books, 1980 ed.

——. *In the Days of McKinley*. New York, NY: Harper and Brothers, 1959.

Leiserson, Avery. *Parties and Politics: An Institutional and Behavioral Approach*. New York, NY: Alfred A. Knopf, 1958.

Lemay, J. A. Leo, and P. M. Zall (eds.). *Benjamin Franklin's Autobiography: An Authoritative Text, Backgrounds, Criticism*. 1791. New York, NY: W. W. Norton and Co., 1986 ed.

Lemire, Elise. *Black Walden: Slavery and Its Aftermath in Concord, Massachusetts*. Philadelphia, PA: University of Pennsylvania Press, 2009.

Lerner, Max. *America as a Civilization - Vol. 2: Culture and Personality*. 1957. New York, NY: Simon and Schuster, 1961 ed.

Levin, Mark R. *Liberty and Tyranny: A Conservative Manifesto*. New York, NY: Threshold, 2009.

Lewis, Lloyd. *Myths After Lincoln*. 1929. New York, NY: The Press of the Reader's Club, 1941 ed.

Lincoln, Abraham. *The Autobiography of Abraham Lincoln* (selected from the *Complete Works of Abraham Lincoln*, 1894, by John G. Nicolay and John Hay). New York, NY: Francis D. Tandy Co., 1905.

Lincoln, Abraham, and Stephen A. Douglas. *Political Debates Between Abraham Lincoln and Stephen A. Douglas*. Cleveland, OH: Burrows Brothers Co., 1894.

Lind, Michael (ed.). *Hamilton's Republic: Readings in the American Democratic Nationalist Tradition*. New York, NY: Free Press, 1997.

Livingstone, William. *Livingstone's History of the Republican Party*. 2 vols. Detroit, MI: William Livingstone, 1900.

Locke, John. *Two Treatises of Government* (Mark Goldie, ed.). 1924. London, UK: Everyman, 1998 ed.

Lodge, Henry Cabot (ed.). *The Works of Alexander Hamilton*. 12 vols. New York, NY: G. P. Putnam's Sons, 1904.

Long, George (ed.). *The Penny Cyclopedia of Society for the Diffusion of Useful Knowledge*. 27 vols. London, UK: Charles Knight and Co., 1843.

Long, John D. (ed.). *The Republican Party: Its History, Principles, and Policies*. New York, NY: M. W. Hazen Co., 1898.

Lorenzkowski, Barbara. *Sounds of Ethnicity: Listening to German North America, 1850-1914*. Winnipeg, Canada: University of Manitoba Press, 2010.

Lytle, Andrew Nelson. *Bedford Forrest and His Critter Company*. New York, NY: G. P. Putnam's Sons, 1931.

MacDonald, William. *A New Constitution for a New America*. New York, NY: B. W. Huebsch,

1921.

Mackay, Charles. *Life and Liberty in America, or Sketches of a Tour in the United States and Canada in 1857-58*. New York, NY: Harper and Brothers, 1859.

Macy, Jesse. *Political Parties in the United States, 1846-1861*. London, UK: Macmillan 1900.

Madison, James. *Letters and Other Writings of James Madison, Fourth President of the United States*. 4 vols. Philadelphia, PA: J. B. Lippincott and Co., 1865.

Magliocca, Gerard N. *The Tragedy of William Jennings Bryan: Constitutional Law and the Politics of Backlash*. New Haven, CT: Yale University Press, 2011.

Maihafer, Harry J. *War of Words: Abraham Lincoln and the Civil War Press*. Dulles, VA: Brassey's, 2001.

Main, Jackson Turner. *The Anti-Federalists: Critics of the Constitution, 1781-1788*. 1961. New York, NY: W. W. Norton and Co., 1974 ed.

——. *Political Parties Before the Constitution*. Chapel Hill, NC: University of North Carolina Press, 1973.

Malone, Laurence J. *Opening the West: Federal Internal Improvements Before 1860*. Westport, CT: Greenwood Press, 1998.

Maltsev, Yuri N. (ed.). *Requiem for Marx*. Auburn, AL: Ludwig von Mises Institute, 1993.

Mandel, Bernard. *Labor, Free and Slave: Workingmen and the Anti-Slavery Movement in the United States*. New York, NY: Associated Authors, 1955.

Marcus, Jacob Rader. *United States Jewry, 1776-1985*. 3 vols. Detroit, MI: Wayne State University Press, 1993.

Marshall, John. *The Life of George Washington, Commander in Chief of the American Forces*. 2 vols. Philadelphia, PA: James Crissy, and Thomas, Cowperthwait and Co., 1839.

Martin, Kingsley. *French Liberal Thought in the Eighteenth Century: A Study of Political Ideas From Bayle to Condorcet*. 1929. New York, NY: Harper and Row, 1962 ed.

Marx, Karl, and Frederick Engels. *Manifesto of the Communist Party*. Chicago, IL: Charles H. Kerr and Co., 1906.

Mayer, David N. *The Constitutional Thought of Thomas Jefferson*. Charlottesville, VA: University of Virginia Press, 1995.

Mayer, Henry. *All on Fire: William Lloyd Garrison and the Abolition of Slavery*. New York, NY: St. Martin's Press, 1998.

McAfee, Ward M. *Religion, Race, and Reconstruction: The Public School in the Politics of the 1870s*. Albany, NY: State University of New York Press, 1998.

McCabe, James Dabney. *Our Martyred President: The Life and Public Services of Gen. James A. Garfield, Twentieth President of the United States*. Philadelphia, PA: National Publishing Co., 1881.

McCarty, Burke (ed.). *Little Sermons in Socialism by Abraham Lincoln*. Chicago, IL: The Chicago Daily Socialist, 1910.

McClure, Alexander Kelly. *Abraham Lincoln and Men of War-Times: Some Personal Recollections of War and Politics During the Lincoln Administration*. Philadelphia, PA: Times Publishing Co., 1892.

——. *Our Presidents and How We Make Them*. New York, NY: Harper and Brothers, 1900.

McCormick, Richard P. *The Second American Party System: Party Formation in the Jacksonian Era*. Chapel Hill, NC: University of North Carolina Press, 1966.

McCullough, David. *John Adams*. New York, NY: Touchstone, 2001.

McDonald, Forrest. *States' Rights and the Union: Imperium in Imperio, 1776-1876*. Lawrence, KS: University Press of Kansas, 2000.

McDonald, Neil A. *The Study of Political Parties*. New York, NY: Random House, 1955.

McElroy, Robert. *Jefferson Davis: The Unreal and the Real*. 1937. New York, NY: Smithmark, 1995 ed.

McGuire, Hunter, and George L. Christian. *The Confederate Cause and Conduct in the War Between the States.* Richmond, VA: L. H. Jenkins, 1907.

McKinley, William. *Speeches and Addresses of William McKinley.* New York, NY: D. Appleton and Co., 1893.

McLaughlin, Andrew Cunningham. *The American Nation: A History* (27 vols): *The Confederation and the Constitution, 1783-1789* (Vol. 10). New York, NY: Harper and Brothers, 1905.

McLaughlin, Andrew Cunningham, and Albert Bushnell Hart (eds.). *Cyclopedia of American Government.* 3 vols. New York, NY: D. Appleton and Co., 1914.

McManus, Edgar J. *A History of Negro Slavery in New York.* Syracuse, NY: Syracuse University Press, 1966.

——. *Black Bondage in the North.* Syracuse, NY: Syracuse University Press, 1973.

McMaster, John Bach. *A History of the People of the United States, From the Revolution to the Civil War.* 5 vols. New York, NY: D. Appleton and Co., 1891.

——. *Our House Divided: A History of the People of the United States During Lincoln's Administration.* 1927. New York, NY: Premier, 1961 ed.

McMillan, Duncan Cameron. *The Elective Franchise in the United States.* New York, NY: G. P. Putnam's Sons, 1878.

McNitt, Frank (ed.). *Navaho Expedition: Journal of a Military Reconnaissance From Santa Fe to New Mexico, to the Navaho Country.* 1964. Norman, OK: University of Oklahoma Press, 2003 ed.

McPherson, Edward. *The Political History of the United States of America, During the Great Rebellion (From November 6, 1860, to July 4, 1864).* Washington, D.C.: Philp and Solomons, 1865.

——. *The Political History of the United States of America, During the Period of Reconstruction, (From April 15, 1865, to July 15, 1870,) Including a Classified Summary of the Legislation of the Thirty-ninth, Fortieth, and Forty-first Congresses.* Washington, D.C.: Solomons and Chapman, 1875.

McPherson, James M. *The Struggle for Equality: Abolitionists and the Negro in the Civil War and Reconstruction.* 1964. Princeton, NJ: Princeton University Press, 1992 ed.

——. *The Negro's Civil War: How American Negroes Felt and Acted During the War for the Union.* 1965. Chicago, IL: University of Illinois Press, 1982 ed.

——. *Abraham Lincoln and the Second American Revolution.* New York, NY: Oxford University Press, 1991.

——. *Battle Cry of Freedom: The Civil War Era.* Oxford, UK: Oxford University Press, 2003.

——. *The Atlas of the Civil War.* Philadelphia, PA: Courage Books, 2005.

McPherson, James M., and the staff of the *New York Times.* *The Most Fearful Ordeal: Original Coverage of the Civil War by Writers and Reporters of the New York Times.* New York, NY: St. Martin's Press, 2004.

McPherson, Stephanie Sammartino. *Political Parties: From Nominations to Victory Celebrations.* Minneapolis, MN: Lerner, 2016.

McRee, Griffith John. *Life and Correspondence of James Iredell.* 2 vols. New York, NY: D. Appleton and Co., 1857.

Mendel, Arthur P. (ed.). *Essential Works of Marxism.* New York, NY: Bantam, 1961.

Meriwether, Elizabeth Avery (pseudonym, "George Edmonds"). *Facts and Falsehoods Concerning the War on the South, 1861-1865.* Memphis, TN: A. R. Taylor and Co., 1904.

Merriam, Charles E. *The American Political Party System: An Introduction to the Study of Political Parties.* New York, NY: Macmillan, 1949.

Message of the President of the United States and Accompanying Documents to the Two Houses of Congress at the Commencement of the Third Session of the 40th Congress. Washington, D.C.: Government Printing Office, 1868.

Michels, Robert. *Political Parties: A Sociological Study of the Oligarchical Tendencies of Modern Democracy.* New York, NY: Hearst's International Library Co., 1915.

Miller, Cristanne. *Reading in Time: Emily Dickinson in the Nineteenth Century.* Amherst, MA:

University of Massachusetts Press, 2012.

Miller, John C. *Crisis in Freedom: The Alien and Sedition Acts*. Boston, MA: Little, Brown and Co., 1952.

———. *The Federalist Era, 1789-1801*. New York, NY: Harper and Row, 1960.

———. *Alexander Hamilton and the Growth of the New Nation*. New York, NY: Harper and Row, 1964.

Miller, Marion Mills (ed.). *Great Debates in American History*. 14 vols. New York, NY: Current Literature, 1913.

Miller, Nathan. *Star-Spangled Men: America's Ten Worst Presidents*. New York, NY: Touchstone, 1998.

Ming, John Joseph. *The Characteristics and the Religion of Modern Socialism*. New York, NY: Benziger Brothers, 1908.

Minor, Charles Landon Carter. *The Real Lincoln: From the Testimony of His Contemporaries*. Richmond, VA: Everett Waddey Co., 1904.

Minutes of the Eighth Annual Meeting and Reunion of the United Confederate Veterans, Atlanta, GA, July 20-23, 1898. New Orleans, LA: United Confederate Veterans, 1907.

Minutes of the Ninth Annual Meeting and Reunion of the United Confederate Veterans, Charleston, SC, May 10-13, 1899. New Orleans, LA: United Confederate Veterans, 1907.

Minutes of the Twelfth Annual Meeting and Reunion of the United Confederate Veterans, Dallas, TX, April 22-25, 1902. New Orleans, LA: United Confederate Veterans, 1907.

Mish, Frederick C. (ed.). *Webster's Ninth New Collegiate Dictionary*. Springfield, MA: Merriam-Webster, 1984.

Mitchell, Margaret. *Gone With the Wind*. 1936. New York, NY: Avon, 1973 ed.

Mitgang, Herbert (ed.). *Lincoln As They Saw Him*. 1956. New York, NY: Collier, 1962 ed.

Monaghan, Jay. *Abraham Lincoln Deals With Foreign Affairs: A Diplomat in Carpet Slippers*. 1945. Lincoln, NE: University of Nebraska Press, 1997 ed.

Moore, Frank (ed.). *The Rebellion Record: A Diary of American Events*. 12 vols. New York, NY: G. P. Putnam, 1861.

Moore, George Henry. *Notes on the History of Slavery in Massachusetts*. New York, NY: D. Appleton and Co., 1866.

Moore, John Henry. *A Study in States Rights*. New York, NY: Neale Publishing Co., 1911.

Moore, John L. *Elections A to Z*. 1999. London, UK: Routledge, 2013 ed.

Moorhead, James H. *American Apocalypse: Yankee Protestants and the Civil War, 1860-1869*. New Haven, CT: Yale University Press, 1971.

Morgan, Edmund S. *The Birth of the Republic, 1763-89*. 1956. Chicago, IL: University of Chicago Press, 1967 ed.

Morgan, Howard Wayne. *The Gilded Age: A Reappraisal*. Syracuse, NY: Syracuse University Press, 1963.

———. *From Hayes to McKinley: National Party Politics, 1877-1896*. Syracuse, NY: Syracuse University Press, 1969.

Morison, Samuel Eliot, and Henry Steele Commager. *The Growth of the American Republic*. 2 vols. 1930. New York, NY: Oxford University Press, 1965 ed.

Morse, Joseph Laffan (ed.). *Funk and Wagnalls New Encyclopedia*. 1971. New York, NY: Funk and Wagnalls, 1973 ed.

Muzzey, David Saville. *The United States of America: Vol. 1, To the Civil War*. Boston, MA: Ginn and Co., 1922.

———. *The American Adventure: Vol. 2, From the Civil War*. 1924. New York, NY: Harper and Brothers, 1927 ed.

Napolitano, Andrew P. *The Constitution in Exile: How the Federal Government has Seized Power by Rewriting the Supreme Law of the Land*. Nashville, TN: Nelson Current, 2006.

Neely, Mark E., Jr. *The Fate of Liberty: Abraham Lincoln and Civil Liberties.* New York, NY: Oxford University Press, 1991.

Neilson, William Allan (ed.). *Webster's Biographical Dictionary.* Springfield, MA: G. and C. Merriam Co., 1943.

Nelson, Michael (ed.). *Guide to the Presidency.* 1996. London, UK: Routledge, 2015 ed.

Nevins, Allan. *Grover Cleveland: A Study in Courage.* New York, NY: Dodd, Mead and Co., 1932.

Nevins, Allan, and Henry Steele Commager. *A Pocket History of the United States.* 1942. New York, NY: Pocket Books, 1981 ed.

Newsome, Albert R. *The Presidential Election of 1824 in North Carolina.* Chapel Hill, NC: University of North Carolina Press, 1939.

Nichols, John. *Th S Word: A Short History of an American Tradition . . . Socialism.* London, UK: Verso, 2011.

Nichols, Roy F. *The Invention of the American Political Parties.* New York, NY: Macmillan, 1967.

Nicolay, John G., and John Hay (eds.). *Abraham Lincoln: A History.* 10 vols. New York, NY: The Century Co., 1890.

——. *Complete Works of Abraham Lincoln.* 12 vols. 1894. New York, NY: Francis D. Tandy Co., 1905 ed.

——. *Abraham Lincoln: Complete Works.* 12 vols. 1894. New York, NY: The Century Co., 1907 ed.

Nivola, Pietro S., and David H. Rosenbloom (eds.). *Classic Readings in American Politics.* New York, NY: St. Martin's Press, 1986.

Norton, Mary Beth, David M. Katzman, Paul D. Escott, Howard P. Chudacoff, Thomas G. Paterson, and William M. Tuttle Jr. *A People and a Nation: A History of the United States - Vol. 2: Since 1865.* Boston, MA: Houghton Mifflin, 1986.

Norwood, Thomas Manson. *A True Vindication of the South.* Savannah, GA: Citizens and Southern Bank, 1917.

Nye, Russel B. *William Lloyd Garrison and the Humanitarian Reformers.* Boston, MA: Little, Brown and Co., 1955.

Oates, Stephen B. *Abraham Lincoln: The Man Behind the Myths.* New York, NY: Meridian, 1984.

——. *The Approaching Fury: Voices of the Storm, 1820-1861.* New York, NY: Harper Perennial, 1998.

O'Brien, Cormac. *Secret Lives of the U.S. Presidents: What Your Teachers Never Told You About the Men of the White House.* Philadelphia, PA: Quirk, 2004.

O'Brien, Steven G. *American Political Leaders: From Colonial Times to the Present.* Santa Barbara, CA: ABC-CLIO, 1991.

Oglesby, Thaddeus K. *Some Truths of History: A Vindication of the South Against the Encyclopedia Britannica and Other Maligners.* Atlanta, GA: Byrd Printing, 1903.

Olcott, Charles. *The Life of William McKinley.* 2 vols. Boston, MA: Houghton Mifflin, 1916.

Olmsted, Frederick Law. *A Journey in the Seaboard Slave States, With Remarks on Their Economy.* New York, NY: Dix and Edwards, 1856.

——. *A Journey Through Texas; or a Saddle-Trip on the Western Frontier.* New York, NY: Dix and Edwards, 1857.

——. *A Journey in the Back Country.* New York, NY: Mason Brothers, 1860.

——. *The Cotton Kingdom: A Traveler's Observations on Cotton and Slavery in the American Slave States.* 2 vols. London, UK: Sampson Low, Son, and Co., 1862.

ORA (full title: *The War of the Rebellion: A Compilation of the Official Records of the Union and Confederate Armies*). 70 vols. Washington, DC: Government Printing Office, 1880.

Ormsby, Robert McKinley. *A History of the Whig Party.* Boston, MA: Crosby, Nichols and Co., 1860.

ORN (full title: *Official Records of the Union and Confederate Navies in the War of the Rebellion*). 30

vols. Washington, DC: Government Printing Office, 1894.

Owsley, Frank Lawrence. *King Cotton Diplomacy: Foreign Relations of the Confederate States of America*. 1931. Chicago, IL: University of Chicago Press, 1959 ed.

Page, Melvin E. (ed.). *Colonialism: An International, Social, Cultural, and Political Encyclopedia*. 2 vols. Santa Barbara, CA: ABC Clio, 2003.

Page, Thomas Nelson. *Robert E. Lee, Man and Soldier*. New York, NY: Charles Scribner's Sons, 1911.

Paine, Thomas. *The Age of Reason: Being an Investigation of True and Fabulous Theology*. New York, NY: G. P. Putnam's Sons, 1890.

Palin, Sarah. *Going Rogue: An American Life*. New York, NY: Harper Collins, 2009.

Palmer, R. R., and Joel Colton. *A History of the Modern World*. 1950. New York, NY: Alfred A. Knopf, 1965 ed.

Patrick, Rembert W. *Jefferson Davis and His Cabinet*. Baton Rouge, LA: Louisiana State University Press, 1944.

Pearson, Henry Greenleaf. *The Life of John A. Andrew, Governor of Massachusetts, 1861-1865*. 2 vols. Boston, MA: Houghton, Mifflin and Co., 1904.

Pendleton, Louis Beauregard. *Alexander H. Stephens*. Philadelphia, PA: George W. Jacobs and Co., 1907.

Peterson, Merrill D. (ed.). *James Madison, A Biography in His Own Words*. (First published posthumously in 1840.) New York, NY: Harper and Row, 1974 ed.

——. (ed.). *Thomas Jefferson: Writings, Autobiography, A Summary View of the Rights of British America, Notes on the State of Virginia, Public Papers, Addresses, Messages and Replies, Miscellany, Letters*. New York, NY: Literary Classics, 1984.

Phillips, Wendell. *Speeches, Letters, and Lectures*. Boston, MA: Lee and Shepard, 1894.

Pickett, William Passmore. *The Negro Problem: Abraham Lincoln's Solution*. New York, NY: G. P. Putnam's Sons, 1909.

Platt, George Washington. *A History of the Republican Party*. Cincinnati, OH: C. J. Krehbiel and Co., 1904.

Pollard, Edward A. *Southern History of the War*. 2 vols. in 1. New York, NY: Charles B. Richardson, 1866.

——. *The Lost Cause*. 1867. Chicago, IL: E. B. Treat, 1890 ed.

——. *The Lost Cause Regained*. New York, NY: G. W. Carlton and Co., 1868.

——. *Life of Jefferson Davis, With a Secret History of the Southern Confederacy, Gathered "Behind the Scenes in Richmond."* Philadelphia, PA: National Publishing Co., 1869.

Porter, Kirk Harold. *National Party Platforms*. New York, NY: Macmillan, 1924.

Potter, David M. *The Impending Crisis: 1848-1861*. New York, NY: Harper and Row, 1976.

Powell, Edward Payson. *Nullification and Secession in the United States: A History of the Six Attempts During the First Century of the Republic*. New York, NY: G. P. Putnam's Sons, 1897.

Rable, George C. *The Confederate Republic: A Revolution Against Politics*. Chapel Hill, NC: University of North Carolina Press, 1994.

Randall, Henry Stephens. *The Life of Thomas Jefferson*. 3 vols. New York, NY: Derby and Jackson, 1858.

Randall, James Garfield. *Lincoln: The Liberal Statesman*. New York, NY: Dodd, Mead and Co., 1947.

Randall, James Garfield, and Richard N. Current. *Lincoln the President: Last Full Measure*. 1955. Urbana, IL: University of Illinois Press, 2000 ed.

Randolph, Thomas Jefferson (ed.). *Memoir, Correspondence, and Miscellanies, from the Papers of Thomas Jefferson*. 4 vols. Charlottesville, VA: F. Carr and Co., 1829.

Ranney, Austin, and Willmoore Kendall. *Democracy and the American Party System*. New York, NY: Harcourt, Brace, and World, 1956.

Ransom, Roger L. *Conflict and Compromise: The Political Economy of Slavery, Emancipation, and the American Civil War*. Cambridge, UK: Cambridge University Press, 1989.

Rawle, William. *A View of the Constitution of the United States of America*. Philadelphia, PA: Philip H. Nicklin, 1829.

Rayner, B. L. *Sketches of the Life, Writings, and Opinions of Thomas Jefferson*. New York, NY: Alfred Francis and William Boardman, 1832.

Reichstein, Andreas. *German Pioneers on the American Frontier: The Wagners in Texas and Illinois*. Denton, TX: University of North Texas Press, 2001.

Remini, Robert V. *The Election of Andrew Jackson*. Philadelphia, PA: J. B. Lippincott Co., 1964.

Remsburg, John B. *Abraham Lincoln: Was He a Christian?* New York, NY: The Truth Seeker Co., 1893.

Reports of Committees of the Senate of the United States (for the Thirty-eighth Congress). Washington, D.C.: Government Printing Office, 1864.

Report of the Joint Committee on Reconstruction (at the First Session, Thirty-ninth Congress). Washington, D.C.: Government Printing Office, 1866.

Reports of Committees of the Senate of the United States (for the Second Session of the Forty-second Congress). Washington, D.C.: Government Printing Office, 1872.

Rhodes, James Ford. *History of the United States from the Compromise of 1850 to the Final Restoration of Home Rule at the South in 1877*. 7 vols. 1895. New York, NY: Macmillan Co., 1907 ed.

Richardson, Heather Cox. *To Make Men Free: A History of the Republican Party*. New York, NY: Basic Books, 2014.

Richardson, James Daniel (ed.). *A Compilation of the Messages and Papers of the Confederacy*. 2 vols. Nashville, TN: United States Publishing Co., 1905.

Richardson, John Anderson. *Richardson's Defense of the South*. Atlanta, GA: A. B. Caldwell, 1914.

Risjord, Norman K. *The Old Republicans: Southern Conservatism in the Age of Jefferson*. New York, NY: Columbia University Press, 1965.

Rives, John (ed.). *Abridgement of the Debates of Congress: From 1789 to 1856* (Vol. 13). New York, NY: D. Appleton and Co., 1860.

Roba, William. *German-Iowa Studies: Selected Essays*. New York, NY: Peter Lang, 2004.

Roberts, Paul M. *United States History: Review Text*. 1966. New York, NY: Amsco School Publications, 1970 ed.

Robinson, William A. *Jeffersonian Democracy in New England*. New Haven, CT: Yale University Press, 1916.

Rosenbaum, Robert A., and Douglas Brinkley (eds.). *The Penguin Encyclopedia of American History*. New York, NY: Viking, 2003.

Rossiter, Clinton. *Parties and Politics in America*. Ithaca, NY: Cornell University Press, 1964.

Rothman, David. *Politics and Power: The United States Senate, 1869-1901*. Cambridge, MA: Harvard University Press, 1966.

Rouse, Adelaide Louise (ed.). *National Documents: State Papers So Arranged as to Illustrate the Growth of Our Country From 1606 to the Present Day*. New York, NY: Unit Book Publishing Co., 1906.

Rove, Karl. *The Triumph of William McKinley: Why the Election of 1896 Still Matters*. New York, NY: Simon and Schuster, 2015.

Rowan, Steven (ed.). *Memoirs of a Nobody: The Missouri Years of an Austrian Radical, 1849-1866*. St. Louis, MO: Missouri Historical Society Press, 1997.

Rowland, Dunbar (ed.). *Jefferson Davis, Constitutionalist: His Letters, Papers, and Speeches*. 10 vols. Jackson, MS: Mississippi Department of Archives and History, 1923.

Rubenzer, Steven J., and Thomas R. Faschingbauer. *Personality, Character, and Leadership in the White House: Psychologists Assess the Presidents*. Dulles, VA: Brassey's, 2004.

Rubino, Rich M. *The Political Bible of Little Known Facts in American Politics*. Cambridge, MA: self-published.

Ruffin, Edmund. *The Diary of Edmund Ruffin: Toward Independence: October 1856-April 1861*. Baton Rouge, LA: Louisiana State University Press, 1972.

Russell, Phillips. *Emerson: The Wisest American*. New York, NY: Blue Ribbon, 1929.

Rutherford, Mildred Lewis. *Four Addresses*. Birmingham, AL: The Mildred Rutherford Historical Circle, 1916.

——. *A True Estimate of Abraham Lincoln and Vindication of the South*. N.p., n.d.

——. *Truths of History: A Fair, Unbiased, Impartial, Unprejudiced and Conscientious Study of History*. Athens, GA: n.p., 1920.

——. *The South Must Have Her Rightful Place In History*. Athens, GA: n.p., 1923.

Rutland, Robert Allen. *The Birth of the Bill of Rights, 1776-1791*. 1955. Boston, MA: Northeastern University Press, 1991 ed.

Sachsman, David B., S. Kittrell Rushing, and Roy Morris, Jr. (eds.). *Words at War: The Civil War and American Journalism*. West Lafayette, IN: Purdue University Press, 2008.

Samuel, Bunford. *Secession and Constitutional Liberty*. 2 vols. New York, NY: Neale Publishing, 1920.

Sandburg, Carl. *Abraham Lincoln: The War Years*. 4 vols. New York, NY: Harcourt, Brace and World, 1939.

Sargent, F. W. *England, the United States, and the Southern Confederacy*. London, UK: Sampson Low, Son, and Co., 1863.

Sarna, Jonathan D., and Benjamin Shapell. *Lincoln and the Jews: A History*. New York, NY: St. Martin's Press, 2015.

Schachner, Nathan. *Aaron Burr*. Cranbury, NJ: A. S. Barnes, 1961.

Schapiro, Leonard. *The Communist Party of the Soviet Union*. New York, NY: Alfred A Knopf, 1960.

Schlüter, Herman. *Lincoln, Labor and Slavery: A Chapter from the Social History of America*. New York, NY: Socialist Literature Co., 1913.

Schurz, Carl. *Life of Henry Clay*. 2 vols. 1887. Boston, MA: Houghton, Mifflin and Co., 1899 ed.

Schwartz, Barry. *Abraham Lincoln and the Forge of National Memory*. Chicago, IL: University of Chicago Press, 2000.

Scott, James Brown. *James Madison's Notes of Debates in the Federal Convention of 1787, and Their Relation to a More Perfect Society of Nations*. New York, NY: Oxford University Press, 1918.

Seabrook, Lochlainn. *Abraham Lincoln: The Southern View*. 2007. Franklin, TN: Sea Raven Press, 2013 ed.

——. *A Rebel Born: A Defense of Nathan Bedford Forrest*. 2010. Franklin, TN: Sea Raven Press, 2011 ed.

——. *Everything You Were Taught About the Civil War is Wrong, Ask a Southerner!* 2010. Franklin, TN: Sea Raven Press, revised 2014 ed.

——. *The Quotable Jefferson Davis: Selections From the Writings and Speeches of the Confederacy's First President*. Franklin, TN: Sea Raven Press, 2011.

——. *Lincolnology: The Real Abraham Lincoln Revealed In His Own Words*. Franklin, TN: Sea Raven Press, 2011.

——. *The Unquotable Abraham Lincoln: The President's Quotes They Don't Want You To Know!* Franklin, TN: Sea Raven Press, 2011.

——. *Honest Jeff and Dishonest Abe: A Southern Children's Guide to the Civil War*. Franklin, TN: Sea Raven Press, 2012 Sesquicentennial Civil War Edition.

——. *The Great Impersonator: 99 Reasons to Dislike Abraham Lincoln*. Spring Hill, TN: Sea Raven Press, 2012.

——. *The Alexander H. Stephens Reader: Excerpts From the Works of a Confederate Founding Father.* Spring Hill, TN: Sea Raven Press, 2013.

——. *The Articles of Confederation Explained: A Clause-by-Clause Study of America's First Constitution.* Spring Hill, TN: Sea Raven Press, 2014.

——. *Everything You Were Taught About American Slavery War is Wrong, Ask a Southerner!* Spring Hill, TN: Sea Raven Press, 2015.

——. *Confederacy 101: Amazing Facts You Never Knew About America's Oldest Political Tradition.* Spring Hill, TN: Sea Raven Press, 2015.

——. *Slavery 101: Amazing Facts You Never Knew About America's "Peculiar Institution."* Spring Hill, TN: Sea Raven Press, 2015.

——. *The Great Yankee Coverup: What the North Doesn't Want You to Know About Lincoln's War!* Spring Hill, TN: Sea Raven Press, 2015.

——. *Confederate Flag Facts: What Every American Should Know About Dixie's Southern Cross.* Spring Hill, TN: Sea Raven Press, 2016.

——. *Nathan Bedford Forrest and the Ku Klux Klan: Yankee Myth, Confederate Fact.* Spring Hill, TN: Sea Raven Press, 2016.

——. *Everything You Were Taught About African-Americans and the Civil War is Wrong, Ask a Southerner!* Spring Hill, TN: Sea Raven Press, 2016.

——. *Lincoln's War: The Real Cause, the Real Winner, the Real Loser.* Spring Hill, TN: Sea Raven Press, 2016.

——. *The Unholy Crusade: Lincoln's Legacy of Destruction in the American South.* Spring Hill, TN: Sea Raven Press, 2017.

Seward, William Henry. *Life and Public Services of John Quincy Adams, Sixth President of the United States.* New York, NY: Miller, Orton and Mulligan, 1856.

Shenkman, Richard. *Legends, Lies and Cherished Myths of American History.* New York, NY: Perennial, 1988.

Shenkman, Richard, and Kurt Edward Reiger. *One-Night Stands with American History: Odd, Amusing, and Little-Known Incidents.* 1980. New York, NY: Perennial, 2003 ed.

Sherman, William Tecumseh. *Memoirs of General William T. Sherman.* 2 vols. 1875. New York, NY: D. Appleton and Co., 1891 ed.

Shirer, William L. *The Rise and Fall of the Third Reich: A History of Nazi Germany.* New York, NY: Simon and Schuster, 1960.

Shorto, Russell. *Thomas Jefferson and the American Ideal.* Hauppauge, NY: Barron's, 1987.

Shotwell, Walter G. *Life of Charles Sumner.* New York, NY: Thomas Y. Crowell and Co., 1910.

Silverman, Jason H. *Lincoln and the Immigrant.* Carbondale, IL: Southern Illinois University Press, 2015.

Simkins, Francis Butler. *A History of the South.* New York, NY: Random House, 1972.

Simmons, Henry E. *A Concise Encyclopedia of the Civil War.* New York, NY: Bonanza Books, 1965.

1. Simon, John Y. (ed.). *The Papers of Ulysses S. Grant.* 9 vols. Carbondale, IL: Southern Illinois University Press, 1982.

Simpson, Lewis P. (ed.). *I'll Take My Stand: The South and the Agrarian Tradition.* 1930. Baton Rouge, LA: University of Louisiana Press, 1977 ed.

Skidmore, Max J. *Presidential Performance: A Comprehensive Review.* Jefferson, NC: McFarland and Co., 2004.

Smelser, Marshall. *American Colonial and Revolutionary History.* 1950. New York, NY: Barnes and Noble, 1966 ed.

——. *The Democratic Republic, 1801-1815.* New York, NY: Harper and Row, 1968.

Smith, Emma Peters, David Saville Muzzey, and Minnie Lloyd. *World History: The Struggle for Civilization.* Boston, MA: Ginn and Co., 1946.

Smith, Hedrick. *Reagan: The Man, The President.* Oxford, UK: Pergamon Press, 1980.

Smith, James Allen. *The Spirit of American Government: A Study of the Constitution: Its Origin, Influence and Relation to Democracy.* New York, NY: Macmillan Co., 1907.

Smith, James Morton. *Freedom's Fetters: The Alien and Sedition Laws and American Civil Liberties.* Ithaca, NY: Cornell University Press, 1956.

Smith, Page. *America Enters the World: A People's History of the Progressive Era and World War I.* New York, NY: McGraw-Hill, 1985.

Smucker, Samuel M. *The Life and Times of Thomas Jefferson.* Philadelphia, PA: J. W. Bradley, 1859.

Snay, Mitchell. *Horace Greeley and the Politics of Reform in Nineteenth-Century America.* Lanham, MD: Rowman and Littlefield, 2011.

Snider, Denton J. *Lincoln at Richmond: A Dramatic Epos of the Civil War.* St. Louis, MO: Sigma, 1914.

Sobel, Robert (ed.). *Biographical Directory of the United States Executive Branch, 1774-1898.* Westport, CT: Greenwood Press, 1990.

Sorauf, Frank J. *Political Parties in the American System.* Boston, MA: Little, Brown and Co., 1964.

Sorrel, Gilbert Moxley. *Recollections of a Confederate Staff Officer.* New York, NY: Neale Publishing Co., 1905.

Sotheran, Charles. *Horace Greeley and Other Pioneers of American Socialism.* 1892. New York, NY: Mitchell Kennerley, 1915 ed.

Southern Historical Society Papers, Vol. 14, January-December, 1886. Richmond, VA: Rev. J. William Jones, 1886.

Spaeth, Harold J., and Edward Conrad Smith. *The Constitution of the United States.* 1936. New York, NY: Harper Collins, 1991 ed.

Spargo, John. *Karl Marx: His Life and Work.* New York, NY: B. W. Huebsch, 1910.

Sparks, Jared. *The Life of Gouverneur Morris, With Selections From His Correspondence and Miscellaneous Papers.* 3 vols. Boston, MA: Gray and Bowen, 1832.

——. *The Works of Benjamin Franklin.* 10 vols. Chicago, IL: Townsend Mac Coun, 1882.

Speer, Albert. *Inside the Third Reich.* 1969. New York, NY: Avon, 1971 ed.

Spence, James. *On the Recognition of the Southern Confederation.* Ithaca, NY: Cornell University Library, 1862.

Spingola, Deanna. *The Ruling Elite: A Study in Imperialism, Genocide and Emancipation.* Bloomington, ID: Trafford, 2011.

Spooner, Lysander. *No Treason* (only Numbers 1, 2, and 6 were published). Boston, MA: Lysander Spooner, 1867-1870.

Sprout, John G. *"The Best Men": Liberal Reformers in the Gilded Age.* New York, NY: Oxford University Press, 1968.

Stanton, Elizabeth Cady, Susan B. Anthony, and Matilda Joslyn Gage (eds.). *History of Woman Suffrage.* 2 vols. New York, NY: Fowler and Wells, 1881.

Stanwood, Edward. *A History of the Presidency: From 1788 to 1897.* Boston, MA: Houghton Mifflin Co., 1912.

Starr, John W., Jr. *Lincoln and the Railroads: A Biographical Study.* New York, NY: Dodd, Mead and Co., 1927.

Staudenraus, P. J. *The African Colonization Movement, 1816-1865.* New York, NY: Columbia University Press, 1961.

Stavrianos, Leften Stavros. *The World Since 1500: A Global History.* 1966. Englewood Cliffs, NJ: Prentice Hall, 1991 ed.

Stebbins, Rufus Phineas. *An Historical Address Delivered At the Centennial Celebration of the Incorporation of the Town of Wilbraham, June 15, 1863.* Boston, MA: George C. Rand and

Avery, 1864.

Stedman, Edmund Clarence, and Ellen Mackay Hutchinson (eds.). *A Library of American Literature From the Earliest Settlement to the Present Time.* 10 vols. New York, NY: Charles L. Webster and Co., 1888.

Steele, Joel Dorman, and Esther Baker Steele. *Barnes' Popular History of the United States of America.* New York, NY: A. S. Barnes and Co., 1904.

Steiner, Bernard. *The History of Slavery in Connecticut.* Baltimore, MD: Johns Hopkins University Press, 1893.

Steiner, Lewis Henry. *Report of Lewis H. Steiner: Inspector of the Sanitary Commission, Containing a Diary Kept During the Rebel Occupation of Frederick, MD, September, 1862.* New York, NY: Anson D. F. Randolph, 1862.

Stephens, Alexander Hamilton. *Speech of Mr. Stephens, of Georgia, on the War and Taxation.* Washington, D.C.: J & G. Gideon, 1848.

——. *A Constitutional View of the Late War Between the States; Its Causes, Character, Conduct and Results.* 2 vols. Philadelphia, PA: National Publishing, Co., 1870.

——. *Recollections of Alexander H. Stephens: His Diary Kept When a Prisoner at Fort Warren, Boston Harbour, 1865.* New York, NY: Doubleday, Page, and Co., 1910.

Stephenson, Nathaniel Wright. *Lincoln: An Account of His Personal Life, Especially of Its Springs of Action as Revealed and Deepened by the Ordeal of War.* Indianapolis, IN: Bobbs-Merrill, 1922.

Sterling, Dorothy (ed.). *Speak Out in Thunder Tones: Letters and Other Writings by Black Northerners, 1787-1865.* 1973. Cambridge, MA: Da Capo, 1998 ed.

Stern, Philip Van Doren (ed.). *The Life and Writings of Abraham Lincoln.* 1940. New York, NY: Modern Library, 2000 ed.

Stevens, Harry R. *The Early Jackson Party in Ohio.* Durham, NC: Duke University Press, 1957.

Stevenson, Louise L. *Lincoln in the Atlantic World.* New York, NY: Cambridge University Press, 2015.

Stewart, Donald H. *The Opposition Press of the Federalist Period.* Albany, NY: State University of New York Press, 1969.

Stites, Bill. *The Republican Party in the Late 1800s: A Changing Role for American Government.* New York, NY: Rosen Publishing, 2004.

Stonebraker, J. Clarence. *The Unwritten South: Cause, Progress and Results of the Civil War - Relics of Hidden Truth After Forty Years.* Seventh ed., n.p., 1908.

Stovall, Pleasant A. *Robert Toombs: Statesman, Speaker, Soldier, Sage.* New York, NY: Cassell Publishing, 1892.

Strode, Hudson. *Jefferson Davis: American Patriot.* 3 vols. New York, NY: Harcourt, Brace and World, 1955, 1959, 1964.

Sturge, Joseph. *A Visit to the United States in 1841.* London, UK: Hamilton, Adams, and Co., 1842.

Summers, Mark W. *The Plundering Generation: Corruption and the Crisis of the Union, 1849-1861.* New York, NY: Oxford University Press, 1988.

Sumner, Charles. *The Crime Against Kansas: The Apologies for the Crime - The True Remedy.* Boston, MA: John P. Jewett, 1856.

Swift, Lindsay. *Brook Farm: Its Members, Scholars, and Visitors.* New York, NY: Macmillan, 1900.

Sword, Wiley. *The Confederacy's Last Hurrah: Spring Hill, Franklin, and Nashville.* New York, NY: HarperCollins, 1992.

——. *Southern Invincibility: A History of the Confederate Heart.* New York, NY: St. Martin's Press, 1999.

Sydnor, Charles S. *American Revolutionaries in the Making.* New York, NY: Macmillan, 1965.

Tagg, Larry. *The Unpopular Mr. Lincoln: The Story of America's Most Reviled President.* New York, NY: Savas Beatie, 2009.

Tarbell, Ida Minerva. *The Life of Abraham Lincoln.* 4 vols. New York, NY: Lincoln History Society, 1895-1900.

Tatalovich, Raymond, and Byron W. Daynes. *Presidential Power in the United States.* Monterey, CA: Brooks/Cole, 1984.

Taylor, Richard. *Destruction and Reconstruction: Personal Experiences of the Late War in the United States.* New York, NY: D. Appleton, 1879.

Taylor, Susie King. *Reminiscences of My Life in Camp With the 33rd United States Colored Troops Late 1st S. C. Volunteers.* Boston, MA: Susie King Taylor, 1902.

Taylor, Walter Herron. *General Lee: His Campaigns in Virginia, 1861-1865, With Personal Reminiscences.* Norfolk, VA: Nusbaum Book and News Co., 1906.

Tenney, William Jewett. *The Military and Naval History of the Rebellion in the United States.* New York, NY: D. Appleton and Co., 1865.

Terkel, Studs. *Hard Times: An Oral History of the Great Depression.* New York, NY: Avon, 1970.

Testimony Taken By the Joint Select Committee to Inquire Into the Condition of Affairs in the Late Insurrectionary States. 13 vols. Washington, D.C.: Government Printing Office, 1872.

The Civil War Society. *Civil War Battles: An Illustrated Encyclopedia.* 1997. New York, NY: Gramercy, 1999 ed.

——. *The Civil War Society's Encyclopedia of the Civil War.* New York, NY: Wings Books, 1997.

Thompson, Arthur R. *To the Victor Go the Myths and Monuments: The History of the First 100 Years of the War Against God and the Constitution, 1776-1876, and Its Modern Impact.* Appleton, WI: American Opinion Foundation Publishing, 2016.

Thompson, Holland. *The New South: A Chronicle of Social and Industrial Evolution.* New Haven, CT: Yale University Press, 1920.

Tinkcom, H. M. *Republicans and Federalists in Pennsylvania, 1790-1801.* Harrisburg, PA: Pennsylvania Historical and Museum Commission, 1950.

The American Annual Cyclopedia and Register of Important Events of the Year 1861. New York, NY: D. Appleton and Co., 1868.

The American Annual Cyclopedia and Register of Important Events of the Year 1862. New York, NY: D. Appleton and Co., 1869.

The American Annual Cyclopedia and Register of Important Events of the Year 1863. New York, NY: D. Appleton and Co., 1864.

The Collegiate Encyclopedia. 1963. New York, NY: Grolier, 1970 ed.

The Congressional Globe, Containing Sketches of the Debates and Proceedings of the First Session of the Twenty-Eighth Congress (Vol. 13). Washington, D.C.: The Globe, 1844.

The Great Issue to be Decided in November Next: Shall the Constitution and the Union Stand or Fall, Shall Sectionalism Triumph? Washington, D.C.: National Democratic Executive Committee, 1860.

The National Almanac and Annual Record for the Year 1863. Philadelphia, PA: George W. Childs, 1863.

The Oxford English Dictionary. Compact edition, 2 vols. 1928. Oxford, UK: Oxford University Press, 1979 ed.

The Quarterly Review (Vol. 111). London, UK: John Murray, 1862.

The Standard American Encyclopedia. 1916. Chicago, IL: Standard American Corp., 1937 ed.

The World Book Encyclopedia. 1928. Chicago, IL: Field Enterprises Educational Corp., 1966 ed.

Thompson, Robert Means, and Richard Wainwright (eds.). *Confidential Correspondence of Gustavus Vasa Fox, Assistant Secretary of the Navy, 1861-1865.* 2 vols. 1918. New York, NY: Naval History Society, 1920 ed.

Thorndike, Rachel Sherman (ed.). *The Sherman Letters.* New York, NY: Charles Scribner's Sons, 1894.

Thornton, Brian. *101 Things You Didn't Know About Lincoln: Loves and Losses, Political Power Plays,*

White House Hauntings. Avon, MA: Adams Media, 2006.

Thornton, Gordon. *The Southern Nation: The New Rise of the Old South*. Gretna, LA: Pelican Publishing Co., 2000.

Thornton, John. *Africa and Africans in the Making of the Atlantic World, 1400-1800*. 1992. Cambridge, UK: Cambridge University Press, 1999 ed.

Thornton, Mark, and Robert B. Ekelund, Jr. *Tariffs, Blockades, and Inflation: The Economics of the Civil War*. Wilmington, DE: Scholarly Resources, 2004.

Tilley, John Shipley. *Lincoln Takes Command*. 1941. Nashville, TN: Bill Coats Limited, 1991 ed.

——. *Facts the Historians Leave Out: A Confederate Primer*. 1951. Nashville, TN: Bill Coats Limited, 1999 ed.

Tocqueville, Alexis de. *Democracy in America*. 2 vols. New York, NY: George Adlard, 1839.

Toland, John. *Adolf Hitler*. 1976. New York, NY: Ballantine, 1987 ed.

Tourgee, Albion W. *A Fool's Errand By One of the Fools*. London, UK: George Routledge and Sons, 1883.

Townsend, Mary Bobbitt. *Yankee Warhorse: A Biography of Major General Peter Osterhaus*. Columbia, MO: University of Missouri Press, 2010.

Tracy, Gilbert A. (ed.). *Uncollected Letters of Abraham Lincoln*. Boston, MA: Houghton Mifflin Co., 1917.

Trumbull, Lyman. *Speech of Honorable Lyman Trumbull, of Illinois, at a Mass Meeting in Chicago, August 7, 1858*. Washington, D.C.: Buell and Blanchard, 1858.

Tucker, George. *The Life of Thomas Jefferson, Third President of the United States*. 2 vols. London, UK: Charles Knight and Co., 1837.

Turner, Frederick J. *Rise of the New West, 1819-1829*. New York, NY: Collier-Macmillan, 1962.

Turner, Lynn W. *William Plumer of New Hampshire*. Chapel Hill, NC: University of North Carolina Press, 1962.

Tyler, Lyon Gardiner. *The Letters and Times of the Tylers*. 3 vols. Williamsburg, VA: N.p., 1896.

——. *Propaganda in History*. Richmond, VA: Richmond Press, 1920.

——. *The Gray Book: A Confederate Catechism*. Columbia, TN: Gray Book Committee, SCV, 1935.

Unger, Irwin. *These United States: The Questions of Our Past, Vol. 2: Since 1865*. 1978. Englewood Cliffs, NJ: Prentice Hall, 1992 ed.

Upshur, Abel Parker. *A Brief Enquiry Into the True Nature and Character of Our Federal Government*. Philadelphia, PA: John Campbell, 1863.

Vallandigham, Clement Laird. *Speeches, Arguments, Addresses, and Letters of Clement L. Vallandigham*. New York, NY: J. Walter and Co., 1864.

Van Buren, G. M. *Abraham Lincoln's Pen and Voice: Being a Complete Compilation of His Letters, Civil, Political, and Military*. Cincinnati, OH: Robert Clarke and Co., 1890.

Van Buren, Martin. *Inquiry Into the Origin and Course of Political Parties in the United States*. New York, NY: Hurd and Houghton, 1867.

Vandenberg, Arthur Hendrick. *The Greatest American: Alexander Hamilton*. New York, NY: G. P. Putnam's Sons, 1922.

Van Loon, Hendrik Willem. *The Story of America*. 1927. Cleveland, OH: The World Publishing Co., 1942 ed.

Varhola, Michael O. *Life in Civil War America*. Cincinnati, OH: Family Tree Books, 1999.

Ver Steeg, Clarence Lester, and Richard Hofstadter. *A People and a Nation*. New York, NY: Harper and Row, 1977.

Villard, Henry. *Memoirs of Henry Villard, Journalist and Financier, 1835-1900*. 2 vols. Boston, MA: Houghton, Mifflin and Co., 1904.

Wagstaff, Henry M. (ed.). *The Papers of John Steele*. 2 vols. Raleigh, NC: Edwards and Broughton Printing Co., 1924.

Walters, Raymond, Jr. *Albert Gallatin: Jeffersonian Financier and Diplomat*. Pittsburgh, PA:

University of Pittsburgh Press, 1969.

Ward, John William. *Andrew Jackson: Symbol for an Age*. 1953. London, UK: Oxford University Press, 1955 ed.

Waring, George Edward, Jr. *Whip and Spur*. New York, NY: Doubleday and McClure, 1897.

Warner, Ezra J. *Generals in Gray: Lives of the Confederate Commanders*. 1959. Baton Rouge, LA: Louisiana State University Press, 1989 ed.

——. *Generals in Blue: Lives of the Union Commanders*. 1964. Baton Rouge, LA: Louisiana State University Press, 2006 ed.

Washington, Booker T. *Up From Slavery: An Autobiography*. 1901. Garden City, NY: Doubleday, Page and Co., 1919 ed.

Washington, Henry Augustine. (ed.). *The Writings of Thomas Jefferson: Being His Autobiography, Correspondence, Reports, Messages, Addresses, and Other Writings, Official and Private*. 9 vols. New York, NY: John C. Riker, 1854.

Watson, Harry L. *Andrew Jackson vs. Henry Clay: Democracy and Development in Antebellum America*. New York, NY: St. Martin's Press, 1998.

Watts, Peter. *A Dictionary of the Old West*. 1977. New York, NY: Promontory Press, 1987 ed.

Wayne, Stephen J., G. Calvin MacKenzie, and Richard L. Cole. *Conflict and Consensus in American Politics*. Belmont, CA: Thomson Wadsworth, 2007.

Weintraub, Max. *The Blue Book of American History*. New York, NY: Regents Publishing Co., 1960.

Welles, Gideon. *Diary of Gideon Welles, Secretary of the Navy Under Lincoln and Johnson* (Vol. 1). Boston, MA: Houghton Mifflin, 1911.

Wells, H. G. *The Outline of History: Being a Plain History of Life and Mankind*. 2 vols. 1920. Garden City, NY: Garden City Books, 1961 ed.

West, Willis Mason (ed.). *A Source Book in American History to 1787*. Boston, MA: Allyn and Bacon, 1913.

White, Leonard D. *The Federalists: A Study in Administrative History*. New York, NY: Macmillan, 1956.

——. *The Jeffersonians: A Study in Administrative History, 1801-1829*. New York, NY: Macmillan, 1959.

Wilbur, Henry Watson. *President Lincoln's Attitude Towards Slavery and Emancipation: With a Review of Events Before and Since the Civil War*. Philadelphia, PA: W. H. Jenkins, 1914.

Wiley, Bell Irvin. *Southern Negroes: 1861-1865*. 1938. New Haven, CT: Yale University Press, 1969 ed.

——. *The Life of Johnny Reb: The Common Soldier of the Confederacy*. 1943. Baton Rouge, LA: Louisiana State University Press, 1978 ed.

——. *The Plain People of the Confederacy*. 1943. Columbia, SC: University of South Carolina, 2000 ed.

——. *The Life of Billy Yank: The Common Soldier of the Union*. 1952. Baton Rouge, LA: Louisiana State University Press, 2001 ed.

Wilkens, J. Steven. *America: The First 350 Years*. Monroe, LA: Covenant Publications, 1998.

Williams, Charles Richard. *The Life of Rutherford Birchard Hayes, Nineteenth President of the United States*. 2 vols. Boston, MA: Houghton Mifflin Co., 1914.

Williams, James. *The South Vindicated*. London, UK: Longman, Green, Longman, Roberts, and Green, 1862.

Williams, Richard Hal. *The Democratic Party and California Politics, 1880-1896*. Stanford, CA: Stanford University Press, 1973.

——. *Realigning America: McKinley, Bryan and the Remarkable Election of 1896*. Lawrence, KS: University Press of Kansas, 2010.

Williamson, Chilton. *American Suffrage from Property to Democracy, 1760-1860*. Princeton, NJ:

Princeton University Press, 1960.

Wilson, Clyde N. *Why the South Will Survive: Fifteen Southerners Look at Their Region a Half Century After I'll Take My Stand*. Athens, GA: University of Georgia Press, 1981.

——. (ed.) *The Essential Calhoun: Selections From Writings, Speeches, and Letters*. New Brunswick, NJ: Transaction Publishers, 1991.

——. *A Defender of Southern Conservatism: M.E. Bradford and His Achievements*. Columbia, MO: University of Missouri Press, 1999.

——. *From Union to Empire: Essays in the Jeffersonian Tradition*. Columbia, SC: The Foundation for American Education, 2003.

——. *Defending Dixie: Essays in Southern History and Culture*. Columbia, SC: The Foundation for American Education, 2005.

Wilson, James Harrison. *The Life of Charles A. Dana*. New York, NY: Harper and Brothers, 1907.

Wilson, William Lyne (ed.). *The National Democratic Party: Its History, Principles, Achievements, and Aims*. Philadelphia, PA: Hubbard Brothers, 1889.

Wilson, Woodrow. *Division and Reunion: 1829-1889*. 1893. New York, NY: Longmans, Green, and Co., 1908 ed.

——. *A History of the American People*. 5 vols. 1902. New York, NY: Harper and Brothers, 1918 ed.

Winsor, Justin (ed.). *Narrative and Critical History of America*. 8 vols. Boston, MA: Houghton, Mifflin and Co., 1884.

Wittke, Carl Frederick. *Refugees of Revolution: The German Forty-Eighters in America*. Philadelphia, PA: University of Pennsylvania Press, 1952.

——. *The German-Language Press in America*. Lexington, KY: University Press of Kentucky, 1957.

Wolfe, John H. *Jeffersonian Democracy in South Carolina*. Chapel Hill, NC: University of North Carolina Press, 1940.

Wood, W. J. *Civil War Generalship: The Art of Command*. 1997. New York, NY: Da Capo Press, 2000 ed.

Woodburn, James Albert. *The Life of Thaddeus Stevens*. Indianapolis, IN: Bobbs-Merrill, 1913.

Woods, Thomas E., Jr. *The Politically Incorrect Guide to American History*. Washington, D.C.: Regnery, 2004.

Woodward, William E. *Meet General Grant*. 1928. New York, NY: Liveright Publishing, 1946 ed.

Woodworth, Steven E. *Jefferson Davis and His Generals: The Failure of Confederate Command in the West*. Lawrence, KS: University Press of Kansas, 1990.

Young, Alfred. *The Democratic Republicans of New York: The Origins, 1763-1797*. Chapel Hill, NC: University of North Carolina Press, 1967.

Young, James Sterling. *The Washington Community, 1800-1828*. New York, NY: Columbia University Press, 1966.

Young, John Russell. *Around the World With General Grant*. 2 vols. New York, NY: American News Co., 1879.

Zall, Paul M. (ed.). *Lincoln on Lincoln*. Lexington, KY: University Press of Kentucky, 1999.

Zavodnyik, Peter. *The Age of Strict Construction: A History of the Growth of Federal Power, 1789-1861*. Washington, D.C.: Catholic University of America Press, 2007.

Zinn, Howard. *A People's History of the United States: 1492-Present*. 1980. New York, NY: Harper Collins, 1995.

Zucker, A. E. (ed.). *The Forty-Eighters: Political Refugees of the German Revolution of 1848*. New York, NY: Columbia University Press, 1950.

Zuczek, Richard (ed.). *Encyclopedia of the Reconstruction Era*. 2 vols. Westport, CT: Greenwood Press, 2006.

INDEX

MEET THE AUTHOR

LOCHLAINN SEABROOK, a neo-Victorian, is a well respected man of letters, a Kentucky Colonel, and the winner of the prestigious Jefferson Davis Historical Gold Medal for his "masterpiece," *A Rebel Born: A Defense of Nathan Bedford Forrest*. A classic littérateur and an unreconstructed Southern historian, he is an award-winning author, Civil War scholar, Bible authority, and a traditional Southern Agrarian of Scottish, English, Irish, Dutch, Welsh, German, and Italian extraction.

A child prodigy, Seabrook is today a true Renaissance Man whose occupational titles also include encyclopedist, lexicographer, musician, artist, graphic designer, genealogist, photographer, and award-winning poet. Also a songwriter and a screenwriter, he has a 40 year background in historical nonfiction writing and is a member of the Sons of Confederate Veterans, the Civil War Trust, and the National Grange.

Known to his many fans as the "voice of the traditional South," due to similarities in their writing styles, ideas, and literary works, Seabrook is also often referred to as the "new Shelby Foote," the "Southern Joseph Campbell," and the "American Robert Graves" (his English cousin). Seabrook coined the terms "South-shaming" and "Lincolnian liberalism," and holds the world's record for writing the most books on Nathan Bedford Forrest: nine. In addition, Seabrook is the first Civil War scholar to connect the early American nickname for the U.S., "The Confederate States of America," with the Southern Confederacy that arose eight decades later, and the first to note that in 1860 the party platforms of the two major political parties were the opposite of what they are today (Victorian Democrats were conservatives, Victorian Republicans were liberals).

Above, Colonel Lochlainn Seabrook, "the voice of the traditional South," award-winning Civil War scholar and unreconstructed Southern historian. America's most popular and prolific pro-South author, his many books have introduced hundreds of thousands to the truth about the War for Southern Independence. He coined the phrase "South-shaming" and holds the world's record for writing the most books on Nathan Bedford Forrest: nine.

The grandson of an Appalachian coal-mining family, Seabrook is a seventh-generation Kentuckian, co-chair of the Jent/Gent Family Committee (Kentucky), founder and director of the Blakeney Family Tree Project, and a board member of the Friends of Colonel Benjamin E. Caudill. Seabrook's literary works have been endorsed by leading authorities, museum curators, award-winning historians, bestselling authors, celebrities, noted scientists, well regarded educators, TV show hosts and producers, renowned military artists, esteemed Southern organizations, and distinguished academicians from around the world.

Seabrook has authored over 50 popular adult books on the American Civil War, American and international slavery, the U.S. Confederacy (1781), the Southern Confederacy (1861), religion, theology, thealogy, Jesus, the Bible, the Apocrypha, the Law of Attraction, alternative health, spirituality, ghost stories, the paranormal, ufology, social issues, and cross-cultural studies of the family and marriage. His Confederate biographies, pro-South studies, genealogical monographs, family histories, military encyclopedias, self-help guides, and etymological dictionaries have received wide acclaim.

Seabrook's eight children's books include a Southern guide to the Civil War, a biography of Nathan Bedford Forrest, a dictionary of religion and myth, a rewriting of the King Arthur legend (which reinstates the original pre-Christian motifs), two bedtime stories for preschoolers, a naturalist's guidebook to owls, a worldwide look at the family, and an examination of the Near-Death Experience.

Of blue-blooded Southern stock through his Kentucky, Tennessee, Virginia, West Virginia, and North Carolina ancestors, he is a direct descendant of European royalty via his 6th great-grandfather, the Earl of Oxford, after which London's famous Harley Street is named. Among his celebrated male Celtic ancestors is Robert the Bruce, King of Scotland, Seabrook's 22nd great-grandfather. The 21st great-grandson of Edward I "Longshanks" Plantagenet), King of England, Seabrook is a thirteenth-generation Southerner through his descent from the colonists of Jamestown, Virginia (1607).

The 2nd, 3rd, and 4th great-grandson of dozens of Confederate soldiers, one of his closest connections to Lincoln's War is through his 3rd great-grandfather, Elias

(Photo © Lochlainn Seabrook)

Jent, Sr., who fought for the Confederacy in the Thirteenth Cavalry Kentucky under Seabrook's 2nd cousin, Colonel Benjamin E. Caudill. The Thirteenth, also known as "Caudill's Army," fought in numerous conflicts, including the Battles of Saltville, Gladsville, Mill Cliff, Poor Fork, Whitesburg, and Leatherwood.

Seabrook is a direct descendant of the families of Alexander H. Stephens, John Singleton Mosby, William Giles Harding, and Edmund Winchester Rucker, and is related to the following Confederates and other 18th- and 19th-Century luminaries: Robert E. Lee, Stephen Dill Lee, Stonewall Jackson, Nathan Bedford Forrest, James Longstreet, John Hunt Morgan, Jeb Stuart, Pierre G. T. Beauregard (approved the Confederate Battle Flag design), George W. Gordon, John Bell Hood, Alexander Peter Stewart, Arthur M. Manigault, Joseph Manigault, Charles Scott Venable, Thornton A. Washington, John A. Washington, Abraham Buford, Edmund W. Pettus, Theodrick "Tod" Carter, John B. Womack, John H. Winder, Gideon J. Pillow, States Rights Gist, Henry R. Jackson, John Lawton Seabrook, John C. Breckinridge, Leonidas Polk, Zachary Taylor, Sarah Knox Taylor (first wife of Jefferson Davis), Richard Taylor, Davy Crockett, Daniel Boone, Meriwether Lewis (of the Lewis and Clark Expedition)

Andrew Jackson, James K. Polk, Abram Poindexter Maury (founder of Franklin, TN), Zebulon Vance, Thomas Jefferson, Edmund Jennings Randolph, George Wythe Randolph (grandson of Jefferson), Felix K. Zollicoffer, Fitzhugh Lee, Nathaniel F. Cheairs, Jesse James, Frank James, Robert Brank Vance, Charles Sidney Winder, John W. McGavock, Caroline E. (Winder) McGavock, David Harding McGavock, Lysander McGavock, James Randal McGavock, Randal William McGavock, Francis McGavock, Emily McGavock, William Henry F. Lee, Lucius E. Polk, Minor Meriwether (husband of noted pro-South author Elizabeth Avery Meriwether), Ellen Bourne Tynes (wife of Forrest's chief of artillery, Captain John W. Morton), South Carolina Senators Preston Smith Brooks and Andrew Pickens Butler, and famed South Carolina diarist Mary Chesnut.

Seabrook's modern day cousins include: Patrick J. Buchanan (conservative author), Cindy Crawford (model), Shelby Lee Adams (Letcher Co., Kentucky, photographer), Bertram Thomas Combs (Kentucky's 50th governor), Edith Bolling (wife of President Woodrow Wilson), and actors Andy Griffith, George C. Scott, Robert Duvall, Reese Witherspoon, Lee Marvin, Rebecca Gayheart, and Tom Cruise.

Seabrook's screenplay, *A Rebel Born*, based on his book of the same name, has been signed with acclaimed filmmaker Christopher Forbes (of Forbes Film). It is now in pre-production, and is set for release in 2017 as a full-length feature film. This will be the first movie ever made of Nathan Bedford Forrest's life story, and as a historically accurate project written from the Southern perspective, is destined to be one of the most talked about Civil War films of all time.

Born with music in his blood, Seabrook is an award-winning, multi-genre, BMI-Nashville songwriter and lyricist who has composed some 3,000 songs (250 albums), and whose original music has been heard in film (*A Rebel Born, Cowgirls 'n Angels, Confederate Cavalry, Billy the Kid: Showdown in Lincoln County, Vengeance Without Mercy, Last Step, County Line, The Mark*) and on TV and radio worldwide. A musician, producer, multi-instrumentalist, and renown performer—whose keyboard work has been variously compared to pianists from Hargus Robbins and Vince Guaraldi to Elton John and Leonard Bernstein—Seabrook has opened for groups such as the Earl Scruggs Review, Ted Nugent, and Bob Seger, and has performed privately for such public figures as President Ronald Reagan, Burt Reynolds, Loni Anderson, and Senator Edward W. Brooke. Seabrook's cousins in the music business include: Johnny Cash, Elvis Presley, Billy Ray and Miley Cyrus, Patty Loveless, Tim McGraw, Lee Ann Womack, Dolly Parton, Pat Boone, Naomi, Wynonna, and Ashley Judd, Ricky Skaggs, the Sunshine Sisters, Martha Carson, and Chet Atkins.

Seabrook lives with his wife and family in historic Middle Tennessee, the heart of Forrest country and the Confederacy, where his conservative Southern ancestors fought valiantly against Liberal Lincoln and the progressive North in defense of Jeffersonianism, constitutional government, and personal liberty.

LochlainnSeabrook.com

If you enjoyed this book you will be interested in Colonel Seabrook's other popular related titles:

- ☛ EVERYTHING YOU WERE TAUGHT ABOUT THE CIVIL WAR IS WRONG, ASK A SOUTHERNER!
- ☛ EVERYTHING YOU WERE TAUGHT ABOUT AMERICAN SLAVERY IS WRONG, ASK A SOUTHERNER!
- ☛ CONFEDERATE FLAG FACTS: WHAT EVERY AMERICAN SHOULD KNOW ABOUT DIXIE'S SOUTHERN CROSS
- ☛ CONFEDERACY 101: AMAZING FACTS YOU NEVER KNEW ABOUT AMERICA'S OLDEST POLITICAL TRADITION

Available from Sea Raven Press and wherever fine books are sold

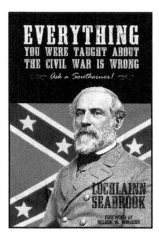

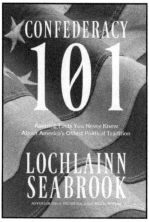

ALL OF OUR BOOK COVERS ARE AVAILABLE AS 11" X 17" POSTERS, SUITABLE FOR FRAMING.

SeaRavenPress.com • NathanBedfordForrestBooks.com

CPSIA information can be obtained
at www.ICGtesting.com
Printed in the USA
LVHW012326140519
617453LV00003B/50/P